Pthreads Programming

Pthreads Programming

Bradford Nichols, Dick Buttlar, and Jacqueline
Proulx Farrell

O'REILLY®

Beijing · Cambridge · Farnham · Köln · Paris · Sebastopol · Taipei · Tokyo

Pthreads Programming
by Bradford Nichols, Dick Buttlar, and Jackie Farrell

Copyright © 1996 O'Reilly & Associates, Inc. All rights reserved.
Printed in the United States of America.

Published by O'Reilly & Associates, Inc., 101 Morris Street, Sebastopol, CA 95472.

Editor: Andy Oram

Production Editor: Nancy Crumpton

Printing History:

September 1996: First Edition

February 1998: Minor corrections

ISBN: 1-56592-115-1

[M]

[10/00]

Table of Contents

Examples

Preface

It's been quite a while since the people from whom we get our project assignments accepted the excuse "Gimme a break! I can only do one thing at a time!" It
used to be such a good excuse, too, when things moved just a bit slower and a
good day was measured in written lines of code. In fact, today we often do many
things at a time. We finish off breakfast on the way into work; we scan the Internet for sports scores and stock prices while our application is building; we'd even
read the morning paper in the shower if the right technology were in place!

Being busy with multiple things is nothing new, though. (We'll just give it a new
computer-age name, like *multitasking*, because computers are happiest when we
avoid describing them in anthropomorphic terms.) It's the way of the natural
world—we wouldn't be able to write this book if all the body parts needed to
keep our fingers moving and our brains engaged didn't work together at the same
time. It's the way of the mechanical world—we wouldn't have been able to get to
this lovely prefabricated office building to do our work if the various, clanking
parts of our automobiles didn't work together (most of the time). It's the way of
the social and business world—three authoring tasks went into the making of this
book, and the number of tasks, all happening at once, grew exponentially as it
went into its review cycles and entered production.

Computer hardware and operating systems have been capable of multitasking for
years. CPUs using a RISC (reduced instruction set computing) microprocessor
break down the processing of individual machine instructions into a number of
separate tasks. By pipelining each instruction through each task, a RISC machine
can have many instructions in progress at the same time. The end result is the her-
alded speed and throughput of RISC processors. Time-sharing operating systems

have been allowing users nearly simultaneous access to the processor for longer than we can remember. Their ability to schedule different tasks (typically called *processes*) really pays off when separate tasks can actually execute simultaneously on separate CPUs in a multiprocessor system.

Although real user applications can be adapted to take advantage of a computer's ability to do more than one thing at once, a lot of operating system code must execute to make it possible. With the advent of threads we've reached an ideal state—the ability to perform multiple tasks simultaneously with as little operating system overhead as possible.

Although threaded programming styles have been around for some time now, it's only recently that they've been adopted by the mainstream of UNIX programmers (not to mention those erstwhile laborers in the vineyards of Windows NT and other operating systems). Software sages swear at the lunchroom table that transaction processing monitors and real-time embedded systems have been using thread-like abstractions for more than twenty years. In the mid-to-late eighties, the general operating system community embarked on several research efforts focused on threaded programming designs, as typified by the work of Tom Doeppner at Brown University and the Mach OS developers at Carnegie-Mellon. With the dawn of the nineties, threads became established in the various UNIX operating systems, such as USL's System V Release 4, Sun Solaris, and the Open Software Foundation's OSF/1. The clash of platform-specific threads programming libraries advanced the need of some portable, platform-independent threads interface. The IEEE has just this year met this need with the acceptance of the IEEE Standard for Information Technology Portable Operating System Interface (POSIX) Part 1: System Application Programming Interface (API) Amendment 2: Threads Extension [C Language]—the Pthreads standard, for short.

This book is about Pthreads—a lightweight, easy-to-use, and portable mechanism for speeding up applications.

Organization

We'll start off Chapter 1, *Why Threads?*, by introducing you to multithreading as a way of performing the many tasks of a program with greater efficiency and speed than would be possible in a serial or multiprocess design. We'll then examine the pitfalls of serial and multiprocess programming, and discuss the concept of potential parallelism, the cornerstone of any decision to write a multitasking program. We'll introduce you to your first Pthreads call—*pthread_create*—and look at those structures by which a thread is uniquely identified. We'll briefly examine the ways in which multiple threads in the same process exchange data, and we'll highlight some synchronization issues.

We'll continue our discussion of planning and structuring a multithreaded program in Chapter 2, *Designing Threaded Programs*. Here, we'll look at the types of applications that can benefit most from multithreading. We'll present the three classic methods for distributing work among threads—the boss/worker model, the peer model, and the pipeline model. We'll also compare two strategies for creating threads—creation on demand versus thread pools. After a brief discussion of thread data-buffering techniques, we'll introduce the ATM server application example that we'll use as the proving ground for thread concepts we'll examine throughout the rest of the book.

In Chapter 3, *Synchronizing Pthreads*, we'll look at the tools that the Pthreads library provides to help you ensure that threads access shared data in an orderly manner. This chapter includes lengthy discussions of mutex variables and condition variables, the two primary Pthreads synchronization tools. It also describes reader/writer locks, a more complex synchronization tool built from mutexes and condition variables. By the end of the chapter, we will have added synchronization to our ATM server example and presented most of what you'll need to know to write a working multithreaded program.

We'll look at the special characteristics of threads and the more advanced features of the Pthreads library in Chapter 4, *Managing Pthreads*. We'll cover some large topics, such as keys (a very handy way for threads to maintain private copies of shared data) and cancellation (a practical method for allowing your threads to be terminated asynchronously without disturbing the state of your program's data and locks). We'll cover some smaller topics, such as thread attributes, including the one that governs the persistence of a thread's internal state. (When you get to this chapter, we promise that you'll know what this means, and you may even value it!) A running theme of this chapter are the various tools that, when combined, allow you to control thread scheduling policies and priorities. You'll find these discussions especially important if your program includes one or more real-time threads.

In Chapter 5, *Pthreads and UNIX*, we'll describe how multithreaded programs interact with features of the UNIX operating system that many serial programs take for granted. First, we'll examine the special challenges UNIX signals pose to multithreaded programs; we'll look at the types of signals threads must worry about and how you can direct certain signals to specific threads. We'll then focus on the requirements the Pthreads library imposes on system calls and libraries to allow them to work correctly when multiple threads from the same process are using them at the same time. Finally, we'll show you what the UNIX *fork* and *exec* calls do to threads. (It isn't always pretty.)

After we've dealt with the fundamentals of Pthreads programming in the earlier chapters, we turn to the more basic issues you'll face in deploying a multithreaded application in Chapter 6, *Practical Considerations*. The theme of this chapter is speed. We'll look at those performance concerns over which you have little control—those that are inherent in a given platform's Pthreads implementation. Here, we'll profile the three major ways implementors design a Pthreads-compliant platform, listing the advantages and drawbacks of each. We'll move on to a discussion of debugging threads, where we'll illustrate a number of debugging strategies using a thread-capable debugger. Finally, we'll look at various alternatives for improving our program's performance. We'll run some tests on various versions of our ATM server to test their performance as contention and workload increase.

We've also included three brief appendixes:

- Appendix A, *Pthreads and DCE*, shows how a multithreaded program might be written using the Open Software Foundation's Distributed Computing Environment (DCE).

- Appendix B, *Pthreads Draft 4 vs. the Final Standard*, lists the differences between Draft 4 of the Pthreads standard and Draft 10, its final version.

- Appendix C, *Pthreads Quick Reference*, is meant to help you find the syntax of any Pthreads library call quickly, without the need for another book.

Example Programs

You can obtain the source code for the examples presented in this book from O'Reilly & Associates through their Internet server.

The example programs in this book are available electronically by FTP.

FTP

To use FTP, you need a machine with direct access to the Internet. A sample session is shown, with what you should type in boldface.

```
% ftp ftp.oreilly.com
Connected to ftp.oreilly.com.
220 FTP server (Version 6.21 Tue Mar 10 22:09:55 EST 1992) ready.
Name (ftp.oreilly.com:yourname) : anonymous
331 Guest login ok, send domain style e-mail address as password.
Password: yourname@domain.name (use your user name and host here)
230 Guest login ok, access restrictions apply.
ftp> cd /work/nutshell/pthread
250 CWD command successful.
ftp> binary (Very important! You must specify binary transfer for
compressed files.)
200 Type set to I.
```

```
ftp> get examples.tar.gz
200 PORT command successful.
150 Opening BINARY mode data connection for examples.tar.gz.
226 Transfer complete.
ftp> quit
221 Goodbye.
%
```

The file is a *gzip* compressed tar archive; extract the files from the archive by typing:

```
% gzcat examples.tar.gz | tar xvf -
```

System V systems require the following tar command instead:

```
% gzcat examples.tar.gz | tar xof -
```

If *gzcat* is not available on your system, use separate *gunzip* and *tar* or *shar* commands.

```
% gunzip examples.tar.gz
% tar xvf examples.tar
```

Typographical Conventions

The following font conventions are used in this book:

- *Italic* is used for function names, filenames, program names, commands, and variables. It's also used to identify new terms and concepts when they are introduced.

- Constant Width is used for code examples and for the system output portion of interactive examples.

- **Constant Bold** is used in interactive examples to show commands or other text that would be typed literally by the user.

- *Constant Italic* identifies programmer-supplied variables in the C language function bindings that appear in Appendix C, *Pthreads Quick Reference*.

Acknowledgments

First of all, we'd like to thank Andy Oram, our editor at O'Reilly & Associates. He stuck with us through the long haul, and the book benefits from his attentive reviews, technical expertise, and sheer professionalism on this book beyond measure. We're also indebted to our technical reviewers: Jeff Denham, Bill Gallmeister, and Dean Brock. Jeff, Greg Nichols, and Bernard Farrell read and commented on early drafts of the book. Thank you all!

Brad: "The inspiration for this book came from a threads programming seminar I developed back in 1991 for the Institute for Software Advancement (ISA). I'd like to express my appreciation to Rich Mitchell of ISA and Nick Uginow of DEC for setting me on this track, as well as the good folks at DECwest in Seattle and DEC software engineering in Nashua, New Hampshire, who attended my seminars and helped the course evolve. I'd like to acknowledge the support and encouragement of my former colleagues at DEC: Andy Kegal, Fred Glover, Ed Cande, and Steve Strange. On the personal side, I'd like to acknowledge my grandmother, Natalie Bunker, for the desire to write a book, my wife Susan for supporting me through the long project, and my friend Paul Silva for modeling the determination needed to complete it."

Dick: "I'd like to thank Kathleen Johnson, Thomas Doeppner, Stan Amway, Cheryl Wiecek, Steve Fiorelli, and Dave Long. Each can lay a claim to some flavor and vintage of threads information I filed away somewhere in my head just in case someone asked. Special thanks to Ruth Goldenberg (the most technical and generous of writers), Mike Etzel, and Howard Littlefield. I want to especially thank Connie, my wife, for her love, patience, and permission to skip this year's spring cleanup. (Another book for the snow-shovelling season, Brad and Jackie?) Finally, love to my kids: Jenn (who wants a giraffe on the cover), Maggie (a doggie), and Tom (a lobster...on a pirate's shoulder...with one leg....).

Jackie: "I'd like to thank Bernard, who is not only a superb technical resource but an absolutely wonderful, supportive husband. I'd also like to thank Mark Sanders and Jonathan Swartz for my first introductions to threads concepts. Thanks also to the whole DECthreads team, and Peter Portante in particular, for helping refine my understanding of the practical matters of programming with Pthreads."

1

Why Threads?

When describing how computers work to someone new to PCs, it's often easiest to haul out the old notion that a program is a very large collection of instructions that are performed from beginning to end. Our notion of a program can include certain eccentricities, like loops and jumps, that make a program more resemble a game of Chutes and Ladders than a piano roll. If programming instructions were squares on a game board, we can see that our program has places where we stall, squares that we cross again and again, and spots we don't cross at all. But we have one way into our program, regardless of its spins and hops, and one way out.

Not too many years ago, single instructions were how we delivered work to computers. Since then, computers have become more and more powerful and grown more efficient at performing the work that makes running our programs possible. Today's computers can do many things at once (or very effectively make us believe so). When we package our work according to the traditional, serial notion of a program, we're asking the computer to execute it close to the humble performance of a computer of yesterday. If all of our programs run like this, we're very likely not using our computer to its fullest capabilities.

One of those capabilities is a computing system's ability to perform *multitasking*. Today, it's frequently useful to look at our program (our very big task) as a collection of subtasks. For instance, if our program is a marine navigation system, we could launch separate tasks to perform each sounding and maintain other tasks that calculate relative depth, correlate coordinates with depth measurements, and display charts on a screen. If we can get the computer to execute some of these subtasks at the same time, with no change in our program's results, our overall task will continue to get as much processing as it needs, but it will complete in a shorter period of time. On some systems, the execution of subtasks will be interleaved on a single processor; on others, they can run in parallel. Either way, we'll see a performance boost.

Up until now, when we divided our program into multiple tasks, we had only one way of delivering them to the processor—processes. Specifically, we started designing programs in which parent processes forked child processes to perform subtasks. In this model, each subtask must exist within its own process. Now, we've been given an alternative that's even more efficient and provides even better performance for our overall program—threads. In the threads model, multiple subtasks exist as individual streams of control within the same process.

The threads model takes a process and divides it into two parts:

- One contains resources used across the whole program (the processwide information), such as program instructions and global data. This part is still referred to as the *process*.

- The other contains information related to the execution state, such as a program counter and a stack. This part is referred to as a *thread*.

To compare and contrast multitasking between cooperating processes and multitasking using threads, let's first look at how the simple C program in Example 1-1 can be represented as a process (Figure 1-1), a process with a single thread (Figure 1-2), and, finally, as a process with multiple threads (Figure 1-3).

Example 1–1: A Simple C Program (simple.c)

```
#include <stdio.h>
void do_one_thing(int *);
void do_another_thing(int *);
void do_wrap_up(int, int);

int r1 = 0, r2 = 0;

extern int
```

Example 1–1: A Simple C Program (simple.c) (continued)

```
main(void)
{
  do_one_thing(&r1);
  do_another_thing(&r2);
  do_wrap_up(r1, r2);
  return 0;
}

void do_one_thing(int *pnum_times)
{
  int i, j, x;

  for (i = 0;  i < 4; i++) {
    printf("doing one thing\n");
    for (j = 0; j < 10000; j++) x = x + i;
    (*pnum_times)++;
  }
}

void do_another_thing(int *pnum_times)
{
  int i, j, x;

  for (i = 0;  i < 4; i++) {
    printf("doing another \n");
    for (j = 0; j < 10000; j++) x = x + i;
    (*pnum_times)++;
  }
}

void do_wrap_up(int one_times, int another_times)
{
 int total;

 total = one_times + another_times;
 printf("wrap up: one thing %d, another %d, total %d\n",

 one_times, another_times, total);
}
```

Figure 1-1 shows the layout of this program in the virtual memory of a process, indicating how memory is assigned and which resources the process consumes. Several regions of memory exist:

- A read-only area for program instructions (or "text" in UNIX parlance)

- A read-write area for global data (such as the variables *r1* and *r2* in our program)

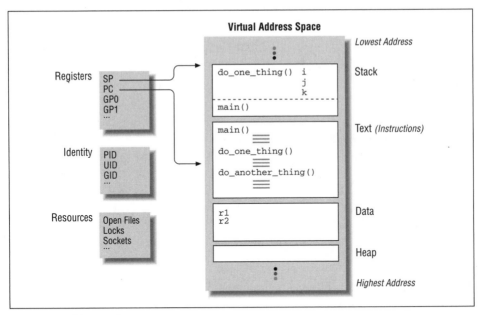

Figure 1-1: The simple program as a process

- A heap area for memory that is dynamically allocated through *malloc* system calls

- A stack on which the automatic variables of the current procedure are kept (along with function arguments and other information needed to link it to the procedure that called it), just below similar information for the procedure that called it, just below similar information for the procedure that called it, and so on and so on. Each of these procedure-specific areas is known as a *stack frame*, and one exists for each procedure in the program that remains active. In the stack area of this illustration you can see the stack frames of our procedures *do_one_thing* and *main*.

To complete our inventory of system resources needed to sustain this process, notice:

- Machine registers, including a program counter (PC) to the currently executing instruction and a pointer (SP) to the current stack frame

- Process-specific include tables, maintained by the operating system, to track system-supplied resources such as open files (each requiring a file descriptor), communication end points (sockets), locks, and signals

Figure 1-2 shows the same C program as a process with a single thread. Here, the machine registers (program counter, stack pointer, and the rest) have become part of the thread, leaving the rest as the process. As far as the outside observer of the program is concerned, nothing much has changed. As a process with a single thread, this program executes in exactly the same way as it does when modeled as a nonthreaded process. It is only when we design our program to take advantage of multiple threads in the same process that the thread model really takes off.

Figure 1-3 shows our program as it might execute if it were designed to operate in two threads in a single process. Here, each thread has its own copy of the machine registers. (It's certainly very handy for a thread to keep track of the instruction it is currently executing and where in the stack area it should be pushing and popping its procedure-context information.) This allows Thread 1 and Thread 2 to execute at different locations (or exactly the same location) in the program's text. Thread 1, the thread in which the program was started, is executing *do_one_thing*, while Thread 2 is executing *do_another_thing*. Each thread can refer to global variables in the same data area. (*do_one_thing* uses *r1* as a counter; *do_another_thing* uses *r2*.) Both threads can refer to the same file descriptors and other resources the system maintains for the process.

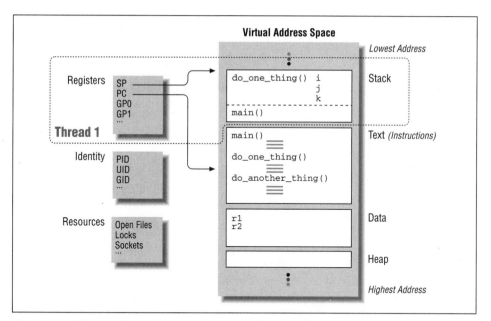

Figure 1–2: The simple program as a process with a thread

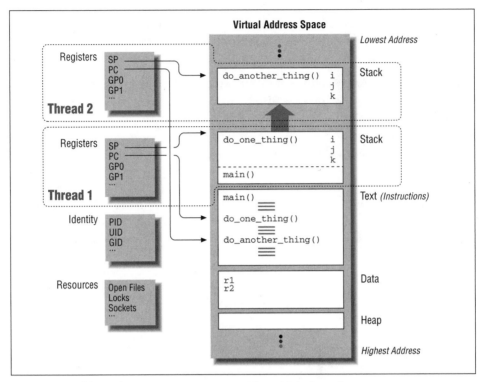

Figure 1–3: The simple program as a process with multiple threads

What Are Pthreads?

How do you design a program so that it executes in multiple threads within a process? Well, for starters, you need a thread creation routine and a way of letting the new thread know where in the program it should begin executing. But at this point, we've passed beyond the ability to generalize.

Up to this point, we've discussed the basics of threads and thread creation at a level common to all thread models. As we move on to discuss specifics (as we will in the remainder of this book), we encounter differences among the popular thread packages. For instance, Pthreads specifies a thread's starting point as a procedure name; other thread packages differ in their specification of even this most elementary of concepts. Differences such as this motivated IEEE to create the Pthreads standard.

Pthreads is a standardized model for dividing a program into subtasks whose execution can be interleaved or run in parallel. The "P" in Pthreads comes from POSIX

(Portable Operating System Interface), the family of IEEE operating system interface standards in which Pthreads is defined (POSIX Section 1003.1c to be exact). There have been and still are a number of other threads models—Mach Threads and NT Threads, for example. Programmers experience Pthreads as a defined set of C language programming types and calls with a set of implied semantics. Vendors usually supply Pthreads implementations in the form of a header file, which you include in your program, and a library, to which you link your program.

Potential Parallelism

If we return to the simple program in our examples, we see that it has three tasks to complete. The three tasks are represented by the routines *do_one_thing*, *do_another_thing*, and *do_wrap_up*. The *do_one_thing* and *do_another_thing* tasks are simply loops that print out slightly different messages and then perform some token calculations to while away the time. The *do_wrap_up* task adds together the return values from the other two tasks and prints the result. Many real programs can be split, in a similar way, into individual tasks representing different CPU-based and I/O-based activities. For instance, a program that retrieves blocks of data from a file on disk and then performs computations based on their contents is an eminent candidate for multitasking.

When we run the program, it executes each routine serially, always completely finishing the first before starting the second, and completely finishing the second before starting the third. If we take a closer look at the program, we see that the order in which the first two routines execute doesn't affect the third, as long as the third runs after both of them have completed. This property of a program—that statements can be executed in any order without changing the result—is called *potential parallelism.*

To illustrate parallelism, Figure 1-4 shows some possible sequences in which the program's routines could be executed. The first sequence is that of the original program; the second is similar but with the first two routines exchanged. The third shows interleaved execution of the first routines; the last, their simultaneous execution. All sequences produce exactly the same result.

An obvious reason for exploiting potential parallelism is to make our program run faster on a multiprocessor. However, there are additional reasons for investigating a program's potential parallelism:

Overlapping I/O

If one or more tasks represent a long I/O operation that may block while waiting for an I/O system call to complete, there may be performance advantages in allowing CPU-intensive tasks to continue independently. For example,

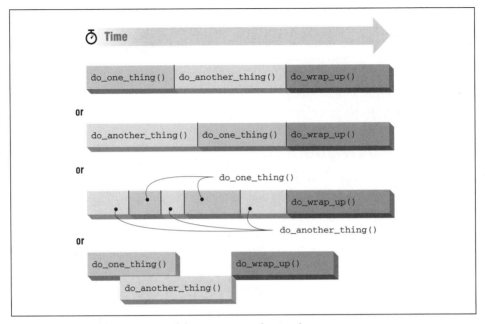

Figure 1–4: Possible sequences of the routines in the simple program

a word processor could service print requests in one thread and process a user's editing commands in another.

Asynchronous events

If one or more tasks is subject to the indeterminate occurrence of events of unknown duration and unknown frequency, such as network communications, it may be more efficient to allow other tasks to proceed while the task subject to asynchronous events is in some unknown state of completion. For example, a network-based server could process in-progress requests in one group of threads while another thread waits for the asynchronous arrival of new requests from clients through network connections.

Real-time scheduling

If one task is more important than another, but both should make progress whenever possible, you may wish to run them with independent scheduling priorities and policies. For example, a stock information service application could use high priority threads to receive and update displays of online stock prices and low priority threads to display static data, manage background printing, and perform other less important chores.

Threads are a means to identify and utilize potential parallelism in a program. You can use them in your program design both to enhance its performance and to efficiently structure programs that do more than one thing at a time. For instance, handling signals, handling input from a communication interface, and managing I/O are all tasks that can be done—and done very well—by multiple threads executing simultaneously.

Specifying Potential Parallelism in a Concurrent Programming Environment

Now that we know the orderings that we desire or would allow in our program, how do we express potential parallelism at the programming level? Those programming environments that allow us to express potential parallelism are known as *concurrent programming environments*. A concurrent programming environment lets us designate tasks that can run in parallel. It also lets us specify how we would like to handle the communication and synchronization issues that result when concurrent tasks attempt to talk to each other and share data.

Because most concurrent programming tools and languages have been the result of academic research or have been tailored to a particular vendor's products, they are often inflexible and hard to use. Pthreads, on the other hand, is designed to work across multiple vendors' platforms and is built on top of the familiar UNIX C programming interface. Pthreads gives you a simple and portable way of expressing multithreading in your programs.

UNIX Concurrent Programming: Multiple Processes

Before looking at threads further, let's examine the concurrent programming interface that UNIX already supports: allowing user programs to create multiple processes and providing services the processes can use to communicate with each other.

Example 1-2 recasts our earlier single-process program as a program in which multiple processes execute its procedures concurrently. The *main* routine starts in a single process (which we will refer to as the *parent* process). The parent process then creates a *child* process to execute the *do_one_thing* routine and another to execute the *do_another_thing* routine. The parent waits for both children to finish (as parents of the human kind often do), calls the *do_wrap_up* routine, and exits.

Example 1-2: A Simple C Program with Concurrent Processes

```
#include <stdlib.h>
#include <stdio.h>
#include <unistd.h>
#include <sys/types.h>
#include <sys/ipc.h>
#include <sys/shm.h>
#include <sys/wait.h>
```

Example 1–2: A Simple C Program with Concurrent Processes (continued)

```
void do_one_thing(int *);
void do_another_thing(int *);
void do_wrap_up(int, int);

int    shared_mem_id;
int    *shared_mem_ptr;
int    *r1p;
int    *r2p;
extern int
main(void)
{
  pid_t  child1_pid, child2_pid;
  int  status;

  /* initialize shared memory segment */
  shared_mem_id = shmget(IPC_PRIVATE, 2*sizeof(int), 0660);
  shared_mem_ptr = (int *)shmat(shared_mem_id, (void *)0, 0);
  r1p = shared_mem_ptr;
  r2p = (shared_mem_ptr + 1);

  *r1p = 0;
  *r2p = 0;

  if ((child1_pid = fork()) == 0) {
    /* first child */
    do_one_thing(r1p);
    exit(0);
  }

  /* parent */
  if ((child2_pid = fork()) == 0) {
    /* second child */
    do_another_thing(r2p);
    exit(0);
  }

  /* parent */
  waitpid(child1_pid, &status, 0);
  waitpid(child2_pid, &status, 0);

  do_wrap_up(*r1p, *r2p);
  return 0;

}
```

Creating a new process: fork

The UNIX system call that creates a new process is *fork*. The *fork* call creates a child process that is identical to its parent process at the time the parent called *fork* with the following differences:

- The child has its own process identifier, or PID.

- The *fork* call provides different return values to the parent and the child processes.

Figure 1-5 shows a process as it forks. Here, both parent and child are executing at the point in the program just following the *fork* call. Interestingly, the child begins executing as if it were returning from the *fork* call issued by its parent. It can do so because it starts out as a nearly identical copy of its parent. The initial values of all of its variables and the state of its system resources (such as file descriptors) are the same as those of its parent.

If the *fork* call returns to both the parent and child, why don't the parent and child execute the same instructions following the *fork*? UNIX programmers specify different code paths for parent and child by examining the return value of the *fork* call. The *fork* call always returns a value of 0 to the child and the child's PID to the parent. Because of this semantic we almost always see *fork* used as shown in Example 1-3.

Example 1–3: A fork Call (simple_processes.c)

```
if ((pid = fork()) < 0 ) {
            /* Fork system call failed */
            .

            .

            .
            perror("fork"), exit(1);
}else if (pid == 0) {
            /* Child only, pid is 0 */
            .

            .

            .
            return 0;
}else {
            /* Parent only , pid is child's process ID */
            .

            .

            .
}
```

After the program forks into two different processes, the parent and child execute independently unless you add explicit synchronization. Each process executes its own instructions serially, although the way in which the statements of each may be interwoven by concurrency is utterly unpredictable. In fact, one process could completely finish before the other even starts (or resumes, in the case in which the parent is the last to the finish line). To see what we mean, let's look at the output from some test runs of our program in Example 1-2.

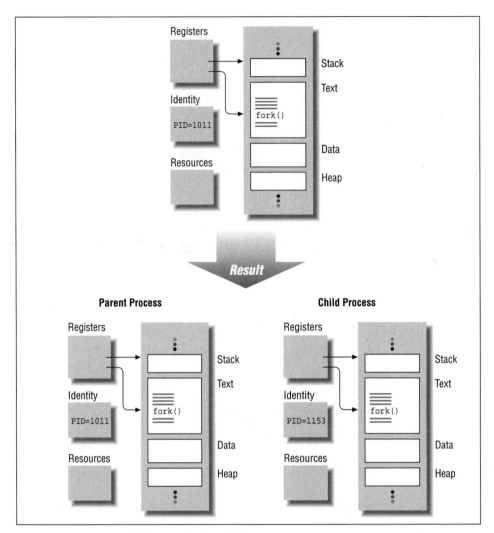

Figure 1–5: A program before and after a fork

```
# simple_processes
doing another
doing one thing
doing another
doing one thing
doing another
doing one thing
doing one thing
doing another
wrap up: one thing 4, another 4, total 8
# simple_processes
doing another
```

```
doing another
doing one thing
doing another
doing one thing
doing one thing
doing another
doing one thing
wrap up: one thing 4, another 4, total 8
#
```

This program is a good example of parallelism and it works—as do the many real UNIX programs that use multiple processes. When looking for concurrency, then, why choose multiple threads over multiple processes? The overwhelming reason lies in the single largest benefit of multithreaded programming: threads require less program and system overhead to run than processes do. The operating system performs less work on behalf of a multithreaded program than it does for a multi-process program. This translates into a performance gain for the multithreaded program.

Pthreads Concurrent Programming: Multiple Threads

Now that we've seen how UNIX programmers traditionally add concurrency to a program, let's look at a way of doing so that employs threads. Example 1-4 shows how our single-process program would look if multiple threads execute its procedures concurrently. The program starts in a single thread, which, for reasons of clarity, we'll refer to as the *main* thread. For the most part, the operating system does not recognize any thread as being a parent or master thread—from its viewpoint, all threads in a process are equal.

Using Pthreads function calls, the creator thread spawns a thread to execute the *do_one_thing* routine and another to execute the *do_another_thing* routine. It waits for both threads to finish, calls the *do_wrap_up* routine, and exits. In the same way that the processes behave in our multiprocess version of the program, each thread executes independently unless you add explicit synchronization.

Example 1-4: A Simple C Program with Concurrent Threads (simple_threads.c)

```
#include <stdio.h>
#include <pthread.h>

void do_one_thing(int *);
void do_another_thing(int *);
void do_wrap_up(int, int);

int r1 = 0, r2 = 0;

extern int
```

Example 1-4: A Simple C Program with Concurrent Threads (simple_threads.c) (continued)

```
main(void)
{
  pthread_t          thread1, thread2;

  pthread_create(&thread1,
          NULL,
          (void *) do_one_thing,
          (void *) &r1);

  pthread_create(&thread2,
          NULL,
          (void *) do_another_thing,
          (void *) &r2);

  pthread_join(thread1, NULL);
  pthread_join(thread2, NULL);

  do_wrap_up(r1, r2);
  return 0;
}
```

Creating a new thread: pthread_create

Whereas you create a new process by using the UNIX *fork* system call, you create a new thread by calling the *pthread_create* Pthreads function. You provide the following arguments:

*   A pointer to a buffer to which *pthread_create* returns a value that identifies the newly created thread. This value, or handle, is of type *pthread_t*.* You can use it in all subsequent calls to refer to this specific thread.

*   A pointer to a structure known as a *thread attribute object*. A thread attribute object specifies various characteristics for the new thread. In the example program, we pass a value of NULL for this argument, indicating that we accept the default characteristics for the new thread.

*   A pointer to the routine at which the new thread will start executing.

*   A pointer to a parameter to be passed to the routine at which the new thread starts.

Like most Pthreads functions, *pthread_create* returns a value that indicates whether it has succeeded or failed. A zero value represents success, and a nonzero value indicates and identifies an error.

---

* The *pthread_t* type may look a little strange to you if you're used to the data types returned by C language system calls on many UNIX systems. Because many of these types (like *int*) reveal quite a bit about the underlying architecture of a given platform (such as whether its addresses are 16, 32, or 64 bits long), POSIX prefers to create new data types that conceal these fundamental differences. By convention, the names of these data types end in *_t*.

The formal prototype of a start routine is (void*)routine(void*arg). In our code example, we are adding threads to an existing program (a not atypical scenario) and using the (void *) cast to quit the compiler. In later examples, we redeclare the routine to the correct prototype where possible.

Threads are peers

In the multiprocess version of our example (Example 1-2), we could refer to the caller of *fork* as the parent process and the process it creates as the child process. We could do so because UNIX process management recognizes a special relationship between the two. It is this relationship that, for instance, allows a parent to issue a *wait* system call to implicitly wait for one of its children.

The Pthreads concurrent programming environment maintains no such special relationship between threads. We may call the thread that creates another thread the *creator* thread and the thread it creates the *spawned* thread, but that's just semantics. Creator threads and spawned threads have exactly the same properties in the eyes of the Pthreads. The only thread that has slightly different properties than any other is the first thread in the process, which is known as the *main* thread. In this simple program, none of the differences have any significance.

Once the two *pthread_create* calls in our example program return, three threads exist concurrently. Which will run first? Will one run to completion before the others, or will their execution be interleaved? It depends on the default scheduling policies of the underlying Pthreads implementation. It could be predictable, but then again, it may not be. The output on our system looks like this:

```
# simple_threads
doing another
doing one thing
doing another
doing one thing
doing another
doing one thing
doing another
doing one thing
wrap up: one thing 4, another 4, total 8
# simple_threads
doing another
doing one thing
doing another
doing one thing
doing one thing
doing another
doing one thing
doing another
wrap up: one thing 4, another 4, total 8
#
```

Parallel vs. Concurrent Programming

Let's make a distinction between concurrent and parallel programming for the remainder of the book. We'll use *concurrent programming* in a general sense to refer to environments in which the tasks we define can occur in any order. One task can occur before or after another, and some or all tasks can be performed at the same time. We'll use *parallel programming* to specifically refer to the simultaneous execution of concurrent tasks on different processors. Thus, all parallel programming is concurrent, but not all concurrent programming is parallel.

The Pthreads standard specifies concurrency; it allows parallelism to be at the option of system implementors. As a programmer, all you can do is define those tasks, or threads, that can occur concurrently. Whether the threads actually run in parallel is a function of the operating system and hardware on which they run. Because Pthreads was designed in this way, a Pthreads program can run without modification on uniprocessor as well as multiprocessor systems.

Okay, so portability is great, but what of performance? All of our Pthreads programs will be running with specific Pthreads libraries, operating systems, and hardware. To squeeze the best performance out of a multithreaded application, you must understand the specifics of the environment in which it will be running—especially those details that are beyond the letter of the standard. We'll spend some time in the later sections of this book identifying and describing the implementation-specific issues of Pthreads.

Synchronization

Even in our simple program, in Examples 1-1 through 1-4, some parts can be executed in any order and some cannot. The first two routines, *do_one_thing* and *do_another_thing*, can run concurrently because they update separate variables and therefore do not conflict. But the third routine, *do_wrap_up*, must read those variables, and therefore must ensure that the other routines have finished using them before it can read them. We must force an order upon the events in our program, or *synchronize* them, to guarantee that the last routine executes only after the first two have completed.

In threads programming, we use synchronization to make sure that one event in one thread happens before another event in another thread. A simple analogy would involve two people working together to jump start a car, one attaching the cables under the hood and one in the car getting ready to turn the key. The two must use some signal between them so that the person connecting the cables completes the task before the other turns the key. This is real life synchronization.

In general, cooperation between concurrent procedures leads to the sharing of data, files, and communication channels. This sharing, in turn, leads to a need for synchronization. For instance, consider a program that contains three routines. Two routines write to variables and the third reads them. For the final routine to read the right values, you must add some synchronization. It's telling that, of all the function calls supplied in a Pthreads library, only one—*pthread_create*—is used to enable concurrency. Almost all of the other function calls are there to replace the synchronization that was inherent in the program when it executed serially—and slowly!

In the multiprocess version of our program, Example 1-2, we used the UNIX *waitpid* system call to prevent the parent process from executing the *do_wrap_up* routine before the other two processes completed the *do_one_thing* and *do_another_thing* routines and exited. The *waitpid* call provides synchronization by suspending its caller until a child process exits. (Notice that we use the *waitpid* call only in the code path of the parent.) In the Pthreads version of our program (Example 1-4), we use the *pthread_join* call to synchronize the threads' execution. The *pthread_join* call provides synchronization for threads similar to that which *waitpid* provides for processes, suspending its caller until another thread exits. Unlike *waitpid*, which is specifically intended for parent and child processes, you can use *pthread_join* between any two threads in a program.

Both the multiprocess and multithreaded versions of our program use coarse methods to synchronize. One process or thread just stalled until the others caught up and finished. In later sections of this book we'll go into great detail on the finer methods of Pthreads synchronization, namely mutex variables and condition variables. The finer methods allow you to synchronize thread activity on a thread's access to one or more variables, rather than blocking the execution of an entire routine and thread in which it executes. Using the finer synchronization techniques, threads can spend less time waiting on each other and more time accomplishing the tasks for which they were designed.

As a quick introduction to mutex variables, let's make a slight modification to the Pthreads version of our simple program. In Example 1-5, we'll add a new variable, *r3*. Because all routines will read from and write to this variable, we'll need some synchronization to control access to it. For this, we'll define a mutex variable (of type *pthread_mutex_t*) and initialize it. (Just as a thread can have a thread attribute object, a mutex can have a *mutex attribute object* that indicates its special characteristics. Here, too, we'll pass a value of NULL for this argument, indicating that we accept the default characteristics for the new mutex.)

Example 1-5: A Simple C Program with Concurrent Threads and a Mutex (simple_mutex.c)

```
#include <stdio.h>
#include <pthread.h>

void do_one_thing(int *);
void do_another_thing(int *);
void do_wrap_up(int, int);

int r1 = 0, r2 = 0, r3 = 0;
pthread_mutex_t r3_mutex=PTHREAD_MUTEX_INITIALIZER;
extern int
main(int argc, char **argv)
{
  pthread_t         thread1, thread2;

  r3 = atoi(argv[1]);

  pthread_create(&thread1,
          NULL,
          (void *) do_one_thing,
          (void *) &r1);

  pthread_create(&thread2,
          NULL,
          (void *) do_another_thing,
          (void *) &r2);

  pthread_join(thread1, NULL);
  pthread_join(thread2, NULL);

  do_wrap_up(r1, r2);
  return 0;
}
```

We'll also make changes to the routines that will read from and write to *r3*. We'll synchronize their access to *r3* by using the mutex we created in the main thread. When we're finished, the code for *do_another_thing* and *do_wrap_up* will resemble the code in *do_one_thing* in Example 1-6.

Example 1-6: Concurrent Threads and a Mutex: do_one_thing Routine

```
void do_one_thing(int *pnum_times)
{
  int i, j, x;

  pthread_mutex_lock(&r3_mutex);
  if (r3 > 0) {
     x = r3;
     r3--;
  }else {
     x = 1;
  }
  pthread_mutex_unlock(&r3_mutex);
```

Example 1-6: Concurrent Threads and a Mutex: do_one_thing Routine (continued)

```
    for (i = 0;  i < 4; i++) {
      printf("doing one thing\n");
      for (j = 0; j < 10000; j++) x = x + i;
      (*pnum_times)++;
    }
  }
```

The mutex variable acts like a lock protecting access to a shared resource—in this case the variable *r3* in memory. Whichever thread obtains the lock on the mutex in a call to *pthread_mutex_lock* has the right to access the shared resource it protects. It relinquishes this right when it releases the lock with the *pthread_mutex_unlock* call. The mutex gets its name from the term *mutual exclusion*—all threads have a mutual relationship with regard to the mutex variable; whichever thread holds the lock excludes all others from access.

You'll notice in Example 1-6 that you must make special Pthreads calls to manipulate mutexes. You can't just invent mutexes in your C code by testing and setting some sort of synchronization flag. If your code tests the mutex and then sets it, you leave a tiny (but potentially fatal) length of time during which another thread could also test and set the same mutex. Pthreads implementors avoid this window of vulnerability by taking advantage of operating system services or special machine instructions.

Sharing Process Resources

From a programming standpoint, the major difference between the multiprocess and multithreaded concurrency models is that, by default, all threads share the resources of the process in which they exist. Independent processes share nothing. Threads share such process resources as global variables and file descriptors. If one thread changes the value of any such resource, the change will be evident to any other thread in the process, if anyone cares to look. The sharing of process resources among threads is one of the multithreaded programming model's major performance advantages, as well as one of its most difficult programming aspects. Having all of this context available to all threads in the same memory facilitates communication between threads. However, at the same time, it makes it easy to introduce errors of the sort in which one thread affects the value of a variable used by another thread in ways the other thread did not expect.

In Example 1-6, because the *do_one_thing* and *do_another_thing* routines simply place their results into global variables, the main thread can also access them should it need to. Because shared data calls for synchronization, the program uses the *pthread_join* call to enforce the order in which different threads write to and read from these global variables. The way this works is pretty simple. The two spawned threads know that, as long as they are running, the main thread has not passed its *pthread_join* call and, so, won't look at their output values. The main thread knows that, once it has passed the second *pthread_join* call, no other threads are active. The values of the output parameters are set to their final value and can be used.

The processes in the multiprocess version of our program also use shared memory, but the program must do something special so that they can use it. We used the System V shared memory interface. Before it creates any child processes, the parent initializes a region of shared memory from the system using the *shmget* and *shmat* calls. After the *fork* call, all the processes of the parent and its children have common access to this memory, using it in the same way as the multithreaded version uses global variables, and all the parent and children processes can see whatever changes any of them may make to it.

Communication

When two concurrent procedures communicate, one writing data and one reading data, they must adopt some type of synchronization so that the reader knows when the writer has completed and the writer knows that the reader is ready for more data. Some programming environments provide explicit communication mechanisms such as message passing. The Pthreads concurrent programming environment provides a more implicit (some would call it primitive) mechanism. Threads share all global variables. This affords threads programmers plenty of opportunities for synchronization.

Multiple processes can use any of the many other UNIX Interprocess Communication (IPC) mechanisms: sockets, shared memory, and messages, to name a few. The multiprocess version of our program uses shared memory, but the other methods are equally valid. Even the *waitpid* call in our program could be used to exchange information, if the program checked its return value. However, in the multiprocess world, all types of IPC involve a call into the operating system—to initialize shared memory or a message structure, for instance. This makes communication between processes more expensive than communication between threads.

Scheduling

We can also order the events in our program by imposing some type of scheduling policy on them. Unless our program is running on a system with an infinite number of CPUs, it's a safe bet that, sooner or later, there will be more concurrent tasks ready to run in our program than there are CPUs available to run them. The operating system uses its scheduler to select from the pool of ready and runnable tasks those that it will run. In a sense, the scheduler synchronizes the tasks' access to a shared resource: the system's CPUs.

Neither the multithreaded version of our program nor the multiprocess version imposes any specific scheduling requirements on its tasks. POSIX defines some scheduling calls as an optional part of its Pthreads package, allowing you to select scheduling policies and priorities for threads.

Who Am I? Who Are You?

When you create a thread, *pthread_create* returns a thread handle of type *pthread_t*. You can save this handle and use it to determine a thread's identity using the *pthread_self* and *pthread_equal* function calls. The *pthread_self* call returns the thread handle of the calling thread and *pthread_equal* compares two thread handles.* You might use the two calls to identify a thread when it enters a routine, as shown in Example 1-7.

Example 1-7: Code that Examines the Identity of the Calling Thread (ident.c)

```
    .
    .
    .
pthread_t io_thread;
    .
    .
extern int
main(void)
{
        .
        .
        .
        pthread_create(&io_thread,
                        .... );
        .
        .
        .
}

void routine_x(void)
{
pthread_t thread;
        .
        .
        .
```

---

* The Pthreads standard leaves the exact definition of the *pthread_t* type up to system implementors. Because a system implementor might define a thread handle to be a structure, you should always use *pthread_equal* to compare threads. A direct comparison (such as *io_thread* == *thread*) may not work.

Example 1-7: Code that Examines the Identity of the Calling Thread (ident.c) (continued)

```
        thread = pthread_self();
        if (pthread_equal(io_thread, thread)) {
        .
        .
        .
        }
        .
        .
        .
    }
```

Terminating Thread Execution

A process terminates when it comes to the end of *main*. At that time the operating system reclaims the process's resources and stores its exit status. Similarly, a thread exits when it comes to the end of the routine in which it was started. (By the way, all threads expire when the process in which they run exits.) When a thread terminates, the Pthreads library reclaims any process or system resources the thread was using and stores its exit status. A thread can also explicitly exit with a call to *pthread_exit*. You can terminate another thread by calling *pthread_cancel*. In any of these cases, the Pthreads library runs any routines in its cleanup stack and any destructors in keys in which it has store values. We'll describe these features in Chapter 4, *Managing Pthreads*.

Exit Status and Return Values

The Pthreads library may or may not save the exit status of a thread when the thread exits, depending upon whether the thread is joinable or detached. A *joinable* thread, the default state of a thread at its creation, does have its exit status saved; a *detached* thread does not. Detaching a thread gives the library a break and lets it immediately reclaim the resources associated with the thread. Because the library will not have an exit status for a detached thread, you cannot use a *pthread_join* to join it. We'll show you how to dynamically set the state of a thread to detached in Chapter 2, *Designing Threaded Programs*, when we introduce the *pthread_detach* call. In Chapter 4, we'll show you how to create a thread in the detached state by specifying attribute objects.

What is the exit status of a thread? You can associate an exit status with a thread in either of two ways:

*   If the thread terminates explicitly with a call to *pthread_exit*, the argument to the call becomes its exit status.

- If the thread does not call *pthread_exit,* the return value of the routine in which it started becomes its exit status.

As defined by the Pthreads standard, the thread-start routine (specified in the *pthread_create* call) returns a *(void *)* type. However, you'll often find that your thread-start routines must return something other than an address—e.g., a binary TRUE/FALSE indicator. They can do this quite easily as long as you remember to cast the return value as a *(void *)* type and avoid using a value that conflicts with PTHREAD_CANCELED, the only status value that the Pthreads library itself may return. (Pthreads implementations cannot define PTHREAD_CANCELED as a valid address or as NULL, so you're always safest when returning an address.) Of course, if the thread running the thread-start routine cannot be canceled (peek ahead to Chapter 4 to learn a bit about cancellation), you can ignore this restriction.

In Example 1-8, we've defined three possible exit status values and elected to have *routine_x* return pointers to integer constants with these values. We use *pthread_exit* and 'return interchangeably.

Example 1-8: Specifying a Thread's Exit Status (exit_status_alternative.c)

```
#include <stdio.h>
#include <pthread.h>

pthread_t thread;
static int arg;
static const int internal_error = -12;
static const int normal_error = -10;
static const int success = 1;

void * routine_x(void *arg_in)
{
  int *arg = (int *)arg_in;
  .

  .

  .
  if ( /* something that shouldn't have happened */) {
    pthread_exit((void *) &real_bad_error);
  }else if ( /* normal failure */ ) {
    return ((void *) &normal_error);
  }else {
    return ((void *) &success);
  }
}
extern int
main(int argc, char **argv)
{
  pthread_t thread;
  void *statusp;
  .

  .

  .
```

Example 1-8: Specifying a Thread's Exit Status (exit_status_alternative.c) (continued)

```
        pthread_create(&thread, NULL, routine_x, &arg);
        pthread_join(thread, &statusp);
        if (*statusp == PTHREAD_CANCELED) {
          printf("Thread was canceled.\n");
        }else {
          printf("Thread completed and exit status is %ld.\n", *(int *)statusp);
        }
        return 0;
    }
```

A final note on *pthread_join* is in order. Its purpose is to allow a single thread to wait on another's termination. The result of having multiple threads concurrently call *pthread_join* is undefined in the Pthreads standard.

Pthreads Library Calls and Errors

Most Pthreads library calls return zero on success and an error number otherwise.[*] Errors numbers are defined in the *errno.h* header file. The Pthreads standard doesn't require library calls to set 'errno, the global variable traditionally used by UNIX and POSIX.1 calls to deliver an error to their callers.

You can use code similar to that in Example 1-9 to perform error checking on a Pthreads call.

Example 1-9: Full Error-Checking for a Pthreads Library Call

```
    #include <errno.h>
    #include <stdio.h>
    .
    .
    .
    if (rtn = pthread_create(...)) {
       /* error has occurred */
       fprintf(stderr,"Error: pthread_create, ");
       if (rtn == EAGAIN)
          fprintf(stderr,"Insufficent resources\n");
          else if (rtn == EINVAL)
                  fprintf(stderr, "Invalid arguments\n");
       exit(1);
    }
    /* no error */
    .
    .
    .
```

---

[*] The two Pthreads library calls that don't return an error code upon failure are *pthread_getspecific* and *pthread_self*. A *pthread_getspecific* call returns NULL if it's unsuccessful. A *pthread_self* call always succeeds.

If your platform supports a routine to convert error numbers to a readable string such as the XPG4 call, *strerror,* your code could be simplified as in Example 1-10.

Example 1-10: Full Error-Checking for a Pthreads Library Call, Simplified

```
#include <string.h>
#include <stdio.h>
  .
  .
  .
if (rtn = pthread_create(...))
    fprintf(stderr, "Error: pthread_create, %s\n", strerror(rtn)), exit(1);

/* no error */
  .
  .
  .
```

In both examples, we made the rather typical decision to terminate the entire program rather than the individual thread that encountered the error (that is, we called *exit* rather than *pthread_exit*). What you do depends upon what your program is doing and what type of error it encounters.

As you may have noticed, we normally don't test the return values of the Pthreads library calls we make in the code examples in this book. We felt that doing so would get in the way of the threads programming practices the examples are meant to illustrate. If we were writing this code for a commercial product, we would diligently perform all required error checking.

Why Use Threads Over Processes?

If both the process model and threads model can provide concurrent program execution, why use threads over processes?

Creating a new process can be expensive. It takes time. (A call into the operating system is needed, and if the process creation triggers process rescheduling activity, the operating system's context-switching mechanism will become involved.) It takes memory. (The entire process must be replicated.) Add to this the cost of interprocess communication and synchronization of shared data, which also may involve calls into the operating system kernel, and threads provide an attractive alternative.

Threads can be created without replicating an entire process. Furthermore, some, if not all, of the work of creating a thread is done in user space rather than kernel space. When processes synchronize, they usually have to issue system calls, a relatively expensive operation that involves trapping into the kernel. But threads can synchronize by simply monitoring a variable—in other words, staying within the user address space of the program.

We'll spell out the advantages of threads over the multiprocess model of multitasking in our performance measurements in Chapter 6, *Practical Considerations*. In the meantime, we'll show you how to build a multithreaded program.

A Structured Programming Environment

Revisiting the techniques used to obtain concurrency that we discussed earlier—potential parallelism, overlapping I/O, asynchronous events, and real-time scheduling—we find that UNIX offers many disjointed mechanisms to accomplish them between processes. They include the *select* system call, signals, nonblocking I/O, and the *setjmp/longjmp* system call pair, plus many calls for real time (such as *aio_read* and *aio_write*) and parallel processing. Pthreads offers a clean, consistent way to address all of these motivations. If you're a disciplined programmer, designing and coding a multithreaded program should be easier than designing and coding a multiprocess program.

Now, we know that the example program we've been looking at in this chapter is far too simple to convince anyone that a particular programming style is more structured or elegant than another. Subsequent examples will venture into more complex territory and, in doing so, illustrate Pthreads mechanisms for a more practical set of coding problems. We hope that they may make the case for Pthreads.

Choosing Which Applications to Thread

The major benefit of multithreaded programs over nonthreaded ones is in their ability to concurrently execute tasks. However, in providing concurrency, multithreaded programs introduce a certain amount of overhead. If you introduce threads in an application that can't use concurrency, you'll add overhead without any performance benefit.

So what makes concurrency possible? First, of course, your application must consist of some independent tasks—tasks that do not depend on the completion of other tasks to proceed. Secondly, you must be confident that concurrent execution of these tasks would be faster than their serial execution.

On a uniprocessing system, the concurrent execution of independent tasks will be faster than their serial execution if at least one of these tasks issues a lot of I/O requests and must wait for the device to complete each request. On a multiprocessor, even CPU-bound tasks can benefit from concurrency because they can truly proceed in parallel.

If you are writing an application for a uniprocessor, look at overlapping I/O and asynchronous events as the motivation for threading an application. If your program is hung up in doing a lot of disk, file, or network accesses when it could be doing other useful things, threads offer a means of doing them while the thread that handles the I/O is waiting.[*] If your program must deal with many asynchronous events, such as the receipt of an out-of-band message, threads give you an efficient way to structure its event handling where the only alternatives for a single-threaded process would be to either abruptly change context or put off handling the event to a more convenient time. The server portion of a client/server program often meets both of these criteria for concurrency: it must handle asynchronous requests and wait while retrieving and storing data in secondary storage.

If your application has been designed to use multiple processes, it's likely that it would benefit from threading. A common design model for a UNIX server daemon is to accept requests and fork a child image of itself to process the request. If the benefits of concurrency outweighed the overhead of using separate processes in the application, threading is bound to improve its performance because threads involve less overhead.

The remaining class of applications that can benefit from threads are those that execute on multiprocessing systems. Purely CPU-bound applications can achieve a performance boost with threads. A matrix-multiply program (or similar analytical program) with independent computational tasks but no excessive I/O requirements would not benefit from threads on a uniprocessing system. However, on a multiprocessor, this same application could speed up dramatically as the threads performed their computations in parallel.

As we'll see in Chapter 6, there are commonly three different types of Pthreads implementations. To take full advantage of a multiprocessing system, you'll need an implementation that's sophisticated enough to allow multiple threads in a single process to access multiple CPUs.

---

[*] A side benefit is that your code is ready to take advantage of multiprocessing systems in the future. Multiprocessing UNIX hosts are not restricted to exotic scientific number crunching anymore as two- to four-CPU server and desktop platforms have become commonplace.

2

Designing Threaded Programs

So far you've seen only a couple of Pthreads calls, but you know enough about the programming model to start considering real design issues. In this chapter we'll examine a number of broad questions. How much work is worth the overhead of creating a thread? How can I subdivide my program into threads? What relationship do the threads have to the functions in my program?

To give us a sample application worth threading, we'll introduce an application that will take us through most of the book: a server for automatic teller machines (ATMs). We'll try out our design ideas on this server.

Suitable Tasks for Threading

To find the places in your program where you can use threads, you essentially must look for the properties we identified in Chapter 1, *Why Threads?*: potential parallelism, overlapping I/O, asynchronous events, and real-time scheduling. Whenever a task has one or more of these properties, consider running it in a thread. You can identify a task that is suitable for threading by applying to it the following criteria:

- It is independent of other tasks.

  Does the task use separate resources from other tasks? Does its execution depend on the results of other tasks? Do other tasks depend on its results? We want to maximize concurrency and minimize the need for synchronization. The more tasks depend on each other and share resources, the more the threads executing them will end up blocked waiting on each other.

- It can become blocked in potentially long waits.

  Can the task spend a long time in a suspended state? A program can typically perform millions of integer operations in the time it would take to perform a single I/O operation. If you dedicate a thread to the I/O task, the rest of the program could accomplish a lot more work in less time.

- It can use a lot of CPU cycles.

  Does the task perform long computations, such as matrix crunching, hashing, or encryption? Time-consuming calculations that are independent of activities elsewhere in the program are good candidates for threading. In a multiprocessing environment, you might let a thread executing on one CPU process a long computation while other threads on other CPUs handle input.

- It must respond to asynchronous events.

  Must the task handle events that occur at random intervals, such as network communications or interrupts from hardware and the operating system? Use threads to encapsulate and synchronize the servicing of these events, apart from the rest of your application.

- Its work has greater or lesser importance than other work in the application.

  Must the task perform its work in a given amount of time? Must it run at specific times or specific time intervals? Is its work more time critical than that of other tasks? Scheduling considerations are often a good reason for threading a program. For instance, a window manager application would assign a high priority thread to user input and a much lower priority thread to memory garbage collection.

Server programs—such as those written for database managers, file servers, or print servers—are ideal applications for threading. They must be continuously responsive to asynchronous events—requests for services coming over communications channels from a number of client programs. Processing these requests typically requires I/O to secondary storage.

Computational and signal-processing applications that will run on multiprocessing systems are another good candidate for threading. They contain many CPU-intensive tasks that can be spread out over a number of available CPUs.

Finally, real-time developers are attracted to threads as a model for servers and multiprocessing applications. Multithreaded applications are more efficient than multiprocess applications. The threads model also allows the developers to set specific scheduling policies for threads. What's more, threads eliminate some of the complexity that comes with asynchronous programming. Threads wait for events whereas a serial program would be interrupted and would jump from context to context.

Models

There are no set rules for threading a program. Every program is different, and when you first try to thread a program, you'll likely discover that it's a matter of trial and error. You may initially dedicate a thread to a particular task only to find that your assumptions about its activity have changed or weren't true in the first place.

Over time a few common models for threaded programs have emerged. These models define how a threaded application delegates its work to its threads and how the threads intercommunicate. Because the Pthreads standard imposes little structure on how programmers use threads, you would do well to start your multi-threaded program design with a close look at each model. Although none has been explicitly designed for a specific type of application, you'll find that each model tends to be better suited than the others for certain types. We discuss:

- The boss/worker model
- The peer model
- The pipeline model

Boss/Worker Model

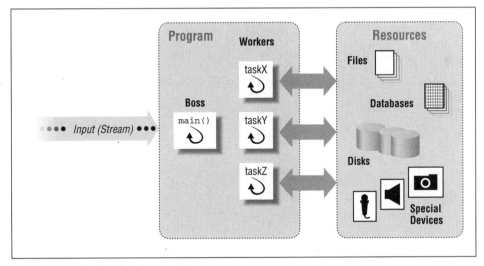

Figure 2–1: The boss/worker model

Figure 2-1 depicts the boss/worker model. A single thread, the *boss*, accepts input for the entire program. Based on that input, the boss passes off specific tasks to one or more *worker* threads.

The boss creates each worker thread, assigns it tasks, and, if necessary, waits for it to finish. In the pseudocode in Example 2-1, the boss dynamically creates a new worker thread when it receives a new request. In the *pthread_create* call it uses to create each worker thread, the boss specifies the task-related routine the thread will execute. After creating each worker, the boss returns to the top of its loop to process the next request. If no requests are waiting, the boss loops until one arrives.

Once finished, each worker thread can be made responsible for any output resulting from its task, or it can synchronize with the boss and let it handle its output.

Example 2-1: Boss/Worker Model Program (Pseudocode)

```
main()

/* The boss */
{
    forever {
            get a request
            switch request
            case X : pthread_create( ... taskX)
            case Y : pthread_create( ... taskY)
            .
            .
            .

    }
}
taskX() /* Workers processing requests of type X */
{
    perform the task, synchronize as needed if accessing shared resources
    done
}

taskY() /* Workers processing requests of type Y */
{
    perform the task, synchronize as needed if accessing shared resources
    done
}
.
.
.
```

If the boss creates its workers dynamically when requests arrive, as it does in our pseudocode, there will be as many concurrent worker threads as there are concurrent requests. Alternatively, the boss could save some run-time overhead by creating all worker threads up front. In this variant of the boss/worker model, known as a *thread pool* and shown in Example 2-2, the boss creates all worker threads at program initialization. Each worker immediately suspends itself to wait for a wakeup call from the boss when a request arrives for it to process. The boss advertises work by queuing requests on a list from which workers retrieve them.

Example 2–2: Boss/Worker Model Program with a Thread Pool (Pseudocode)

```
main()

/* The boss */
{
 for the number of workers
        pthread_create( ... pool_base )

 forever {
        get a request
        place request in work queue
        signal sleeping threads that work is available
 }
}
pool_base() /* All workers */
{
 forever {
        sleep until awoken by boss
        dequeue a work request
        switch
          case request X: taskX()
          case request Y: taskY()
            .
            .
            .

 }
}
```

The boss/worker model works well with servers (database servers, file servers, window managers, and the like). The complexities of dealing with asynchronously arriving requests and communications are encapsulated in the boss. The specifics of handling requests and processing data are delegated to the workers. In this model, it is important that you minimize the frequency with which the boss and workers communicate. The boss can't spend its time being blocked by its workers and allow new requests to pile up at the inputs. Likewise, you can't create too many interdependencies among the workers. If every request requires every worker to share the same data, all workers will suffer a slowdown.

Peer Model

Unlike the boss/worker model, in which one thread is in charge of work assignments for the other threads, in the peer model, illustrated in Figure 2-2, all threads work concurrently on their tasks without a specific leader.

In the peer model, also known as the *workcrew* model, one thread must create all the other peer threads when the program starts. However, unlike the boss thread in the boss/worker model, this thread subsequently acts as just another peer thread that processes requests, or suspends itself waiting for the other peers to finish.

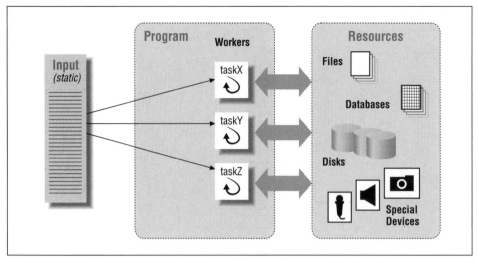

Figure 2-2: The peer model

Whereas the boss/worker model employs a stream of input requests to the boss, the peer model makes each thread responsible for its own input. A peer knows its own input ahead of time, has its own private way of obtaining its input, or shares a single point of input with other peers. The structure of such a program is shown in Example 2-3.

Example 2-3: Peer Model Program (Pseudocode)

```
main()
{
    pthread_create( ... thread1 ... task1 )
    pthread_create( ... thread2 ... task2 )
    .
    .
    .
    signal all workers to start
    wait for all workers to finish
    do any clean up
}

task1()
{
    wait for start
    perform task, synchronize as needed if accessing shared resources
    done
}

task2()
{
    wait for start
```

Example 2-3: Peer Model Program (Pseudocode) (continued)

```
    perform task, synchronize as needed if accessing shared resources
    done
}
```

The peer model is suitable for applications that have a fixed or well-defined set of inputs, such as matrix multipliers, parallel database search engines, and prime number generators. Well-defined input allows programs to adopt what could be construed as a boss/worker model without the boss. Because there is no boss, peers themselves must synchronize their access to any common sources of input. However, like workers in the boss/worker model, peers can also slow down if they must frequently synchronize to access shared resources.

Consider an application in which a single plane or space is divided among multiple threads, perhaps so they can calculate the spread of a life form (such as in the SimLife computer game) or changes in temperature as heat radiates across geographies from a source. Each thread can calculate one delta of change. However, because the results of each thread's calculations require the adjustment of the bounds of the next thread's calculations, all threads must synchronize afterward to exchange and compare each other's results. This is a classic example of a peer model application.

Pipeline Model

The pipeline model assumes:

- A long stream of input
- A series of suboperations (known as stages or filters) through which every unit of input must be processed
- Each processing stage can handle a different unit of input at a time

An automotive assembly line is a classic example of a pipeline. Each car goes through a series of stages on its way to the exit gates. At any given time many cars are in some stage of completion. A RISC (reduced instruction set computing) processor also fits the pipeline model. The input to this pipeline is a stream of instructions. Each instruction must pass through the stages of decoding, fetching operands, computation, and storing results. That many instructions may be at various stages of processing at the same time contributes to the exceptionally high performance of RISC processors.

In each of these examples, a pipeline improves throughput because it can accomplish the many different stages of a process on different input units (be they cars or instructions) concurrently. Instead of taking each car or instruction from start to finish before starting the next, a pipeline allows as many cars or instructions to be worked on at the same time as there are stages to process them. It still takes the same amount of time from start to finish for a specific car (that red one, for instance) or instruction to be processed, but the overall throughput of the assembly line or computer chip is greatly increased.

Figure 2-3 shows a thread pipeline.

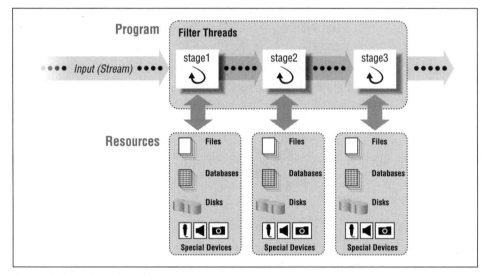

Figure 2-3: A thread pipeline

As the pseudocode in Example 2-4 illustrates, a single thread receives input for the entire program, always passing it to the thread that handles the first stage of processing. Similarly a single thread at the end of the pipeline produces all final output for the program. Each thread in between performs its own stage of processing on the input it received from the thread that performed the previous stage, and passes its output to the thread performing the next. Applications in which the pipeline might be useful are image processing and text processing or any application that can be broken down into a series of filter steps on a stream of input.

Example 2-4: Pipeline Model Program (pseudocode)

```
main()
{
    pthread_create( ... stage1 )
    pthread_create( ... stage2 )
    .
    .
    .
```

Example 2–4: Pipeline Model Program (pseudocode) (continued)

```
        wait for all pipeline threads to finish
        do any clean up
}

stage1()
{
    forever {
            get next input for the program
            do stage 1 processing of the input
            pass result to next thread in pipeline
            }
}

stage2()
{
    forever {
            get input from previous thread in pipeline
            do stage 2 processing of the input
            pass result to next thread in pipeline
            }
}

stageN()
{
    forever {
            get input from previous thread in pipeline
            do stage N processing to the input
            pass result to program output
            }
}
```

We could add multiplexing or demultiplexing to this pipeline, allowing multiple threads to work in parallel on a particular stage. We could also dynamically configure the pipeline at run time, having it create and terminate stages (and the threads to service them) as needed.

Note that the overall throughput of a pipeline is limited by the thread that processes its slowest stage. Threads that follow it in the pipeline cannot perform their stages until it has completed. When designing a multithreaded program according to the pipeline model, you should aim at balancing the work to be performed across all stages; that is, all stages should take about the same amount of time to complete.

Buffering Data Between Threads

The boss/worker, peer, and pipeline are models for complete multithreaded programs. Within any of these models threads transfer data to each other using buffers. In the boss/worker model, the boss must transfer requests to the workers. In the pipeline model, each thread must pass input to the thread that performs the next stage of processing. Even in the peer model, peers may often exchange data.

A thread assumes either of two roles as it exchanges data in a buffer with another thread. The thread that passes the data to another is known as the *producer*; the one that receives that data is known as the *consumer*. Figure 2-4 depicts this relationship.

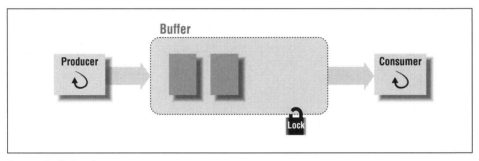

Figure 2–4: Producer-consumer

The ideal producer/consumer relationship requires:

A buffer

   The buffer can be any data structure accessible to both the producer and the consumer. This is a simple matter for a multithreaded program, for a such a shared buffer need only be in the process's global data region. The buffer can be just big enough to hold one data item or it can be larger, depending upon the application.

A lock

   Because the buffer is shared, the producer and consumer must synchronize their access to it. With Pthreads, you would use a mutex variable as a lock.

A suspend/resume mechanism

   The consumer may suspend itself when the buffer contains no data for it to consume. If so, the producer must be able to resume it when it places a new item in the buffer. With Pthreads, you would arrange this mechanism using a condition variable.

State information

Some flag or variable should indicate how much data is in the buffer.

In the pseudocode in Example 2-5, the producer thread takes a lock on the shared buffer, places a work item in it, releases the lock, and resumes the consumer thread. The consumer thread is more complex. It first takes a lock on the shared buffer. If it finds the buffer empty, it releases the lock (thus giving the producer a chance to populate it with work) and hibernates. When the consumer thread awakens, it reacquires the lock, and removes a work item from the buffer.

Example 2-5: Producer/Consumer Threads (Pseudocode)

```
producer()
{
    .

    .

    .
    lock shared buffer
    place results in buffer
    unlock buffer
    wake up any consumer threads
    .

    .

    .
}

consumer()
{
    .

    .

    .
    lock shared buffer
    while state is not full {
            release lock and sleep
            awake and reacquire lock
            }
    remove contents
    unlock buffer
    .

    .

    .
}
```

If the threads share a buffer that can hold more than one data item, the producer can keep producing new items even if the consumer thread has not yet processed the previous one. In this case the producer and consumer must agree upon a mechanism for keeping track of how many items are currently in the buffer.

You can devise other permutations of the producer/consumer relationship based on the number of producer and consumer threads that access the same buffer. For example, an application that adopts the boss/worker model and uses a thread pool must accommodate a single producer (the boss) and many consumers (the workers).

A more specialized producer/consumer relationship, often used in pipelines for signal processing applications, uses a technique known as *double buffering.* Using double buffering, threads act as both producer and consumer to each other. In the example of double buffering shown in Figure 2-5, one set of buffers contains unprocessed data and another set contains processed data. One thread—the I/O thread—obtains unprocessed data from an I/O device and places it in a shared buffer. (In other words, it's the producer of unprocessed data.) The I/O thread also obtains processed data from another shared buffer and writes it to an I/O device. (That is, it's the consumer of processed data.) A second thread—the calculating thread—obtains unprocessed data from the shared buffer filled by the I/O thread, processes it, and places its results in another shared buffer. The calculating thread is thus the consumer of unprocessed data and the producer of processed data.

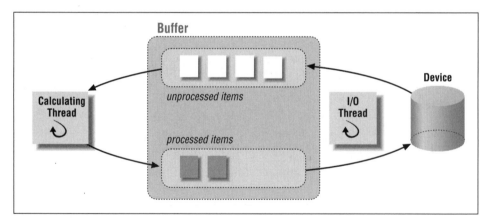

Figure 2-5: Double buffering

Some Common Problems

Regardless of the model you select, a few classes of bugs creep into nearly every threaded application at some point during its development. Avoiding them takes a lot of concentration. Finding them once they've crept in requires patience and persistence. Most bugs result from oversights in the way the application manages its shared resources. Either you forget to keep one thread out of a resource while another is modifying it, or the way in which you attempt to synchronize access to the resource causes your threads to hang. We'll walk through a debugging session for a multithreaded program in Chapter 6, *Practical Considerations*. For the time being, we'll rest content with pronouncing a few basic rules and noting the most common pitfalls.

The basic rule for managing shared resources is simple and twofold:

- Obtain a lock before accessing the resource.

- Release the lock when you are finished with the resource.

Unfortunately, there are many borderline areas of usage where it is difficult to clearly apply this rule. In those applications in which locks and resources must be created dynamically—while multiple threads are already running—you can get into trouble very easily. The symptoms of sharing without proper synchronization are often subtle: incorrect answers and corrupted data. It is often quite hard to track down the point in the program where the error or corruption occurred. Further, the effort of debugging is often exacerbated by difficulties you may have in reproducing the bug. It is much easier to run a single-threaded program with the same inputs and get the same outputs. Programs that take advantage of concurrency aren't like that. A multithreaded program with a synchronization bug may run correctly hundreds of times for every time that it fails.

The other common bug in threaded programs results from assumptions about the "liveliness" of its threads. When a thread attempts to obtain a lock, it assumes that any thread currently holding that lock will eventually let it go. If that thread fails to release the lock for whatever reason—it hangs or it simply forgets—other threads will grind to a halt as they wait for it to release its lock. You can encounter the same problem if you make a thread wait for some variable to reach an unreachable value or wait on a condition variable that is never signaled.

Performance

When considering the performance of a threaded application, note that threads can represent negligible to significant overhead, depending on how they are implemented and how they are used. Before you add threads to a program, be sure that the benefits of threading outweigh the costs. Some of the costs of threading include:

- The memory and CPU cycles required to manage each thread, including the structures the operating system uses to manage them, plus the overhead for the Pthreads library and any special code in the operating system that supports the library.

- The CPU cycles spent for synchronization calls that enforce orderly access to shared data. These calls cost in CPU cycles to execute the calls.

- The time during which the application is inactive while one thread is waiting on another thread. This cost results from too many dependencies among threads and can be allayed by improved program design.

Example: An ATM Server

Example 2-6 is a client/server program that implements an imaginary automated teller machine (ATM) application. This server will give us an opportunity to exercise our thinking about multithreaded program design and explore more realistic—and more complicated—thread handling applications.

As shown in Figure 2-6, the example is made up of a client that provides a user interface[*] and a server that processes requests from the client. On disk, the server stores a database of bank accounts, each including an account ID, password, and balance.

In a typical ATM operation, a customer chooses a withdrawal from a menu presented by the client and enters the amount to be withdrawn. The client packages this information into a request that it sends to the server. The server spawns a thread that checks the user's password against the one in the database, decrements the amount of money in the user's account, and sends back an indication of whether the operation succeeded. The client and server process communicate using UNIX sockets. The client reports any information returned from the server back to the user. Multiple clients can run simultaneously.

We want the server to be capable of overlapping I/O, because the account data is stored in secondary storage and its access will require a significant amount of time. The environment is asynchronous because multiple clients may exist simultaneously, sending requests of unpredictable type, order, and frequency.

In the following sections of this chapter, we'll discuss two different implementations of this program: a serial version and a multithreaded version that uses Pthreads.[†] The multithreaded version of the program uses the boss/worker model inside the server. The boss looks at the first field of each request, then spawns a thread or process to handle that request. When the worker completes the request, it communicates the results directly back to the client program.

---

[*] The client for an ATM application should be an actual machine, but, for the purposes of this book, we'll just make it a command-line program that accepts typed-in requests. (Unfortunately, this type of client isn't realistic enough to spit out ten dollar bills.)

[†] You can obtain the complete source code for all versions of the ATM example, including that for the multiprocess version used in our performance testing in Chapter 6, from our ftp site. Throughout this chapter, we'll show only those interfaces and routines pertinent to the current discussion.

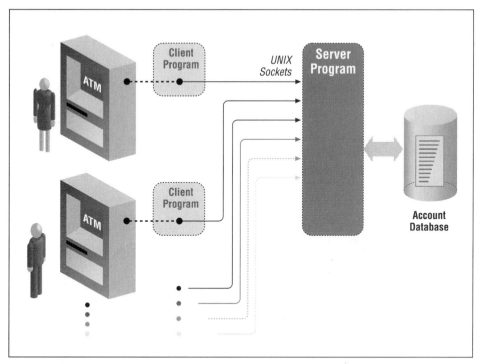

Figure 2-6: The ATM and bank database server example

For simplicity's sake, we've partitioned the client and server into modules. The interfaces between these modules will remain unchanged throughout all versions of our example. We'll change only the dispatch and service routine module from one version to another. Table 2-1 shows the contents of the client and server modules.

Table 2-1: The ATM Example Program Modules

Module	Component	Description
Client program	User interface (*main*)	Prompts a customer for a request, parses the response, and makes a remote procedure call (RPC) to access the server.
	RPC	Includes a procedure for each possible type of request. Each procedure copies its arguments into a buffer and passes the buffer to the communication module for transmission to the server. When a response arrives from the server, the procedure checks its return values.

Table 2-1: The ATM Example Program Modules (continued)

Module	Component	Description
Server program	Communication	Finds and passes buffers to and from the server using UNIX sockets.
	Communication	Receives and transmits buffers to clients using UNIX sockets.
	Dispatch (and service) routines (*main)*	Obtains input buffers from clients by means of the communication module, identifies the request type and copies out arguments, and calls the service routine that handles the requested operation. Together, the dispatch and service routines make up the server-side procedures of the client's RPC. When request processing is complete, the dispatch routine prepares and transmits a response buffer to the client.
	Database routines	Reads from and writes to the account database file using standard file I/O.

The Serial ATM Server

If we didn't have threads, what would be the simplest implementation of the ATM server? One that comes to mind is a program that runs in a loop, processing available requests serially. If a request is available, the program processes it in a request-specific service routine and sends a response to the client. The *main* routine for this version of the server is shown in Example 2-6.

Example 2-6: Serial ATM Server: main Routine (atm_svr_serial.c)

```
extern int
main(argc, argv)
int argc;
char **argv;
{
  char req_buf[COMM_BUF_SIZE], resp_buf[COMM_BUF_SIZE];
  int   conn;
  int   trans_id;
  int   done=0;

  atm_server_init(argc, argv);

  /* loop forever */
  for(;;) {

    server_comm_get_request(&conn, req_buf);
    sscanf(req_buf, "%d", &trans_id);
```

Example 2-6: Serial ATM Server: main Routine (atm_svr_serial.c) (continued)

```
        switch(trans_id) {

          case CREATE_ACCT_TRANS:
               create_account(resp_buf);
               break;

          case DEPOSIT_TRANS:
               deposit(req_buf, resp_buf);
               break;

          case WITHDRAW_TRANS:
               withdraw(req_buf, resp_buf);
               break;

          case BALANCE_TRANS:
               balance(req_buf, resp_buf);
               break;

          case SHUTDOWN:
               if (shutdown_req(req_buf, resp_buf)) done = 1;
               break;

          default:
               handle_bad_trans_id(req_buf, resp_buf);
               break;

          }

        server_comm_send_response(conn, resp_buf);

        if(done) break;

      }

      server_comm_shutdown();
    }
  return 0;
```

The serial version of our ATM server can process only a single request at a time, no matter how many clients are requesting service.

Handling asynchronous events: blocking with select

The server handles the asynchronous arrival of requests from clients by waiting. When the server's *main* routine calls *server_comm_get_request*, the server's communication layer uses a UNIX *select* call to determine which channels have data on them waiting to be read. If none do, the *select* call (and consequently the *server_comm_get_request* call) blocks until data arrives.

Handling file I/O: blocking with read/write

The server in Example 2-6 does nothing but block when performing file operations. When it issues a *read* or *write* call to the file, the server waits until the operating system completes the operation and the call returns.

The server could have used UNIX signals to access the file without blocking. If so, it would need to establish a signal handler that processes the results of its I/O requests and to register this handler with the operating system such that it takes control when the completion of an I/O request is signaled. This would allow the server to make asynchronous I/O calls that return immediately. When the request completes at a later time, the server is interrupted and put into its signal handler to process the results.

The big drawback for using asynchronous I/O in a serial server is in the complicated state management and synchronization problems that arise between the server and its signal handler. The program must keep track of the state of all in-progress requests. It must create and maintain locks for various resources (such as account records) so that they are not simultaneously accessed in program and signal contexts. Finally, the clean division of the program into modules breaks down. The communication, server, and database modules all get mixed together.

All in all, the experiment of using asynchronous I/O in a serial ATM server is a good argument for designing such a server to use threads. It's much cleaner to let a single thread wait for I/O to complete than it is to manage the complexity of signals and synchronization.

The serial version of our ATM server works—in fact, it works quite well—when the input stream of requests is light. However, the performance of the serial server degrades rapidly as more and more clients request access to its data. Clients begin to see longer and longer delays in the processing of their requests because all are blocked by server access to the database. In Chapter 6, we'll run some tests on single-threaded and multithreaded versions of the server that show the point at which it becomes inefficient to use the serial version.

What can we do to improve the performance of our server under load? It can help a lot to allow it to move on to another client request while its I/O to the database is proceeding. The next versions of our server will do just that.

The Multithreaded ATM Server

Let's add threads to our example. We'll begin by identifying those tasks we want individual threads to process. Having each request processed by a separate thread may or may not be a good starting point.

Before we pursue our design, let's step back and look again at the general criteria for selecting tasks for threads. In general we'd like to select tasks for our ATM server's threads based on whether:

- They are independent of each other.

  If we assume that simultaneous accesses to the same account are rare, it makes sense to have each request processed by a separate thread. Threads will not compete for account data. No individual thread will rely on the work accomplished by another thread to complete its work.

- They can become blocked in potentially long waits.

  This is true of all requests to our server, because any access to the account database could involve disk access to a file.

- They can use a lot of CPU cycles.

  Our server contains no tasks that can be defined as compute intensive.

- They must respond to asynchronous events.

  This is true of the manner in which the communication layer of our server accepts client requests.

- They require scheduling.

  In our first pass at a multithreaded version of our ATM server we won't use scheduling. But we can imagine that certain operations could be given higher priority than others. A thread handling a shutdown request might be given priority over other requests. If we used the database to generate monthly account statements, we could give those requests lower priority than direct customer requests to bank accounts.

We must also bear in mind some key constraints our ATM server places on our program design:

- We must maintain correctness.

  For the multithreaded version of our ATM server to produce correct and consistent results, we must ensure that two threads don't corrupt an account by writing information to it simultaneously. Thus, we'll use locks to protect the account data.

- We must maintain the liveliness of the threads.

  We must avoid those types of programming bugs in which a worker thread obtains a lock on account data and then exits without releasing the lock. Other worker threads that subsequently attempt to obtain the lock on the same data will deadlock, waiting forever.

- We must minimize overhead.

  Our threads can't spend all their time synchronizing with each other or they are not worth their overhead. As a simplification, we'll start out in our example by allocating a thread for each request. We can later enhance it by allowing threads to remain active, waiting for new requests (that is, we could use a thread pool).

Model: boss/worker model

Because it's a classic server program, we'll use the boss/worker model for our ATM server. A boss thread accepts input from remote clients through the communication module. Worker threads handle each client account request.

Figure 2-7 shows the structure of our ATM example program using the boss/worker ATM server. The boss thread is neatly encapsulated by the server's *main* routine. Each worker thread runs one service routine: deposit, withdraw, and so on.

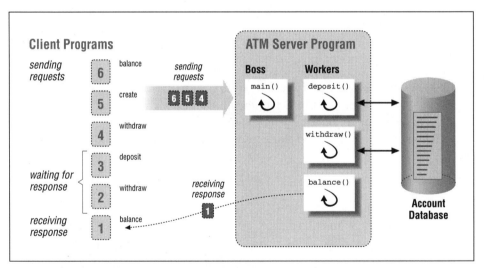

Figure 2–7: The boss/worker Pthreads ATM server

The boss thread

We'll start building our multithreaded ATM server's boss thread from our serial server's *main* routine. The boss thread simply manages the receipt of incoming requests using the *server_comm_get_request* routine. After it obtained each request from the communication module, the serial server's *main* routine unpacked it and called the appropriate service routine. The boss thread's *main* routine will create a worker thread to which it will pass the request. The worker thread begins by executing a generic request-processing routine called *process_request*, as shown in Example 2-7.

Example 2-7: Multithreaded ATM Server: Boss Thread (atm_svr.c)

```
typedef struct workorder{
        int conn;
        char req_buf[COMM_BUF_SIZE];
        } workorder_t;
extern int
main(argc, argv)
int argc;
char **argv;
{
  workorder_t *workorderp;
  pthread_t    *worker_threadp;
  int   conn;
  int   trans_id;

  atm_server_init(argc, argv);

  for(;;) {

    /*** Wait for a request ***/
    workorderp = (workorder_t *)malloc(sizeof(workorder_t));
    server_comm_get_request(&workorderp->conn, workorderp->req_buf);

    sscanf(workorderp->req_buf, "%d", &trans_id);  ⟵
    if (trans_id == SHUTDOWN) {
            .
            .
            .
            break;
            }

    /*** Spawn a thread to process this request ***/
    worker_threadp=(pthread_t *)malloc(sizeof(pthread_t));
    pthread_create(worker_threadp, NULL, process_request, (void *)workorderp);

    pthread_detach(*worker_threadp);
    free(worker_threadp);
  }

  server_comm_shutdown();
  return 0;
}
```

Dynamically detaching a thread

In the code for our boss thread's *main* routine, we've introduced a new Pthreads call—*pthread_detach*. The *pthread_detach* function notifies the Pthreads library that we don't want to join our worker threads: that is, we will never request their exit status. If we don't explicitly tell the Pthreads library that we don't care about a thread's exit status, it'll keep the shadow of the thread alive indefinitely after the thread terminates (in the same way that UNIX keeps the status of zombie processes around). Detaching our worker threads frees the Pthreads library from storing this information, thus saving space and time. We are still responsible for freeing any space we dynamically allocated to hold the *pthread_t* itself.

Aside from using *pthread_detach* on an existing thread, you can create threads already in the detached state. We'll discuss this method in Chapter 4, *Managing Pthreads*.

A worker thread

In our multithreaded ATM server, each worker thread begins its life in a new request-parsing routine called *process_request*. This is a generic request-parsing routine that all workers use regardless of which requests they actually process. Because different service routines process different requests, the primary job of *process_request* is to select the proper service routine. We accomplish this by means of a simple case statement, shown in Example 2-8.

Example 2-8: Multithreaded ATM Server: Worker Thread process_request

```
void process_request(workorder_t *workorderp)
{
  char resp_buf[COMM_BUF_SIZE];
  int  trans_id;
  sscanf(workorderp->req_buf, "%d", &trans_id);

  switch(trans_id) {

      case CREATE_ACCT_TRANS:
          create_account(resp_buf);
          break;

      case DEPOSIT_TRANS:
          deposit(workorderp->req_buf, resp_buf);
          break;

      case WITHDRAW_TRANS:
          withdraw(workorderp->req_buf, resp_buf);
          break;

      case BALANCE_TRANS:
          balance(workorderp->req_buf, resp_buf);
          break;

      default:
          handle_bad_trans_id(workorderp->req_buf, resp_buf);
          break;
  }
```

Example 2–8: Multithreaded ATM Server: Worker Thread process_request (continued)

```
        server_comm_send_response(workorderp->conn,
                              resp_buf);

    free(workorderp);

}
```

In our ATM example, the boss thread is always active. It creates worker threads, as needed, to process requests. Each active worker could be processing a request on a different account, or each worker could be performing a separate operation on the same account. It shouldn't matter to our program. The boss thread limits the number of active worker threads in the server.

At any given time in the ATM example, a request could be in one of three places:

- Queued at the server's communication module, waiting to be picked up by the boss thread
- In the boss thread's hands, about to be passed off to a worker thread
- In the hands of a worker thread, being processed

Synchronization: what's needed

So far, we haven't shown any synchronization between the threads in our multi-threaded ATM server. We'll go into the details in Chapter 3, *Synchronizing Pthreads*, and Chapter 4.

Right now we'll just list what synchronization we'll need:

- Accounts

  Now that we have multiple workers accessing the database through the service routines (*deposit, withdraw,* and *balance*), we'll need to deal with the possibility that two routines may try to manipulate the same account balance at the same time. To prevent simultaneous access, we'll protect database accesses with a mutex variable.

- Limiting the number of workers

  To keep from overloading the CPUs, the boss must limit the number of worker threads that can exist concurrently. It must maintain an ongoing count of worker threads and decrement the count as threads exit. We'll do that and add a check for exiting worker threads.

- Server shutdown

  The ATM client lets privileged users shut down the server. To make our server more robust, we must ensure that the server has completed the requests that are already in progress before it stops accepting new requests and shuts itself down. We'll do this by adding code so that the boss can tell when threads are active.

Future enhancements

We'll add the synchronization we discussed to our multithreaded ATM server in Chapter 3. We'll also enhance our server throughout the remainder of this book. Among the design refinements we'll consider are:

- Thread pools

  Our ATM server creates a worker thread each time it receives a request and pays the cost of thread creation each time. What if we allowed our server to reuse worker threads? When the server starts, it can create a predetermined number of workers in an idle state. Each worker thread could take requests off a queue and return to an idle state (instead of exiting) after completing each request. The reduction in overhead would pay off in performance.

- Cancellation

  In a couple of situations it would be useful if the boss thread could interrupt and terminate a worker thread: to cancel an in-progress request that is no longer wanted or to support a quick shutdown.

- Scheduling

  We could give some threads—possibly shutdown threads and deposit threads—priority over other threads. When a CPU becomes available, we could give these threads first crack at it.

Example: A Matrix Multiplication Program

In this section we'll look at a program very different from the ATM client/server example: one that exemplifies how you can break down a program into tasks. Whereas we used the boss/worker model to design our ATM server, we'll use the peer model for this one.

A large class of programs are computationally intensive and work on large sets of data: image processing, statistical analysis, and finite element modeling, to name a few. In some cases these programs may require I/O to databases or to multiple devices. Our example uses a simple matrix-multiply program to look at the peer design model, which is commonly used in these programs.

Matrix multiplication takes two two-dimensional input arrays of data and computes a third. If you remember your matrix algebra, the multiplication goes like this:

$$c_{row,col} = a_{row,1} * b_{1,col} + a_{row,2} * b_{2,col} \cdots + a_{row,n} * b_{n,col}$$

$$\Sigma \; a_{ik} b_{kj}$$

A program that performs a matrix multiplication must compute the value of every element in the result array. If the program is nonthreaded, the total time for the program is the time it takes to compute an individual element multiplied by the number of elements.

For other programs in this class, the operation on each element of input may not be specifically multiplication—perhaps encryption, translation, or comparison. Also, the input data may not always be a well-formed array. However, all will have the characteristic of repeating some basic operation over and over again on subsets of their data. We can improve the performance of these programs using threads in two ways: by providing overlapping I/O and by parallel processing.

If processing the input elements required I/O, threading would allow the program to continue while one thread blocked waiting for I/O completion (see Figure 2-8). If the input and output arrays of our matrix-multiply program were stored on disk (or even were the input from individual remote sensors), threads could block individually on the I/O operations they needed to complete while other threads continued.

When our matrix-multiply program is run on a multiprocessing system, as shown in Figure 2-9, the threads assigned to different elements of the matrix could run in parallel on different CPUs, thus decreasing the time it takes for the program to complete.

Although our matrix-multiply program is a gross simplification of these kinds of programs, it is still a useful example of the benefits of threading. Our program will have small fixed-sized in-memory arrays; it has no I/O, so we won't be demonstrating overlapping I/O in this case. Also, the computation time for an element is so short in comparison to the setup time and overhead of a thread that, even if you ran it on a multiprocessing system, you might not notice a performance improvement.

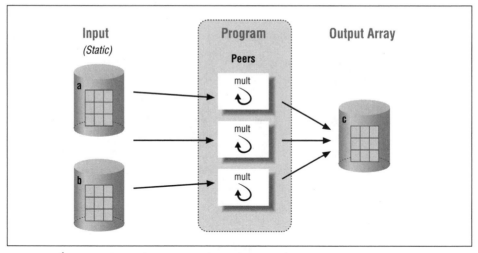

Figure 2-8: Improving performance with overlapping I/O

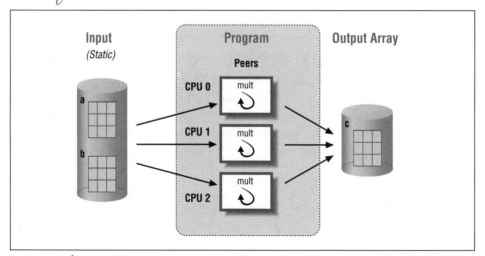

Figure 2-10: Improving performance with parallel processing

The Serial Matrix-Multiply Program

Before we develop a threaded version of this program, let's look at the serial version in Example 2-9.

Example 2-9: Serial Matrix-Multiply Program (matrix_serial.c)

```
#include <stdio.h>
#define ARRAY_SIZE 10

typedef int matrix_t[ARRAY_SIZE][ARRAY_SIZE];
matrix_t MA,MB,MC;

/* Routine to multiply a row by a column and place element in the result matrix. */

void mult(int size,             /* size of the matrix */
          int row,              /* row of result to compute */
          int column,           /* column of result to compute */
          matrix_t MA,          /* input matrix */
          matrix_t MB,          /* input matrix */
          matrix_t MC) {        /* result matrix */

     int position;

     MC[row][column] = 0;
     for(position = 0; position < size; position++) {
          MC[row][column] = MC[row][column] +
            ( MA[row][position]  *  MB[position][column] ) ;
     }
}

/* Main: allocates matrix, assigns values, computes the results */

main() {
     int size = ARRAY_SIZE, row, column;

     /* Fill in matrix values */
      .
      .
      .

     /* Process matrix, by row, column */

     for(row = 0; row < size; row++)     {
       for (column = 0; column < size; column++) {

 mult(size, row, column, MA, MB, MC);
       }
     }
     /* Print matrix */
     printf("MATRIX: The resulting matrix C is:\n");
     for(row = 0; row < size; row ++) {
       for (column = 0; column < size; column++) {
       printf("%5d ",MC[row][column]);
       }
     printf("\n");
     }
}
```

Example 2-9: Serial Matrix-Multiply Program (matrix_serial.c) (continued)

The arrays are named *MA*, *MB*, and *MC* (*MA* × *MB* = *MC*). The *mult* routine computes the result for an individual element in *MC* by multiplying the proper elements of *MA* by *MB* and adds the products. In the main program, a loop calls this routine for each element of *MC*.

The Multithreaded Matrix-Multiply Program

For the threaded version in Example 2-10, we'll use the peer model to organize the program's threads. We'll create a peer thread for each individual element in the result array *MC* and assign it to compute the result. A main thread will also exist— not so much as a peer thread but as a setup and cleanup thread. It performs all of the setup tasks for the program, creates the peer threads, and waits for them to complete. When they do, the main thread prints the results and terminates the program.*

Example 2-10: Multithreaded Matrix-Multiply Program main Routine

```
/* main: allocates matrix, assigns values, computes the results */
.
.
.
typedef struct {
  int       id;
  int       size;
  int       row;
  int       column;
  matrix_t  *MA,
  matrix_t  *MB,
  matrix_t  *MC;
} matrix_work_order_t;
.
.
extern int
main(void) {
      int size = ARRAY_SIZE, row, column;
      matrix_t MA,MB,MC;

      matrix_work_order_t *work_orderp;
      pthread_t peer[size*size];
.
      .
      .
      /* Process Matrix, by row, column */
```

---

* This design might cause a problem on some systems when the number of threads that must be created to handle a very large matrix swamp the system. A more sophisticated solution would be to limit the number of created threads based on the number of available CPUs.

Example 2–10: Multithreaded Matrix-Multiply Program main Routine (continued)

```
    for(row = 0; row < size; row++)      {
      for (column = 0; column < size; column++) {

            id = column + row*10;

            work_orderp =
            (work_order_t *)malloc(sizeof(matrix_work_order_t));
            work_orderp->id = id;
            work_orderp->size = size;
            work_orderp->row = row;
            work_orderp->column = column;
            work_orderp->MA = &MA;
            work_orderp->MB = &MB;
            work_orderp->MC = &MC;

            pthread_create(&(peer[id]), NULL, (void *)peer_mult,
                              (void *)work_orderp);
      }
    }

            /* Wait for peers to exit */
    for (i = 0; i < (size * size); i++) {
        pthread_join(peer[i], NULL);
    }
    .
    .
    return 0;
}
```

In the serial version of our matrix-multiply program (Example 2-9), the *main* routine made a procedure call to invoke the *mult* routine. In the multithreaded version (Example 2-10), the *main* routine creates a peer thread to do the job. There is one complication, though—the *mult* routine as used in the serial version has many arguments, but the *pthread_create* function lets threads start only in routines that are passed a single argument. We'll explain the solution in the next section.

Passing data to a new thread

This limitation of *pthread_create* is annoying, but there is a standard solution that we employ in Example 2-11. We bundle everything the *main* routine wants to pass to its peer threads into a single structure. We call this structure the *matrix_work_order_t*, and it contains fields for all of the arguments passed to the serial program's *mult* routine. Our *main* routine passes each peer thread a pointer to a *matrix_work_order_t* structure as the last argument in the *pthread_create* call.

A common error is not passing the new thread a work order structure that is unique. You may have noticed that our ATM and matrix-multiply programs allocate the data they intend to pass to their threads by using a *malloc* call just prior to the *pthread_create* call. If instead they used a static structure, or placed the *malloc* outside of the "for" loop, the *main* would continuously overwrite the contents of the same structure, and all threads would see values that were intended only for the most recently created thread.

Using the *matrix_work_order_t* structure lets the *main* routine bundle various pieces of information into a single *pthread_create* argument, but the thread's start routine must accept only a single argument. It would be nice to reuse our *mult* routine as a start routine, but its multiple arguments make that impossible. This is common occurrence when trying to use legacy code with threads. Here too we'll use a standard solution. We'll define a new start routine for the peer threads. It'll be a simple wrapper over the preexisting *mult* routine. The *peer_mult* routine takes the pointer to the *matrix_work_order_t* structure that was passed in through *pthread_create* and uses the information from the structure to call the *mult* routine.

Example 2–11: Multithreaded Matrix-Multiply Program peer_mult Routine

```
/*
 * Routine to start off a peer thread
 */

void peer_mult(matrix_work_order_t *work_orderp)
{

  mult(work_orderp->size,
       work_orderp->row,
       work_orderp->column,
       *(work_orderp->MA),
       *(work_orderp->MB),
       *(work_orderp->MC));

  free(work_orderp);
}
```

Synchronization in the matrix-multiply program

Our multithreaded matrix-multiply example doesn't need much unusual synchronization:

* The main thread must wait for the peers to complete. It uses *pthread_join* to do so.

* No data synchronization is required because the peers never write to any shared locations.

- Threads only read the values in the input arrays; we don't have to worry about synchronizing access because someone may change those values.

- The computation of each element in the result array is completely independent of the results for any other element in the result array. We don't need to be concerned about the order in which threads complete the computation of their elements.

Because thread programmers are rarely this lucky, we need to turn the page to Chapter 3.

To do:
- hard copy of ATM server ✓
- hard copy of tpool ✓
- hard copy of linked list ✓
Port ATM Server to Win32. (later)

3

Synchronizing Pthreads

Creating threads is the easy part. It's harder to get them to share data properly. We're tempted to make the obvious analogy to children. To prevent damage to the Nintendo (and the children), we'll only let the one who folds the laundry that evening play Donkey Kong. Similarly, to make threads share data safely, we must ensure that threads that would otherwise behave independently access shared data in an orderly and controlled way. This concept is called *synchronization.* (The other concept is called good parenting.)

Sooner or later, you'll probably make a programming error and fail to synchronize threads. It would be nice if you could get a feel for the symptoms of synchronization failures so that you can react quickly and expertly to such a disaster. Unfortunately, as we'll see, almost any type of quirky behavior might be regarded as a symptom of a synchronization failure. Worse, you may see problems only every so often when you run your program; at other times, if the threads in the program just happen to access data in the right order in a particular run, the program may run fine. So you may notice incorrect output at random times—perhaps in one run out of a hundred. In fact, this come-and-go quality of errors may be the best indicator that your bug is in the way in which you've handled thread synchronization.

Let's suppose we forgot to include synchronization in the ATM server we created in Chapter 2, *Designing Threaded Programs.* When one of our imaginary bank's customers deposits money in an account, she expects that, ultimately, her account balance will be its original value plus the amount she deposited. She probably can't even conceive of anything our bank could do to interfere with her transaction and cause her end balance to be any different than she expects. In other words, she assumes that her deposit is a single, indivisible transaction (if she were a software engineer, she'd know that the word for that type of transaction is *atomic*) that occurs in isolation from other transactions. It's anything but. Her deposit may consist of many, many separate tasks: disk reads, memory reads, calculations, data modifications, memory writes, disk writes, and more. Worse, without synchronization in our ATM server, we'll allow a similar transaction to preempt her deposit at any step—before all of the steps required to make it a deposit have completed.

But it's likely she'll have no problems until, for instance, she tries to withdraw $50 from her account at the same time her husband across town also tries to withdraw $50. This type of problem is known as a *race condition*. A race condition is illustrated in Figure 3-1.

Time	Thread 1	Thread 2	Balance
	(Withdraw $50)	(Withdraw $50)	
	read balance: $125		$ 125
		read balance: $125	$ 125
		set balance: $(125-50)	$ 75
	set balance: $(125-50)		$ 75
	give out cash: $50		$ 75
		give out cash: $50	$ 75

Figure 3-1: ATM race condition with two withdraw threads

In a race condition, two or more threads access the same resource at the same time. In Figure 3-1, Thread 1 and Thread 2 simultaneously attempt a withdrawal from the same bank account. Thread 1 reads the current balance of the account—$125. However, before it can proceed with the other steps that complete the withdrawal (the arithmetic, the storing of the new result, and the dispensing of cash), it is preempted by Thread 2. Thread 2 also reads the account balance—$125, but Thread 2 continues on to complete the transaction. It subtracts $50 from $125, stores the new balance, $75, in the account database, and hands the customer a $50 bill. Sometime thereafter, Thread 1 resumes, subtracts $50 from $125 (which is what it thinks is the account balance), stores the new balance, $75, in the account database, and hands the other customer a $50 bill. Nothing looks wrong to either thread, but in actuality, we've allowed one thread to clobber the write of another. We've subtracted a total of $100 from $125 and have come up with $75. A bank could lose a lot of money if this was allowed to happen.*

The problem with our ATM server is that the three key steps in the withdraw transaction—the reading of the balance, the calculation of the new balance, and the storing of the new balance in the account database—should be atomic. Either all of the steps are performed together without interruption, or none of them are.

[Op1, TP2, Op3] need to be atomic, no interference.

Selecting the Right Synchronization Tool

You can choose from among many Pthreads functions to obtain some type of synchronization:

pthread_join function

> *pthread_join* allows one thread to suspend execution until another has terminated. We discussed the *pthread_join* function in Chapter 1, *Why Threads?*

Mutex variable functions

> A mutex variable acts as a mutually exclusive lock, allowing threads to control access to data. The threads agree that only one thread at a time can hold the lock and access the data it protects. We'll discuss mutex variables in this chapter.

Condition variable functions

> A condition variable provides a way of naming an event in which threads have a general interest. An event can be something as simple as a counter's reaching a particular value or a flag being set or cleared; it may be something more complex, involving a specific coincidence of multiple events. Threads are interested in these events, because such events signify that some condition has been met that allows them to proceed with some particular phase of their execution. The Pthreads library provides ways for threads both to express their interest in a condition and to signal that an awaited condition has been met. We'll discuss condition variables in this chapter.

pthread_once function

> *pthread_once* is a specialized synchronization tool that ensures that initialization routines get executed once and only once when called by multiple threads. We'll discuss the *pthread_once* function in Chapter 4, *Managing Pthreads*.

These synchronization tools provide all that you need to write almost any program you can imagine. We can safely say that you can create whatever complex

---

* Actually, the error just happened to be in the customer's favor because the operations were both withdrawals. If the operations were deposits, the error would be in the bank's favor.

synchronization tools you may need from these basic building blocks. Some of the common synchronization mechanisms are:

Reader/writer exclusion
> Reader/writer locks allow multiple threads to read data concurrently but ensure that any thread writing to the data has exclusive access.

Threadsafe data structures
> You may find it useful to build synchronization primitives into a complex data structure so that each time you access it you don't need to make a separate call to synchronize concurrent access. For instance a queue library may include *enqueue* and *dequeue* functions that transparently include synchronization calls.

Semaphores
> If your platform supports POSIX real-time extensions (POSIX.1b), you can take advantage of yet another common synchronization primitive for concurrent environments—*semaphores*. A *counting semaphore* is like a mutex but is associated with a counter. If your platform supports both the POSIX real-time extensions and Pthreads, you can use semaphores on a per-thread basis in the same way you would use a mutex.* We'll briefly discuss semaphores in Chapter 5, *Pthreads and UNIX*.

Later in this chapter we'll provide examples of a threadsafe linked list and a reader/writer lock implementation. These will give you a idea of what it is like to implement higher-level synchronization facilities on top of the standard Pthreads ones.

Mutex Variables

To protect a shared resource from a race condition, we use a type of synchronization called *mutual exclusion*, or *mutex* for short. Using mutexes, we give threads turns at having exclusive access to data. When one thread has exclusive access to data, other threads cannot simultaneously be accessing the same data.

So far, we've focused almost entirely on providing exclusive access to data. However, we could take a different perspective and provide exclusive access to the code paths or routines that access data. We call that piece of code that must be executed atomically a *critical section*.

---

* A full discussion of semaphores is beyond the scope of this book. For a detailed discussion of all of the POSIX real-time extensions, see the book *POSIX.4: Programming for the Real World* by Bill O. Gallmeister from O'Reilly & Associates.

How large does a critical section have to be to require protection through a mutex? Not very large at all—even a single statement might need to be guarded by a mutex. To answer this question for your program, it's important for you to understand something about what your C language statements might look like at an instruction level. Where your C language program might have a single assignment statement, the compiler might substitute a number of machine instructions operating on one or more memory locations. In a multithreaded environment, the original single statement is no longer atomic at the hardware level. For example:

- Double-precision floating-point multiplies and adds on many systems require multiple loads and stores.

- A platform may have alignment restrictions that cause an integer to be accessed by multiple loads or stores when it straddles an alignment boundary.

Be conservative. Because a platform's machine architecture ultimately decides which operations are performed atomically and which are not, you should always use mutexes to ensure a thread's shared data operations are atomic with respect to other threads. For the time being, you can assume that the Pthreads standard arranges things so that Pthreads library operations (such as mutex locks and unlocks) work properly regardless of the platform you are using and the number of CPUs in the system. We'll provide enough background on this topic in Chapter 5, to make you confident that this is so.

Using mutex variables in Pthreads is quite simple. Here's what you do:

1. Create and initialize a mutex for each resource you want to protect, like a record in a database.

2. When a thread must access the resource, use *pthread_mutex_lock* to lock the resource's mutex. The Pthreads library makes sure that only one thread at a time can lock the mutex; all other calls to the *pthread_mutex_lock* function for the same mutex must wait until the thread currently holding the mutex releases it.

3. When the thread is finished with the resource, unlock the mutex by calling *pthread_mutex_unlock*.

It's up to you to put lock and unlock calls in the right place. Unlike some higher-level programming interfaces, the Pthreads library does not enforce locks. Pthreads locks are merely advisory. If each thread locks the mutex when it's supposed to, the system works; if each thread does what it feels like, the data goes unprotected.

If your locking code is correct, the thread that holds a lock on a mutex can assume that:

- No other thread will write to the data. Data protected by the mutex will not change out from under it.

  This is important because a thread may take some action based on the current value of the data. For instance, the ATM example allows a withdrawal whenever the bank balance is greater than the amount to be withdrawn. You certainly wouldn't want a thread to come in and decrease the balance while another thread is giving out the money.

- No other thread will read the data while it is in some sort of intermediate state. After this thread releases the lock, other threads will see only the final data it has written.

  This is important because a thread might need many steps to process the data. The only way to make the data appear atomic to other threads is to prevent them from seeing its intermediate states.

You can use a single mutex lock in our ATM server example to protect the account database from corruption. We'll globally define the mutex and call it *global_data_mutex*. Our server's *main* routine will statically initialize *global_data_mutex* before it creates any worker threads:

```
pthread_mutex_t global_data_mutex = PTHREAD_MUTEX_INITIALIZER;
```

Once it's initialized, the mutex can be used by any worker thread accessing the database, such as the threads that run the *deposit* routine in Example 3-1.

Example 3-1: Using a Single Mutex Lock for the ATM Database (atm_svr.c)

```
void deposit(char *req_buf, char *resp_buf)
{
  int rtn;
  int temp, id, password, amount;
  account_t *accountp;

  /* Parse input string */
  sscanf(req_buf, "%d %d %d %d ", &temp, &id, &password, &amount);

  /* Check inputs */
  if ((id < 0) || (id >= MAX_NUM_ACCOUNTS)) {
    sprintf(resp_buf, "%d %s", TRANS_FAILURE, ERR_MSG_BAD_ACCOUNT);
    return;
  }

  pthread_mutex_lock(&global_data_mutex);

  /* Retrieve account from database */
  if ((rtn = retrieve_account( id, &accountp)) != 0) {
```

Example 3–1: Using a Single Mutex Lock for the ATM Database (atm_svr.c) (continued)

```
    sprintf(resp_buf, "%d %s", TRANS_FAILURE, atm_err_tbl[-rtn]);
    .
    .
    .
}

pthread_mutex_unlock(&global_data_mutex);
}
```

Although we've shown only the *deposit* routine in Example 3-1, all the routines in our server that access the database work in the same way. They lock the mutex before retrieving the account balance, then release it after they've changed the account balance. This may be the simplest solution for our ATM server, but it's not the best. We've limited access to the entire database to a single thread at a time, thus slowing performance considerably. Later in this chapter, as a performance enhancement, we'll add mutexes for individual account records to our server.

Using Mutexes

Mutex variables are of type *pthread_mutex_t*. Before you can use a mutex in your program, you must initialize it, either dynamically or statically. We previously showed an example of static initialization.

You dynamically initialize a mutex by calling *pthread_mutex_init* as shown in Example 3-2.

Example 3–2: Dynamically Initializing a Single Mutex Lock (atm_svr.c)

```
    pthread_mutex_t *mutexp;
    .
    .
    .
    mutexp=(pthread_mutex_t *)malloc(sizeof(pthread_mutex_t));
    pthread_mutex_init(mutexp, NULL);
```

When Pthreads initializes a mutex, it defines an attribute object for the mutex (*pthread_mutex_attr_t*) that you use to customize its behavior. To assign default attributes to a mutex, pass a NULL attribute argument in the *pthread_mutex_init* call. Unlike the *pthread_attr_t* object, which we introduced in our discussion of *pthread_create* in Chapter 1, the *pthread_mutex_attr_t* object has no mandatory attributes. We'll discuss its optional attributes—a process-shared attribute and two priority-inversion attributes (priority ceiling and priority inheritance)—a bit later.

Because you want to protect data from being accessed by more than one thread at a time, the *main* routine usually initializes all mutexes before it creates additional threads. Sometimes this is impractical—for instance, in a system library (it has no *main!*). When this is the case, use the *pthread_once* function, which we'll cover in Chapter 4.

Once you've initialized a mutex, you can lock it by calling *pthread_mutex_lock* or *pthread_mutex_trylock*. The *pthread_mutex_lock* call blocks the calling thread until it's granted the lock. If the mutex is unlocked at the time of the call, the lock's granted immediately; otherwise, it's granted after it's released by the thread that's holding it. We'll discuss *pthread_mutex_trylock* momentarily.

To release a lock, use *pthread_mutex_unlock*. If you should forget to call *pthread_mutex_unlock* for a locked mutex, a deadlock may occur in which other threads that are requesting the lock wait indefinitely for you to release it.

Error Detection and Return Values

The Pthreads standard allows implementations to define the exact level of error detection and reporting for some library calls. Although this allows vendors to design efficient library calls, it can pose a particular problem when you use mutex library calls.

In general, the Pthreads library reports all errors associated with resource availability and system constraints on function operation. For example, if the library realizes that it cannot initialize a mutex for a thread because the library itself hasn't enough space in its internal tables, it returns a value of EAGAIN or ENOMEM to the caller of *pthread_mutex_init*. However, the library does not have to detect improper uses of a mutex and report any errors that might result. Such improper uses include:

- Locking a mutex that you have not initialized
- Locking a mutex that you already own
- Unlocking a mutex that you don't own

Hopefully, the library you use does detect these misuses. If it does not in its default mode, see if it has a debug mode that provides additional error detection.

Using pthread_mutex_trylock

The *pthread_mutex_trylock* function, like *pthread_mutex_lock*, locks a previously initialized mutex. Unlike *pthread_mutex_lock*, though, it does not suspend its caller if another thread already holds the mutex. Instead, it returns immediately, indicating that the mutex is currently locked. The *pthread_mutex_trylock* function can be useful, but using it is not as simple as it seems.

Be careful.

Philosophically, using *pthread_mutex_trylock* seems contrary to the basics of multithreaded program design. We are calling *pthread_mutex_trylock* to prevent a thread from blocking, but we've designed threads into our program so that some threads could block while others continue. When we see a *pthread_mutex_trylock* call, we often wonder why the program's designer didn't simply create another thread for whatever it is that the thread might do while it would be waiting for the lock. This would make the program easier to understand rather than having the one thread, essentially assigned to more than one task, asynchronously bouncing between tasks based on the availability of locks.

Practically, using *pthread_mutex_trylock* represents a kind of polling for a resource—repeatedly trying and backing off until the resource is obtained. This polling leads to some overhead and, worse, potential resource starvation. If the lock is in high demand, the thread that polls for it may never get it. It's like trying to get tickets for a concert by a really hot band—Pink Floyd, for instance. The line forms well before the tickets go on sale and lasts until they are all gone. If you don't keep your place in line, you may never get your tickets. Similarly, a thread that is not patient enough to block and wait may never try the lock and find it available—there is always at least one other thread blocked waiting for the lock. Somewhat more acceptable is the specialized use of *pthread_mutex_trylock* by real-time programmers to poll for state changes. This practice may be inefficient, but it does allow real-time programs to respond quickly to a condition that warrants speed.

Another situation in which a *pthread_mutex_trylock* is often used is in detecting and avoiding deadlock in locking hierarchies and priority inversion situations. Later in this chapter, we'll discuss a more standard solution to locking hierarchy problems that involves defining an order in which any given thread must pursue locks. In Chapter 4, we'll discuss how you can avoid priority inversion problems by using attributes to assign priorities to mutexes.

When Other Tools Are Better

Mutexes are best used for controlling direct access to data and resources. Although you can use mutexes as building blocks for more complex synchronization mechanisms, Pthreads often provides a more appropriate tool for doing so.

In particular, a common task in thread programming is *event synchronization*: each thread in a program reaches a certain point and must wait for other threads to get there. You might adopt this technique, for instance, when your threads are working on different chunks of an array and must exchange results at regular points. Your best choice to impose this type of synchronization is a condition variable. If condition variables were not available, you'd likely use a counter to let threads know when they've all reached a barrier in your program. Not only would each thread need to lock a mutex to decrement the counter, but it would also have to repeatedly lock the mutex to check if the counter had reached zero. If you find code that polls a counter to determine if all threads have synchronized on an event, it's time to use a condition variable. We'll have more to say about condition variables later in this chapter.

Some Shortcomings of Mutexes

Mutexes are the most restrictive type of access control. When a thread locks a mutex on a resource—even if it's only interested in checking the resource's value—it prevents all other threads from accessing the resource. This is effective synchronization for all situations but may not be the most efficient type of lock for situations that allow less restrictive access.

Sometimes you have many threads that read data but only an occasional thread that writes it. There should be a type of lock that allows any number of readers but works like a mutex whenever a writer enters the scene. That is, the writer should not be allowed access whenever any readers are using the data. But when a writer is using it, neither readers nor other writers are allowed in. Reader/writer locks provide this type of access control. Although Pthreads does not specify them, we'll show you later on how to "roll your own" using mutexes and condition variables.

In some circumstances, it would be useful if we could define a *recursive lock*: that is a lock that can be relocked any number of times by its current holder. It would be nice if we could specify this ability in a mutex attribute object. We can imagine the Pthreads library associating an internal counter with a recursive mutex to count the number of times its current holder has called *pthread_mutex_lock*. Each time the current holder calls *pthread_mutex_unlock*, the library would decrement this counter. The lock would not be released until the call that brings the count down to zero is issued.

A recursive mutex is useful for a thread that makes a number of nested calls to a routine that locks and manipulates a resource. You lock the mutex recursively each time the thread enters the routine and unlock it at all exit points. If the thread already holds the lock, the calls merely increase and decrease the recursive count and don't deadlock the thread. If you did not use a recursive mutex, you'd need to distinguish somehow between the times when the thread already holds the lock when it calls the routine and those when it needs to make a prior mutex lock call.

Contention for a Mutex

If more than one thread is waiting for a locked mutex, which thread is the first to be granted the lock once it's released? The choice is made according to the scheduling priorities of the individual threads.

The thread with the highest priority gets the lock. We'll discuss scheduling policies and priorities in Chapter 4. For now, it's worth noting that they allow you to mark one thread as more important than another.

Many threaded programs, however, don't assign different priorities to different threads. Most of these programs are designed for real-time applications and allow the choice of which thread gets a lock first to be made randomly.

The use of priorities in a multithreaded program can lead to a classic multiprocessing problem: *priority inversion.* Priority inversion involves a low priority thread that holds a lock that a higher priority thread wants. Because the higher priority thread cannot continue until the lower priority thread releases the lock, each thread is actually treated as if it had the inverse of its intended priority.

The best way to avoid priority inversion is to minimize the degree to which threads of different priorities share the same locks. This may not always be possible, though. In Chapter 4, we'll show you how to eliminate the risk of priority inversion by using mutex attributes.

Example: Using Mutexes in a Linked List

Linked lists are common structures in programming—and in programming books! But, when multiple threads become involved, there's a new twist: how do multiple threads access a list without screwing it up? In this version of the venerable linked-list example, we'll have multiple threads accessing a list, searching for a node (that is, reading the list), removing a node, and changing its contents (that is, writing to the list). Our include file for this example is shown in Example 3-3.

Example 3-3: Include File for a Linked List Module (llist.h)

```
/* llist.h */

typedef struct llist_node {
    int             index;
    void            *datap;
    struct llist_node    *nextp;
} llist_node_t;

typedef llist_node_t *llist_t;

int llist_init(llist_t *llistp);
int llist_insert_data(int index; void *datap, llist_t *llistp);
```

Example 3-3: Include File for a Linked List Module (llist.h) (continued)

```
int llist_remove_data(int index; void **datapp, llist_t *llistp);
int llist_find_data(int index,  void **datapp, llist_t *llistp);
int llist_change_data(int index, void *datap, llist_t *llistp);
int llist_show(llist_t *llistp);
```

We've set up calls in our *llist.h* file to initialize a linked list of type *llist_t*, insert nodes, remove nodes, retrieve data from nodes, and set variables in nodes. In this simple example, each node has an integer index that indicates its place in the list. A partial implementation of the module including the initialization routine (*llist_init*) and the insert routine (*llist_insert_data*) is shown in Example 3-4.

Example 3-4: Nonthreaded Linked List Code (llist.c)

```
/* llist.c */

#include "llist.h";

/* Right now, this routine simply ensures that we don't initialize a list
   that has data on it. */

int llist_init(llist_t *llistp)
{
   if (*llistp == NULL)
         return 0;
   else
         return -1;
}

int llist_insert_data(int index, void *datap, llist_t *llistp)
{
   llist_node_t *cur, *prev, *new;
   int found = FALSE;

   for (cur = prev = *llistp; cur != NULL; prev = cur, cur= cur->nextp) {
         if (cur->index == index) {
                   free(cur->datap);
                   cur->datap = datap;
                   found = TRUE;
                   break;
         } else if (cur->index > index) {
                   break;
         }
   }
```

```
1   if (!found) {
2         new = (llist_node_t *)malloc(sizeof(llist_node_t));
3         new->index = index;
4         new->data = datap;
5         new->nextp = cur;
6         if (cur == list)
7                   *llistp = new;
```

Example 3-4: Nonthreaded Linked List Code (llist.c) (continued)

```
8           else
                    prev->nextp = new;
    }

    return 0;
}
```

As we've written it so far, our linked list code would present many opportunities for race conditions if we divided its tasks among multiple threads. If we allowed two or more threads to concurrently execute these routines, unexpected results might arise.

Complex Data Structures and Lock Granularity

When a linked list is being accessed by more than one thread, we're not only concerned about the data it contains, but also about the integrity of its structure. Consider a situation in which two threads are inserting nodes in our list at the same time, with the result that the execution of lines 1 through 8 in Example 3-4 are interleaved. Each thread has passed the test at line 6 and thus thinks that it should insert its node on the top of the list. When it executes line 7, each thread makes the head of the list point to the node it will be inserting. Whichever thread is the last to do so will succeed in inserting its node on the list; the other thread's node will be lost forever, occupying inaccessible memory somewhere on the heap. A similar mishap could result from the race condition in which a thread reads a node that is being concurrently removed by another thread.*

Programmers often want to use a preexisting code library or module with a multi-threaded program only to discover that to do so might create race conditions among the threads. We say that it contains *non-threadsafe*, or *nonreentrant*, code. In our linked list example, we'll rewrite the previous module to make it thread-safe. In other cases, we may not have had the option of rewriting our code, perhaps because we were using a precompiled library of code. If this were the situation, we'd add a mutex as a wrapper around our calls to library functions. We'll discuss the issues that arise from using non-threadsafe code in Chapter 5.

---

* Our expectations on the structure and value of that data are sometimes called *invariants*. When we have a linked list, we expect it to remain well formed as long as our program is executing. It should always have a valid head and tail and correctly linked nodes that don't disappear—no matter which thread in our program references it.

Requirements and Goals for Synchronization

When designing the synchronization for our data structures, we'll keep to two strict requirements:

- Eliminate all race conditions.

- Do not introduce deadlock.

We'll try to meet these requirements with as little impact on the performance of our program as possible.

The lock potentially blocks other threads that must access the resource it protects. You can control this expense to some extent by economizing on the length of time a thread spends in a critical section of code. (It's how long this code takes to complete that determines how long other threads must wait on a mutex.) We'll revisit performance issues in Chapter 6, *Practical Considerations*.

The simplest way to synchronize our program would be have a single mutex protect all types of access to the entire list—insertion, deletion, reading data, and writing data. This approach would eliminate all race conditions for these operations and prevent deadlock, thus meeting our requirements. We'll need to first modify the *llist_t* data structure in our header file, as follows:

```
typedef  struct llist {
    llist_node_t *first;
    pthread_mutex_t mutex;
    } llist_t;
```

We'll then change our initialization and insert routines as shown in Example 3-5.

Example 3-5: Multithreaded Linked List Code (llist_threads.c, llist_threads.h)

```
int llist_init(llist_t *llistp)
{

  llistp->first = NULL;
  pthread_mutex_init(&(llistp->mutex), NULL);
  return 0;
}

int llist_insert_data(int index, void *datap, llist_t *llistp)
{
    llist_node_t *cur, *prev, *new;
    int found = FALSE;

    pthread_mutex_lock(&(llistp->mutex));

    for (cur = prev = llistp->first; cur != NULL; prev = cur, cur= cur->nextp) {
            if (cur->index == index) {
                    free(cur->datap);
                    cur->datap = datap;
```

Example 3-5: Multithreaded Linked List Code (llist_threads.c, llist_threads.b) (continued)

```
                        found = TRUE;
                        break;
                } else if (cur->index > index) {

                        break;
                }
        }

        if (!found) {
                new = (llist_node_t *)malloc(sizeof(llist_node_t));
                new->index = index;
                new->data = datap;
                new->nextp = cur;
                if (cur == llistp->first)
                        llistp->first = new;
                else prev->nextp = new;
        }

        pthread_mutex_unlock(&(llistp->mutex));

        return 0;
}
```

The *llist_t* structure now includes a mutex lock that protects the entire list. The *llist_init* routine initializes the mutex in the *pthread_mutex_init* call that follows the *malloc* that allocates the list. Each routine that accesses the list, like *llist_insert_data* in Example 3-5, must first obtain this mutex (by calling *pthread_mutex_lock*). It releases the mutex (by calling *pthread_mutex_unlock*) just before exiting.

By putting the synchronization inside our module, we've created a threadsafe data type without changing its interface.

Although this solution does meet our design requirements, it may not provide the best possible performance. The mutex controls access to the entire list. That is, while the list is being accessed by any thread, it is unavailable to all other threads. If concurrent accesses to the list are uncommon, this may be fine; but what if this isn't true?

Access Patterns and Granularity

Your choices for optimizing performance in a multithreaded program are tied to how its threads access the shared data on the list. If almost all accesses are reads and writes of existing data nodes, as opposed to insertions and removes, your most efficient approach might be to allow nodes to be individually locked. This would allow threads to read and write different nodes simultaneously. However, if threads often insert and remove nodes to and from the list, this solution would add another layer of complexity.

This basic design decision concerns lock *granularity*—that is, the level at which we apply locks to our shared data (and, thus, the number of locks we use to protect the data). On one hand, we could use *coarse-grain* locking and use a single mutex to control access to all shared data. This is what we've been using up to this point. On the other hand, we could use *fine-grain* locking and place a lock on every individually accessible piece of data. Fine-grain locking may result in improved concurrency, but it requires the most coding and overhead in synchronization calls.

In practice, locking systems adopt a lock granularity design that falls somewhere in between these extremes. The programmer takes anticipated usage into account—for instance, whether it's likely for more than one thread to request withdrawals on the same account at the same time. It's an art to provide the most efficient implementation while ensuring that the application works correctly.

Locking Hierarchies

If your shared data has some hierarchical structure—for instance, it's a tree with some depth to it—you may want to allow threads to lock separate subtrees of the structure simultaneously. This assumes a finer-grain lock design.

Figure 3-2 shows a tree with a root and three levels—L1, L2, and L3. We've assigned a mutex to each level to control access to the sublevels below.

This is all well and good, but beware! If we now allow threads to acquire these locks in any order they please, the kind of deadlock known as a *deadly embrace* can occur. For example, consider two threads that intend to lock the same section of the tree (see Figure 3-3). The first thread tries to obtain the L1, L2, and L3 locks in succession, and the second thread goes after L3, L2, and L1 in the reverse order at the same time. If their execution overlapped, it's quite possible that each would stall waiting for a lock already held by the other. (Here, the first thread blocks waiting for the L3 lock that the second thread holds, and the second thread blocks waiting for the L2 lock that the first thread holds.) Our threads are deadlocked waiting for each other.

To avoid a deadly embrace such as this, we must enforce a fixed locking hierarchy. To access data at any given level, all threads in our program must obtain the lock at each lower level in exactly the same order. If threads always took L1 before L2, and L2 before L3, any thread obtaining L1 can assume that L2 is either unlocked or locked by another thread. It can also assume that the other thread that currently owns L2 will not try to lock L1. Presumably, the second thread will

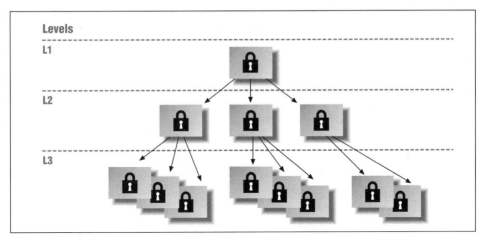

Figure 3-2: Locking in hierarchical data structures

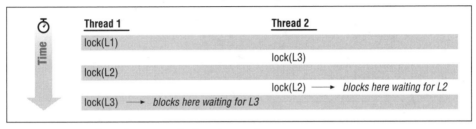

Figure 3-3: Deadly embrace in a locking hierarchy

release L2 sometime, giving the first thread an opportunity to proceed through the hierarchy. Thus, our threads avoid deadlock. Note that this scheme allows a thread with a lock in the hierarchy to release locks of lower levels so that other threads can pursue data off other branches of the subtree.

Some locking systems have built-in support for locking hierarchies—Pthreads isn't one of them. In these systems, you can define each lock's place in the hierarchy to the locking system. When you subsequently try to obtain a lock, the system checks if you own all required prior locks. If not, it gives you an error.

In systems without this support, locking hierarchies must exist entirely in the programmer's head or, perhaps, be written profusely into program comments.

Sharing a Mutex Among Processes

A mutex has a single attribute that determines whether or not it can be seen by threads in other processes: process-shared. (A mutex object also has two attributes that assist in scheduling threads. We'll discuss them in Chapter 4.) If your platform allows you to set the process-shared attribute, the compile-time constant _POSIX_THREAD_PROCESS_SHARED will be TRUE.

When you initialize a mutex dynamically (that is, by calling *pthread_mutex_init*), the Pthreads library creates a mutex attribute object for it. A Pthreads mutex attribute object is of type *pthread_mutex_attr_t*. You initialize and deinitialize it by calling *pthread_mutexattr_init* and *pthread_mutexattr_destroy*, respectively. To set the process-shared attribute, supply the PTHREAD_PROCESS_SHARED constant in a *pthread_mutexattr_setshared* call. To revert to a process-private mutex, specify the PTHREAD_PROCESS_PRIVATE constant. Processes that share a mutex must be able to access it in shared memory (created through System V shared memory mechanisms or through *mmap* calls). The mutex is initialized once by a thread in any of the processes that plan to use it. Example 3-6 shows one way of initializing a process-shared mutex.

Example 3-6: A Process-Shared Mutex (process_shared_mutex.c)

```
#include <stdlib.h>
#include <stdio.h>
#include <unistd.h>
#include <string.h>
#include <sys/types.h>
#include <sys/ipc.h>
#include <sys/shm.h>
#include <sys/wait.h>

#ifndef _POSIX_THREAD_PROCESS_SHARED
#error "This platform does not support process shared mutex"
#endif
int    shared_mem_id;
int    *shared_mem_ptr;
pthread_mutex_t *mptr;
pthread_mutex_attr_t mutex_shared_attr;
extern int
main(void)
{
  pid_t  child_pid;
  int    status;

  /* initialize shared memory segment */
  shared_mem_id = shmget(IPC_PRIVATE, 1*sizeof(pthread_mutex_t), 0660);
  shared_mem_ptr = (int *)shmat(shared_mem_id, (void *)0, 0);
  mptr = shared_mem_ptr;

  pthread_mutexattr_init(&mutex_shared_attr);
  pthread_mutexattr_setshared(&mutex_shared_attr, PTHREAD_PROCESS_SHARED);
  pthread_mutex_init(mptr, &mutex_shared_attr);

  if ((child_pid = fork()) == 0) {
  /* child */
```

Example 3-6: A Process-Shared Mutex (process_shared_mutex.c) (continued)

```
            /* create more threads */
            .
            .
            pthread_mutex_lock(mptr);
            .
            .
    } else {
    /* parent */
            /* create more threads */
            .
            .
            pthread_mutex_lock(mptr);
            .
            .

    }
```

In Example 3-6, we allocate storage for the mutex from the shared memory segment. The main thread in the parent process initializes it, using a mutex attribute object we've set to the PTHREAD_PROCESS_SHARED constant in a call to the function *pthread_mutexattr_setshared*. After it initializes the mutex, the parent process forks. Subsequently, the main threads of both the parent and child processes can create more threads, all of which can use the mutex to synchronize access to mutually shared data. When using a process-shared mutex, consider the following:

- Once a process has multiple threads, forking has many pitfalls. (If you wish to steer this course, see Chapter 5, before going any further.) In Example 3-6, we took care to initialize the mutex before forking and to fork before we created multiple threads from multiple processes.

- For strict, process-to-process synchronization, use System V or POSIX.1b semaphores. For thread-to-thread synchronization across processes, you can use POSIX.1b semaphores as an alternative to process-shared mutexes.

Condition Variables

While a mutex lets threads synchronize by controlling their access to data, a condition variable lets threads synchronize on the value of data. Cooperating threads wait until data reaches a particular state or until a certain event occurs. Condition variables provide a kind of notification system among threads. As mentioned earlier, if Pthreads didn't offer condition variables, but only provided mutexes, threads would need to poll the variable to determine when it reached a certain state.

Example 3-7 shows a simple use of a condition variable. We'll make the global variable *count* a shared resource that two threads increment and create the mutex *count_mutex* (in global scope) to protect it. We'll use the *count_threshold_cv* condition variable to represent an event—the *count* variable's reaching a defined threshold value, WATCH_COUNT.

The *main* routine creates two threads. Each of these threads runs the *inc_count* routine. The *inc_count* routine locks *count_mutex*, increments *count*, reads *count* in a *printf* statement, and tests for the threshold value. If *count* has reached its threshold value, *inc_count* calls *pthread_cond_signal* to notify the thread that's waiting for this particular event. Before exiting, *inc_count* releases the mutex. We'll create a third thread to run the *watch_count* task. The *watch_count* routine waits for *inc_count* to signal our *count_threshold_cv* condition variable.

Example 3-7: A Simple Condition Variable Example (cvsimple.c)

```
#include <stdio.h>
#include <pthread.h>
#define TCOUNT 10
#define WATCH_COUNT 12

int count = 0;
pthread_mutex_t count_mutex = PTHREAD_MUTEX_INITIALIZER;
pthread_cond_t count_threshold_cv = PTHREAD_COND_INITIALIZER;
int  thread_ids[3] = {0,1,2};

extern int
main(void)
{
      int      i;
      pthread_t threads[3];
      pthread_create(&threads[0],NULL,inc_count, &thread_ids[0]);
      pthread_create(&threads[1],NULL,inc_count, &thread_ids[1]);
      pthread_create(&threads[2],NULL,watch_count, &thread_ids[2]);
      for (i = 0; i < 3; i++) {
              pthread_join(threads[i], NULL);
      }
      return 0;
}

void watch_count(int *idp)
{
      pthread_mutex_lock(&count_mutex)
      while (count <= WATCH_COUNT) {
              pthread_cond_wait(&count_threshold_cv,
                              &count_mutex);
              printf("watch_count(): Thread %d,Count is %d\n",
                    *idp, count);
      }
      pthread_mutex_unlock(&count_mutex);
}

void inc_count(int *idp)
{
```

Example 3-7: A Simple Condition Variable Example (cvsimple.c) (continued)

```
    for (i =0; i < TCOUNT; i++) {
            pthread_mutex_lock(&count_mutex);
            count++;
            printf("inc_count(): Thread %d, old count %d,\
                new count %d\n", *idp, count - 1, count );
            if (count == WATCH_COUNT)
                pthread_cond_signal(&count_threshold_cv);
            pthread_mutex_unlock(&count_mutex);
    }
}
```

A condition variable has a data type of *pthread_cond_t*. You can initialize it statically as we do in Example 3-7, or you can initialize it dynamically by calling *pthread_cond_init*, as follows:

```
    pthread_cond_init(&count_threshold_cv, NULL);
```

After you initialize a condition variable, a thread can use it in one of two ways:

- The thread can wait on the condition variable.

  To wait on a condition variable, a thread calls *pthread_cond_wait* or *pthread_cond_timedwait*. Both of these functions suspend the caller until another thread signals* on the condition variable. In addition, the *pthread_cond_timedwait* call lets you specify a timeout argument. If the condition is not signaled in the specified time, the thread is released from its wait.

- It can signal other threads waiting on the condition variable.

  To release threads that are waiting on a condition variable, a thread calls *pthread_cond_signal* or *pthread_cond_broadcast*. The *pthread_cond_signal* function wakes up only one of the potentially many threads waiting on the condition; the *pthread_cond_broadcast* function awakens all of them.

In Example 3-7, the only thread waiting is the one running the *watch_count* task. The threads that signal are running the *inc_count* task.† The thread running *watch_count* first locks the count mutex before checking the count. This is important because, condition or no condition, that counter is still a shared piece of data. We don't want it to change while we're in the middle of checking it. If *count* is not the desired value, the thread calls *pthread_cond_wait* to put itself into a wait on the *count_threshold_cv* condition variable. The *pthread_cond_wait* function

---

* Note that we do not use the term *signals* in the sense used in discussions of UNIX signaling mechanisms. See the section the section called "Condition Variables and UNIX Signals" later in this chapter.

† Although the *pthread_cond_broadcast* function wakes all threads waiting on the condition, they all immediately compete for the associated mutex. Only one of them will succeed in locking the mutex and be able to continue in the code after the *pthread_cond_wait* call. See the discussion in the section called "When Many Threads Are Waiting" coming up.

releases the count mutex while the thread is waiting so other threads have the opportunity to modify *count*. When the condition occurs and it is awakened, the thread running *watch_count* prints a message, unlocks the mutex, and exits. The threads running *inc_count* check the value of the *count* after each increment. If *count* reaches WATCH_COUNT, they use *pthread_cond_signal* to awaken the waiter.

Using a Mutex with a Condition Variable

It is important to use condition variables and mutexes together properly.

A call to *pthread_cond_wait* requires that a locked mutex be passed in along with the condition variable. The system releases the mutex on the caller's behalf when the wait for the condition begins. In concert with the actions of the waiting thread, the thread that issues the *pthread_cond_signal* or *pthread_cond_broadcast* call holds the mutex at the time of the call but must release it after the call. Then, when the system wakes it up, a waiting thread can regain control of the mutex. It too must release the mutex when it's finished with it.

It all sounds complicated, but what if the mutex and the condition variable weren't linked? If the condition were signaled without a mutex, the signaling thread might signal the condition before the waiting thread begins waiting for it—in which case the waiting thread would never wake up. If the system did not release the lock when the waiting thread entered the wait, no other thread could get the mutex and change the value of *count* such that the condition is met. The condition would never be signaled, and the program would deadlock. If the waiting thread didn't release the mutex, no other thread could get the mutex. Here, too, we'd wind up in a deadlock.

When Many Threads Are Waiting

If multiple threads are waiting on a condition variable, who gets awakened first when another thread issues a *pthread_cond_signal* call? As with threads waiting in a lock call to a mutex variable, the waiting threads are released according to their scheduling priority. If all waiting threads are of the same priority, they are released in a first-in first-out order for each *pthread_cond_signal* call that's issued.

The *pthread_cond_broadcast* function releases all threads at once from their waits on the condition variable, but there is a hitch. The system can select only one to which to give possession of the mutex. It does so by applying the same criterion it uses when selecting the thread it wakes when a *phread_cond_signal* call signals a condition—scheduling order. The chosen thread is given the mutex lock and continues in the code following its *pthread_cond_wait* call. The other threads are moved to the queue of threads that are waiting to acquire the mutex. Each will resume as each previous thread in the queue acquires the mutex and then releases it.

Checking the Condition on Wake Up: Spurious Wake Ups

This brings us to another aspect of using condition variables. After it's just been awakened, the waiting thread in our example reenters its *while* loop to check the value of *count* one more time. Is that really necessary, or are we guilty of sloppy coding? After all, *count* must have reached its threshold limit, mustn't it, if the thread is now awake and that was the event on which it was sleeping?

Well, we check the event one more time primarily to ensure correctness: if multiple threads were waiting on the same condition variable, another thread could have already been awakened, perhaps decrementing the count, before our thread was able to run. Second, we want to guard against a condition known as a *spurious wake up*. Perhaps a signaling thread has, in error or due to an unexpected condition, awakened our waiting thread when the expected condition has not in fact been met. In addition, the Pthreads library allows an underlying threads library to issue spurious wake ups to a waiting thread without violating the standard. We need to guard against this possibility as well.

Condition Variable Attributes

When you initialize a condition variable dynamically (that is, by calling the *pthread_cond_init* function), the Pthreads library creates a condition variable attribute object for it. A Pthreads condition variable attribute object is of data type *pthread_condattr_t*. You initialize and deinitialize the condition variable attribute object by calling *pthread_condattr_init* and *pthread_condattr_destroy*, respectively.

A condition variable attribute object has a single, optional attribute that determines whether or not it can be seen by threads in other processes: process-shared. Using the process-shared attribute for condition variables is similar to using it for mutexes and involves many of the same issues. If you can set the process-shared attribute on your platform, _POSIX_THREAD_PROCESS_SHARED, the compile-time constant, will be TRUE. To set the process-shared attribute, supply either the

PTHREAD_PROCESS_SHARED or the PTHREAD_PROCESS_PRIVATE constant in a call to *pthread_condattr_setshared*. To test the attribute's value, issue a call to *pthread_condattr_getshared*.

If you want the default attributes for a condition variable, pass the function *pthread_condattr_init* an attribute argument of NULL.

Condition Variables and UNIX Signals

The Pthreads standard does not define what should happen when a condition variable is signaled from within a UNIX signal handler. We'll provide some detail in Chapter 5, but, for now, let's make this clear: unlike UNIX signals, condition variables are synchronous. You wait on a condition variable, and you start up again when another thread signals you. The signal is not delivered by the system itself, and it is not delivered asynchronously. If you want asynchronous signals, you can certainly use them. In Chapter 5, we'll show how.

Condition Variables and Cancellation

There are also issues with cancellation and waiting on a condition variable. See the section called "The Complication with Cancellation" in Chapter 4.

Reader/Writer Locks

This next example can be a mind-bender if you're not used to synchronization. It takes two synchronization primitives, the mutex and the condition variable, and creates a third—the reader/writer lock.

Let's review the reasons for reader/writer locks and the rules by which they operate. If a thread tries to get a read lock on a resource, it will succeed only if no other thread holds a lock on the resource or if all threads that hold a lock are readers. If another thread holds a write lock on the resource, the would-be reader must wait. Conversely, if a thread tries to get a write lock on the resource, it must wait if any other thread holds a read or write lock.

We'll start by defining a reader/writer variable of type *pthread_rdwr_t* and by creating the functions that operate on it, as listed in Table 3-1.[*]

---

[*] By convention, functions that extend the Pthreads standard should start with *pthread* and end with *np* (for nonportable). We'll follow this convention in this section.

Table 3-1: Reader/Writer Lock Functions

Function	Description
pthread_rdwr_init_np	Initialize reader/writer lock
pthread_rdwr_rlock_np	Obtain read lock
pthread_rdwr_wlock_np	Obtain write lock
pthread_rdwr_runlock_np	Release read lock
pthread_rdwr_wunlock_np	Release write lock

How could threads use this type of lock? We'll modify our linked list program in Example 3-5 to provide Example 3-8.

Example 3-8: Using Reader/Writer Locks (llist_threads_rw.c)

```
typedef struct llist{
   llist_node_t *first;
   pthread_rdwr_t rwlock;
   } llist_t;

.
.
.

int llist_init(llist_t *llistp)
{

  llistp->first = NULL;
  pthread_rdwr_init_np(&(llistp->rwlock), NULL);
  return 0;
}

int llist_insert_data(int index; void *datap, llist_t *llistp)
{
   llist_node_t *cur, *prev, *new;
   int found = FALSE;


   pthread_rdwr_wlock_np(&(llistp->rwlock));


   for (cur = prev = llistp->first; cur != NULL; prev = cur, cur= cur->nextp) {
            if (cur->index == index) {
                    free(cur->datap);
                    .
                    .
                    .
   pthread_rdwr_wunlock_np(&(llistp->rwlock));
   .
   .
   .
}
```

Example 3-8: Using Reader/Writer Locks (llist_threads_rw.c) (continued)

```
int llist_find_data(int index; void **datapp, llist_t *llistp)
{
    llist_node_t *cur, *prev, *new;
    int found = FALSE;

    pthread_rdwr_rlock_np(&(*llistp->rwlock));

    for (cur = prev = *llistp->first; cur != NULL;
                            prev = cur, cur= cur->nextp) {
            if (cur->index == index) {
                            free(cur->datap);
                            .
                            .
                            .
    pthread_rdwr_runlock_np(&(*llistp->rwlock));
    .
    .
    .
}
```

In Example 3-8, our linked list is protected by a reader/writer lock instead of a mutex. The *llist_insert_data* routine obtains a write lock before it modifies the list. The *llist_find_data* routine needs only a read lock.

We show the include file in Example 3-9. We'll define a *pthread_rdwr_t* structure that includes a count of readers, a count of writers, a mutex, and a condition variable. The mutex protects the reader/writer counts in the structure. Threads will wait on the condition variable for a currently held lock to become free. We've effectively hidden both mutex and condition variable in the structure so their use will be transparent to end users of the *pthread_rdwr_t* structure and our reader/writer functions.

Example 3-9: Include File for Reader/Writer Locks (rdwr.h)

```
#include <pthread.h>

typedef struct rdwr_var {
        int readers_reading;
        int writer_writing;
        pthread_mutex_t mutex;
        pthread_cond_t lock_free;
} pthread_rdwr_t;


typedef void *pthread_rdwrattr_t;


#define pthread_rdwrattr_default NULL;
```

Example 3-9: Include File for Reader/Writer Locks (rdwr.h) (continued)

```
int pthread_rdwr_init_np(pthread_rdwr_t *rdwrp, pthread_rdwrattr_t  *attrp);
int pthread_rdwr_rlock_np(pthread_rdwr_t *rdwrp);
int pthread_rdwr_wlock_np(pthread_rdwr_t *rdwrp);
int pthread_rdwr_runlock_np(pthread_rdwr_t *rdwrp);
int pthread_rdwr_wunlock_np(pthread_rdwr_t *rdwrp);
```

Because all thread objects come with attribute objects (threads, mutexes, and so on), we've defined an attribute data type for our reader/writer locks and named it *pthread_rdwrattr_t*. We have no use for it now, but it may come in handy someday. When we pull it out of the closet, it'll act just like the other attribute objects—it'll be initialized in a create call and come with a default value of *pthread_rdwrattr_default*.

The next few pages show how we've implemented the five reader/writer lock functions the threads in Example 3-8 called.

The initialization function (*pthread_rdwr_init_np*), in Example 3-10, simply sets the members of the *rdwr* variable (a *pthread_rdwr_t* structure) to the values they should have when the lock is not held. It initializes the mutex and condition variable to NULL. All other function calls lock the *rdwr* variable's mutex before proceeding to ensure that no other thread is reading or writing the variable's state at the same time.

Example 3-10: Initializing a Reader/Writer Lock (rdwr.c)

```
int pthread_rdwr_init_np(pthread_rdwr_t *rdwrp, pthread_rdwrattr_t  *attrp )
{
        rdwrp->readers_reading = 0;
        rdwrp->writer_writing = 0;
        pthread_mutex_init(&(rdwrp->mutex), NULL);
        pthread_cond_init(&(rdwrp->lock_free), NULL);
        return 0;
}
```

The get-read-lock function (*pthread_rdwr_rlock_np*) checks to see if another thread has a write lock on the *rdwrp* variable. If so, it calls the *pthread_cond_wait* function to wait on the *lock_free* condition variable. When it is awakened and the *rdwrp* variable is no longer write-locked, *pthread_rdwr_rlock_np* increments the number of readers, releases the mutex, and returns. Note that the thread does not care about the actual value of the *readers_reading* member. If it were zero and the function incremented it to 1, the read lock is set and all subsequent writers must wait. If the *readers_reading* count were already greater than 1, the new reader would simply be added to the number of threads already reading. Example 3-11 illustrates how the function would look.

Example 3–11: Read Locking a Reader/Writer Lock (rdwr.c)

```
int pthread_rdwr_rlock_np(pthread_rdwr_t *rdwrp)
{
        pthread_mutex_lock(&(rdwrp->mutex));
        while(rdwrp->writer_writing) {
                pthread_cond_wait(&(rdwrp->lock_free), &(rdwrp->mutex));
        }
        rdwrp->readers_reading++;
        pthread_mutex_unlock(&(rdwrp->mutex));
        return 0;
}
```

The get-write-lock function (*pthread_rdwr_wlock_np*) call, shown in Example 3-12, is similar to *pthread_rdwr_rlock_np*, except that it must check not only for another thread that has a write lock on the *rdwrp* variable, but also for any threads that have read locks. If either is TRUE, the *pthread_rdwr_wlock_np* function calls the *pthread_cond_wait* function to wait on the *lock_free* condition variable. When it is awakened with no readers or writers, *pthread_rdwr_wlock_np* sets the value of *writer_writing* to 1 and releases the mutex. Its caller is now—and will be—the only writer until it calls *pthread_rdwr_wunlock_np* to release the write lock.

Example 3–12: Write Locking a Reader/Writer Lock (rdwr.c)

```
int pthread_rdwr_wlock_np(pthread_rdwr_t *rdwrp)
{
        pthread_mutex_lock(&(rdwrp->mutex));
        while (rdwrp->writer_writing || rdwrp->readers_reading) {
                pthread_cond_wait(&(rdwrp->lock_free), &(rdwrp->mutex));
        }
        rdwrp->writer_writing++;
        pthread_mutex_unlock(&(rdwrp->mutex));
        return 0;
}
```

The unlock-read-lock function (*pthread_rdwr_runlock_np*) reduces the count of readers for a lock, decrementing the value of the *readers_reading* member of the *rdwrp* variable. It checks the *readers_reading* count and, if it is zero, calls *pthread_cond_signal* to tell any threads waiting on the *lock_free* condition variable that the lock has been released and can now be locked. Like all calls that unlock resources, *pthread_rdwr_runlock_np* assumes that it's being used correctly—in this case, by a thread that has previously called *pthread_rdwr_rlock_np*.

Example 3–13: Read Unlocking a Reader/Writer Lock (rdwr.c)

```
int pthread_rdwr_runlock_np(pthread_rdwr_t *rdwrp) {
        pthread_mutex_lock(&(rdwrp->mutex));
        if (rdwrp->readers_reading == 0) {
                pthread_mutex_unlock(&(rdwrp->mutex));
                return -1;
        } else {
```

Example 3-13: Read Unlocking a Reader/Writer Lock (rdwr.c) (continued)

```
                        rdwrp->readers_reading--;
                        if (rdwrp->readers_reading = 0)
                                pthread_cond_signal(&(rdwrp->lock_free));
                        pthread_mutex_unlock(&(rdwrp->mutex));
                        return 0;
                }
        }
```

The unlock-write-lock function (*pthread_rdwr_wunlock_np*) is similar to *pthread_rdwr_runlock_np*. Because only one writer holds the lock at a time, running this routine to release that lock should always result in a signal on the *lock_free* condition as shown in Example 3-14.

Example 3-14: Write Unlocking a Reader/Writer Lock (rdwr.c)

```
        int pthread_rdwr_wunlock_np(pthread_rdwr_t *rdwrp) {
                pthread_mutex_lock(&(rdwrp->mutex));
                if (rdwrp->writer_writing = 0) {
                        pthread_mutex_unlock(&(rdwrp->mutex));
                        return -1;
                } else {
                        rdwrp->writer_writing = 0;
                        pthread_cond_broadcast(&(rdwrp->lock_free));
                        pthread_mutex_unlock(&(rdwrp->mutex));
                        return 0;
                }
        }
```

This implementation doesn't address an important issue in using reader/writer locks. If the lock is currently held by a reader and a writer is already waiting, any reader that comes along next will get the lock before the waiting writer. As long as one or more readers are waiting for the lock, regardless of when they made their requests or where in the waiting lists they're queued relative to any potential writers, the lock will continue to be held for reading. More robust implementations might suspend read lock requests that arrive after a write request is waiting and resume them when there are no more writers. The decision of how to handle incoming reads versus pending writes depends on the priorities of a given system.

Synchronization in the ATM Server

To wrap up our discussion of mutex and condition variables, we'll return to our ATM example. In our discussion of mutexes earlier in this chapter, we added a single mutex to the example to protect the bank account database. As we noted at the time, this isn't the best way to impose synchronization inasmuch as it allows only one thread to access the database at a time.

In this section, we'll provide a more optimal solution to our ATM server's synchronization problems. We'll focus on the following three areas:

- Synchronizing access to the bank account database

- Limiting the number of concurrent worker threads

- Controlling the shutdown of the server

We'll continue to use mutex variables to synchronize access to account data. Imposing a limit on the number of simultaneously active worker threads and controlling server shutdown are event-driven tasks; we'll use both mutexes and condition variables when implementing them.

We first encountered the ATM server example in Chapter 2. We designed it according to the classic boss/worker model for a multithreaded program. In our server, the boss creates a new thread for each request it receives (be it a deposit, withdrawal, or balance inquiry), and the worker thread processes the request independently of the boss or any other worker thread. We've done only half the job by creating threads and adding concurrency to the server. Now we'll finish up by adding robust and efficient synchronization mechanisms.

Synchronizing Access to Account Data

Our multithreaded ATM server must contend with many potential race conditions between worker threads accessing account data. We expect its deposit and withdraw operations to be atomic. Because of this, in Example 3-1 we added a single mutex to the server to protect the integrity of the accounts database.

Although simple, this approach has major performance limitations. Because every worker thread accesses the database and only one at a time can lock the mutex, only one thread can be executing each time an account balance changes. When the server is heavily loaded, the new result is that it behaves very like a single-threaded program. Because different requests frequently access different accounts in the database, multiple requests could often execute at the same time without interfering with each other. In this light, the single-mutex approach is overly conservative.

A much more appropriate solution would be to use finer-grained locking on our data. Thus, we'll associate a mutex with each database account.

The cleanest way to proceed with this decision would be to redesign the ATM server's database module to include mutexes in the account structures themselves. For our purposes, let's assume that the database module is legacy code and we can't—or don't want to—modify it. Instead, we'll place the mutex in a separate structure outside the database module.

In the code fragment in Example 3-15, we'll implement our locking scheme. We'll globally define an array of mutex variables, called *account_mutex*, that has an element for each account. Because accounts have IDs between zero and MAX_NUM_ACCOUNTS, we'll use the account ID as an index into the mutex array. The server's *main* routine will initialize the mutex array by calling *atm_server_init*.

Example 3-15: Initializing per-account locks for the ATM database (atm_svr.c)

```
pthread_mutex_t account_mutex[MAX_NUM_ACCOUNTS];
  .
  .
  .
void atm_server_init(int argc, char **argv)
{
  .
  .
  .
  for (i = 0; i < MAX_NUM_ACCOUNTS; i++)
    pthread_mutex_init(&account_mutex[i], NULL);
  .
  .
  .
}
```

Now, with this set of mutexes, a worker thread need lock only the mutex for the specific account it is accessing. It no longer needs to lock up the entire database; other threads can concurrently lock other mutexes and access other accounts, as shown in Example 3-16.

Example 3-16: Using Per-Account Locks for the ATM Database (atm_svr.c)

```
void deposit(char *req_buf, char *resp_buf)
{
  int rtn;
  int temp, id, password, amount;
  account_t *accountp;

  /* Parse input string */
  sscanf(req_buf, "%d %d %d %d ", &temp, &id, &password, &amount);

  /* Check inputs */
  if ((id < 0) || (id >= MAX_NUM_ACCOUNTS)) {
    sprintf(resp_buf, "%d %s", TRANS_FAILURE, ERR_MSG_BAD_ACCOUNT);
    return;
  }

  pthread_mutex_lock(&account_mutex[id]);

  /* Retrieve account from database */
  if ((rtn = retrieve_account( id, &accountp)) < 0) {
    sprintf(resp_buf, "%d %s", TRANS_FAILURE, atm_err_tbl[-rtn]);
```

Example 3-16: Using Per-Account Locks for the ATM Database (atm_svr.c) (continued)

```
        .
        .
        .
        /* Code to update and access account balance. */

    }

    pthread_mutex_unlock(&account_mutex[id]);

}
```

The thread that runs our *create_open* routine to create a new account poses a special problem. Which mutex should it lock? The account doesn't exist yet, and the worker thread has no account ID to use!

Let's look at how the database layer of our ATM server actually creates a new account.

The database contains a list of potential accounts, each with a flag indicating whether or not it's in use. The *new_account* routine looks for the first account whose in-use flag is clear, sets the flag, and plugs in the information about the new account.

Here is fertile ground for a classic race condition. If two threads execute *new_account* concurrently, they could interleave their flag-reading and flag-setting. Both could return with the same account ID for two different customer accounts—not a good idea. To remove this hazard, we'll need an additional mutex.

The revision of the *create_account* routine in Example 3-17 shows the new mutex. Any thread wishing to add an account must hold this mutex (which we've globally defined) before proceeding.

Example 3-17: A Special Mutex for Opening New Accounts (atm_svr.c)

```
pthread_mutex_t create_account_mutex = PTHREAD_MUTEX_INITIALIZER;
    .
    .
    .
void create_account(char *resp_buf)
{
    int id;
    int rtn;
    account_t *accountp;

    pthread_mutex_lock(&create_account_mutex);

    /* Get a new account */
    if ((rtn = new_account(&id, &accountp)) < 0) {
        sprintf(resp_buf, "%d %d %d %s", TRANS_FAILURE, -1, -1, atm_err_tbl[-rtn]);
        .
```

Example 3-17: A Special Mutex for Opening New Accounts (atm_svr.c) (continued)

```
       .
         .
           .
    }

    pthread_mutex_unlock(&create_account_mutex);
    }
```

Note that deleting an account will work the same way. There is symmetry in creating an object and destroying an object: both require the same kind of protection.

Limiting the Number of Worker Threads

Our next synchronization task will be to limit the number of worker threads that can exist at a single time. There are some good reasons for doing so. On some operating systems, the kernel manages threads as separate contenders for the CPU, just as it manages processes. These systems must limit the number of threads each user may run at a time. Even if your system imposes no limit or an extremely high one, you reach a practical limit at the point you find that you're getting diminishing returns by creating more and more threads.[*] We'll examine this phenomenon further in our performance measurements in Chapter 6.

To limit the number of worker threads, we'll need to keep a count of them. Both boss and worker threads must access this counter. The boss thread increments it when it creates a new worker, and each worker decrements it when it exits. We'll synchronize access to the counter using a mutex.

In Example 3-18, we'll modify our ATM to add a *worker_info* structure. It'll include a counter (*num_active*), a mutex (*num_active_mutex*), and a condition variable (*thread_exit_cv*). The server's*main* routine will set the counter to zero and initialize the mutex and the condition variable.

Example 3-18: Limiting the Number of Worker Threads—Boss (atm_svr.c)

```
    #define MAX_NUM_THREADS 10
    .
    .
    .
    typedef struct {
      int            num_active;
      pthread_cond_t  thread_exit_cv;
      pthread_mutex_t mutex;
    }thread_info_t;

    thread_info_t worker_info;
```

---

[*] Thread pools don't have this problem. The number of worker threads is determined and fixed at initialization. At this point, the worker threads are created, and they live for the duration of the program.

Example 3–18: Limiting the Number of Worker Threads—Boss (atm_svr.c) (continued)

```
      .
      .
extern int
main(argc, argv)
int argc;
char **argv;
{
  workorder_t *workorderp;
  pthread_t   *worker_threadp;
  int   conn;
  int   trans_id;

  atm_server_init(argc, argv);

  for(;;) {

    /*** Wait for a request ***/
    workorderp = (workorder_t *)malloc(sizeof(workorder_t));
    server_comm_get_request(&workorderp->conn, workorderp->req_buf);
      .
      .
      .
    /*** Have we exceeded our limit of active threads ? ***/
    pthread_mutex_lock(&worker_info.mutex);
    while (worker_info.num_active == MAX_NUM_THREADS) {
      pthread_cond_wait(&worker_info.thread_exit_cv,

              &worker_info.mutex);
    }
    worker_info.num_active++;
    pthread_mutex_unlock(&worker_info.mutex);

    /*** Spawn a thread to process this request ***/
    pthread_create(worker_threadp, ...
      .
      .
      .
  }
  server_comm_shutdown();
  return 0;
}
```

Now, when the boss thread receives a request, it locks the *worker_info* mutex and checks the count of active workers before creating a new worker thread. If the number of active workers has not yet reached its limit, the boss increments the counter, unlocks the mutex, and continues. If the limit has been reached, the boss waits on the *thread_exit_cv* condition variable. When the condition is signaled the boss wakes up and rechecks the counter. If the count of active workers is now below the limit, the boss increments the counter, unlocks the mutex, and continues.

In Example 3-19, we'll adjust the *process_request* code our worker threads execute.

Example 3-19: Limiting the Number of Worker Threads— Workers (atm_svr.c)

```
void process_request(workorder_t *workorderp)
{
  char resp_buf[COMM_BUF_SIZE];
  int  trans_id;

  sscanf(workorderp->req_buf, "%d", &trans_id);
  switch(trans_id) {
      case OPEN_ACCT_TRANS:
          open_account(resp_buf);
          break;
          .
          .
          .
      }

  server_comm_send_response(workorderp->conn, resp_buf);

  free(workorderp);

  pthread_mutex_lock(&worker_info.mutex);
  worker_info.num_active--;
  if (worker_info.num_active == (MAX_NUM_THREADS - 1))
     pthread_cond_signal(&worker_info.thread_exit_cv);
  pthread_mutex_unlock(&worker_info.mutex);
}
```

Each worker thread must decrement the active worker count when it exits. It does this in the *process_request* routine. If it finds that it has decremented the counter to one less than the limit, it calls *pthread_cond_signal* to signal the *thread_exit_cv* condition variable to the waiting boss thread.

Synchronizing a Server Shutdown

In the current version of our ATM server, the boss thread runs our program's *main* routine. When the boss thread finishes *main*, the system terminates the process and all its threads, including those worker threads that are still processing active requests. We can't allow this to happen, so our final synchronization task will be to handle server shutdown more gracefully.

To make sure that all worker threads get to complete active tasks before the boss thread exits *main*, we'll reuse the active worker counter and the *thread_exit_cv* condition variable. When we used them to control the number of concurrent workers, the boss thread requested a signal when the active worker count was one less than the active worker limit. This time, the boss will request the signal when the active worker count reaches zero. (Of course, at some time, the boss will stop creating new threads so that this can eventually happen.) We'll modify the *main* routine in the boss thread, as shown in Example 3-20.

Example 3-20: Processing a Shutdown in the Boss Thread (atm_svr.c)

```
extern int
main(argc, argv)
int argc;
char **argv;
{
  workorder_t *workorderp;
  pthread_t   *worker_threadp;
  int   conn;
  int   trans_id;

  atm_server_init(argc, argv);

  for(;;) {

    /*** Wait for a request ***/
    workorderp = (workorder_t *)malloc(sizeof(workorder_t));
    server_comm_get_request(&workorderp->conn, workorderp->req_buf);

    /*** Is it a shutdown request? ***/
    sscanf(workorderp->req_buf, "%d", &trans_id);
    if (trans_id == SHUTDOWN)
      char resp_buf[COMM_BUF_SIZE];

      pthread_mutex_lock(&worker_info.mutex);

      /* Wait for in-progress requests threads to finish */
      while (worker_info.num_active > 0) {
          pthread_cond_wait(&worker_info.thread_exit_cv, &worker_info.mutex);
      }
      pthread_mutex_unlock(&worker_info.mutex);

      /* process it here with main() thread */
      if (shutdown_req(workorderp->req_buf, resp_buf)) {
          server_comm_send_response(workorderp->conn, resp_buf);
          free(workorderp);
          break;
      }
    }

    /*** Have we exceeded our limit of active threads ? ***/
    pthread_mutex_lock(&worker_info.mutex);
      .
      .
      .
  }
  server_comm_shutdown();
  return 0;
}
```

When the boss thread receives a shutdown request, it locks the *worker_info* mutex and checks the active worker counter. If the active worker counter is zero, the boss unlocks the mutex, runs a cleanup function, and leaves the main loop, thus terminating the program. If the counter is greater than zero, the boss must wait for the *thread_exit_cv* condition variable to be signaled. When it's awakened, the boss rechecks the active worker count. If the final worker has exited, the count is zero, and the boss proceeds to shut down the program. If not, the boss must wait on the condition variable again.

We'll modify our *process_request* routine in Example 3-21 so that each worker thread signals the *thread_exit_cv* condition variable before it exits, as well as when it decrements the worker count to one below the limit.

Example 3-21: Processing a Shutdown in the Worker Thread (atm_svr.c)

```
process_request(...)
{
    .
    .
    .
    server_comm_send_response(workorderp->conn, resp_buf);

    free(workorderp);

    pthread_mutex_lock(&worker_info.mutex);
    worker_info.num_active--;
    pthread_cond_signal(&worker_info.thread_exit_cv);
    pthread_mutex_unlock(&worker_info.mutex);
}
```

This works fine but is a bit inefficient. Although the boss can proceed with program shutdown only when the last worker has exited, each exiting worker thread will wake it up (and it will go right back to sleep) until the last worker decrements the active worker counter to 0. If ten worker threads are active when their boss receives the shutdown request, the boss will wake up and reenter its wait nine times before it can finally do something useful! We could fix this. Instead of using the *thread_exit_cv* condition variable for shutdown handling, we could define a new condition variable to indicate when the active worker count reaches zero. As it exits, each worker would call *pthread_cond_signal* on our new condition variable if it notices that the count has become zero. If the boss thread is waiting on the condition, it will wake up and shut down the program.

Thread Pools

We designed our ATM server according to the boss/worker model for multi-threaded programs. The boss creates worker threads on demand. When it receives a request, the boss creates a new worker thread to service that request and that request alone. When the worker completes this request, it exits. This might be ideal if we got a nickel for each thread we created, but it can slow our server in a couple of different ways:

- We don't reuse idle threads to handle new requests. Rather, we create—and destroy—a thread for each request we receive. Consequently, our server spends a lot of time in the Pthreads library.

- We've added to each request's processing time (a request's *latency*, to use a term from an engineering design spec) the time it takes to create a thread. No wonder our ATM customers keep tapping the Enter button and scowling at the camera!

We'll address these performance snags by redesigning our server to use a thread pool, a very common and very important design technique. In a server that uses a thread pool, the boss thread creates a fixed number of worker threads up front. Like their boss, these worker threads survive for the duration of the program. When the boss receives a new request, it places it on a queue. Workers remove requests from the queue and process them. When a worker completes a request, it simply removes another one from the queue.

Figure 3-4 shows the components of a thread pool.

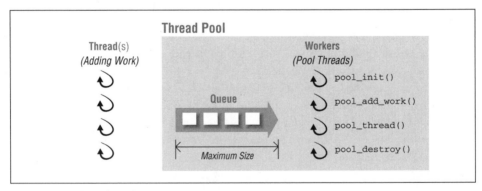

Figure 3-4: Thread pool components

The focal point of a thread pool is the request queue. Each request describes a unit of work. (This description might be the name of a routine; it might be just a flag.) Worker threads continually monitor the queue for new work requests; the boss thread places new requests on the queue.

A thread pool has some basic characteristics:

- Number of worker threads. This limits the number of requests that can be in progress at the same time.

- Request queue size. This limits the number of requests that can be waiting for service.

- Behavior when all workers are occupied and the request queue is full. Some requesters may want to block until their requests can be queued and only then resume execution. Others may prefer immediate notification that the pool is full. (For instance, network-based applications typically depend on a status value to avoid "dropping requests on the floor" when the server is over-loaded.)

An ATM Server Example That Uses a Thread Pool

We'll start on a version of our ATM server that uses a thread pool by adding some definitions to its header file, as shown in Example 3-22.

Example 3-22: Interface to a Thread Pool (tpool.h)

```
typedef struct tpool_work {
        void (*routine)();
        void *arg;
        struct tpool_work *next;
} tpool_work_t;

typedef struct tpool {
        /* pool characteristics */
        int num_threads;
        int max_queue_size;

        int do_not_block_when_full;
        /* pool state */
        pthread_t *threads;
        int cur_queue_size;
        tpool_work_t *queue_head;
        tpool_work_t *queue_tail;
        pthread_mutex_t queue_lock;
        pthread_cond_t  queue_not_empty;
        pthread_cond_t  queue_not_full;
        pthread_cond_t  queue_empty;
        int queue_closed;
        int shutdown;
} *tpool_t;

tpool_init(tpool_t *tpoolp,
           int num_worker_threads,
           int max_queue_size,
           int do_not_block_when_full);
```

Example 3-22: Interface to a Thread Pool (tpool.h) (continued)

```
tpool_add_work(tpool_t tpool,
               void *routine,
               void *arg);

tpool_destroy(tpool_t tpoolp, int finish);
```

We've defined three routines that manipulate a thread pool and two new data types. The routines are *tpool_init*, *tpool_add_work*, and *tpool_destroy*.

- The *tpool_work_t* type represents a single request on the request queue. It includes a pointer to the routine that should be executed by the worker that selects the request, a pointer to this routine's single argument (if any), and a pointer to the next request on the queue. When an external thread (such as the boss) calls *tpool_add_work*, a new request is added to the tail of the queue. When a worker comes along looking for something to do, it removes a request from the queue's head.

- The *tpool_t* type is a pointer to a structure that records the characteristics and state of a single thread pool. It contains pointers to the head and tail of the request queue. Because the queue is a shared data structure that may be accessed by all worker threads (as well as any thread that exists outside of the pool and calls *tpool_add_work*), we'll need to add some synchronization. We'll do so by incorporating a mutex (*queue_lock*) and three condition variables (*queue_not_empty*, *queue_not_full*, and *queue_empty*) in the *tpool_t* structure.

- When a worker looks at the queue and finds it empty, it sleeps on the *queue_not_empty* condition variable. When a caller in *tpool_add_work* adds an item to an empty queue, it wakes up a sleeping worker by signaling the *queue_not_empty* condition. Depending on the *do_not_block_when_full* characteristic of the queue, a thread calling *tpool_add_work* can wait on the *queue_not_full* condition variable. When a worker makes room on the queue by removing a request, it signals the *queue_not_full* condition variable, thus letting the thread in *tpool_add_work* continue.

- Finally, the *tpool_t* structure defines *shutdown* and *queue_closed* flags. Our *tpool_destroy* routine uses these flags to shut down the thread pool. The *queue_closed* flag is used in combination with the *queue_empty* condition variable to support a delayed shutdown. The delayed shutdown allows the currently queued work to complete.

Initializing a thread pool

The *tpool_init* routine, shown in Example 3-23, initializes a thread pool. The routine sets the basic characteristics of the thread pool by copying into the *tpoolt* structure the values of its three input parameters (*num_worker_threads*,

max_queue_size, and *do_not_block_when_full*). It also initializes the thread pool's
state.

Example 3-23: The Thread Pool Initialization Routine (tpool.c)

```
void tpool_init(tpool_t   *tpoolp,
                int       num_worker_threads,
                int       max_queue_size,
                int       do_not_block_when_full)
{
   int i, rtn;
   tpool_t tpool;

   /* allocate a pool data structure */
   if ((tpool = (tpool_t )malloc(sizeof(struct tpool))) == NULL)
     perror("malloc"), exit(-1);

   /* initialize the fields */
   tpool->num_threads = num_worker_threads;
   tpool->max_queue_size = max_queue_size;
   tpool->do_not_block_when_full = do_not_block_when_full;
   if ((tpool->threads =
         (pthread_t *)malloc(sizeof(pthread_t)*num_worker_threads))
          == NULL)
     perror("malloc"), exit(-1);
   tpool->cur_queue_size = 0;
   tpool->queue_head = NULL;
   tpool->queue_tail = NULL;
   tpool->queue_closed = 0;
   tpool->shutdown = 0;
   if ((rtn = pthread_mutex_init(&(tpool->queue_lock), NULL)) != 0)
       fprintf(stderr,"pthread_mutex_init %s",strerror(rtn)), exit(-1);
   if ((rtn = pthread_cond_init(&(tpool->queue_not_empty), NULL)) != 0)
       fprintf(stderr,"pthread_cond_init %s",strerror(rtn)), exit(-1);
   if ((rtn = pthread_cond_init(&(tpool->queue_not_full), NULL)) != 0)
       fprintf(stderr,"pthread_cond_init %s",strerror(rtn)), exit(-1);
   if ((rtn = pthread_cond_init(&(tpool->queue_empty), NULL)) != 0)
       fprintf(stderr,"pthread_cond_init %s",strerror(rtn)), exit(-1);

   /* create threads */
   for (i = 0; i != num_worker_threads; i++) {
       if ((rtn = pthread_create( &(tpool->threads[i]),
                     NULL,
                     tpool_thread,
                     (void *)tpool)) != 0)
           fprintf(stderr,"pthread_create %d",rtn), exit(-1);
   }

   *tpoolp = tpool;
}
```

Checking for work

In Example 3-23, the *tpool_init* routine creates all worker threads, starting each one in the *tpool_thread* routine. The *tpool_thread* routine, in Example 3-24, contains the logic each worker uses to check the queue for work and take appropriate action depending upon whether or not a request is available. It takes a single argument—a pointer to the *tpool_t* structure for the pool to which the thread belongs.

Example 3-24: The Thread Pool Thread (tpool.c)

```
void tpool_thread(tpool_t tpool)
{
    tpool_work_t *my_workp;

    for (;;) {

            pthread_mutex_lock(&(tpool->queue_lock));
            while ( (tpool->cur_queue_size == 0) && (!tpool->shutdown)) {
                    pthread_cond_wait(&(tpool->queue_not_empty),
                    &(tpool->queue_lock));
            }

            if (tpool->shutdown) {
                    pthread_mutex_unlock(&(tpool->queue_lock));
                    pthread_exit(NULL);
            }

            my_workp = tpool->queue_head;
            tpool->cur_queue_size--;
            if (tpool->cur_queue_size == 0)
                    tpool->queue_head = tpool->queue_tail = NULL;
            else
                    tpool->queue->head = my_workp->next;

            if ((!tpool->do_not_block_when_full) &&
              (tpool->cur_queue_size == (tpool->max_queue_size - 1)))
                    pthread_cond_broadcast(&(tpool->queue_not_full));

            if (tpool->cur_queue_size == 0)
                    pthread_cond_signal(&(tpool->queue_empty));
            pthread_mutex_unlock(&(tpool->queue_lock));
            (*(my_workp->routine))(my_workp->arg);
            free(my_workp);
    }
}
```

The body of the routine is a loop in which the worker checks the request queue. If it's empty, the worker sleeps on the *queue_not_empty* condition variable. It can be awakened by either a shutdown request from *tpool_destroy* or a work item placed on its request queue. When awakened by a shutdown request, the worker exits. When awakened by a work request, however, it rechecks the queue, removes the request from the queue's head, and executes the routine specified in the request (using any associated argument). If the worker finds that the queue was full before it removed the node and knows that threads may be blocked waiting to add to the queue (because the pool's *do_not_block_when_full* characteristic is not set), it signals the *queue_not_full* condition. Likewise, if this thread empties the queue, it signals *queue_empty* to allow a delayed shutdown to proceed.

Adding work

In Example 3-25, the *tpool_add_work* routine adds work requests to the queue.

Example 3-25: Adding Work to a Thread Pool (tpool.c)

```
int tpool_add_work(tpool_t tpool, void *routine, void *arg)
{
        tpool_work_t *workp;
        pthread_mutex_lock(&tpool->queue_lock);

        if ((tpool->cur_queue_size == tpool->max_queue_size) &&
                                tpool->do_not_block_when_full) {
                pthread_mutex_unlock(&tpool->queue_lock);
                return -1;
                }
        while ((tpool->cur_queue_size == tpool->max_queue_size) &&
                        (!(tpool->shutdown || tpool->queue_closed))) {
                pthread_cond_wait(&tpool->queue_not_full, &tpool->queue_lock);
                }

        if (tpool->shutdown || tpool->queue_closed) {
                pthread_mutex_unlock(&tpool->queue_lock);
                return -1;
        }

        /* allocate work structure */
        workp = (tpool_work_t *)malloc(sizeof(tpool_work_t));
        workp->routine = routine;
        workp->arg = arg;
        workp->next = NULL;
        if (tpool->cur_queue_size == 0) {
                tpool->queue_tail = tpool->queue_head = workp;
                pthread_cond_broadcast(&tpool->queue_not_empty);
        } else {
                (tpool->queue_tail)->next = workp;
                tpool->queue_tail = workp;
        }
        tpool->cur_queue_size++;
        pthread_mutex_unlock(&tpool->queue_lock);
        return 1;
}
```

The *tpool_add_work* routine checks the *do_not_block_when_full* flag and examines the current size of the request queue. If the queue is full, the routine either returns an error to its caller or suspends itself on the *queue_not_full* condition, depending on the value of the pool's *do_not_block_when_full* flag. In the latter case, the *tpool_add_work* routine resumes when the condition is signaled; it queues the request and returns to its caller.

Deleting a thread pool

The final routine in our thread pool interface, *tpool_destroy* (Example 3-26), deallocates a thread pool. It sets the *shutdown* flag in the *tpool _t* structure to indicate to workers (and threads calling *tpool_add_work*) that the pool is being deactivated. Worker threads exit when they find this flag set; the *tpool_add_work* routine returns a -1 to its caller, as shown in Example 3-26.

Example 3-26: Deleting a Thread Pool (tpool.c)

```
int tpool_destroy(tpool_t    tpool,
                    int        finish)
{
    int           i,rtn;
    tpool_work_t *cur_nodep;

    if ((rtn = pthread_mutex_lock(&(tpool->queue_lock))) != 0)
        fprintf(stderr,"pthread_mutex_lock %d",rtn), exit(-1);

    /* Is a shutdown already in progress? */
    if (tpool->queue_closed || tpool->shutdown) {
        if ((rtn = pthread_mutex_unlock(&(tpool->queue_lock))) != 0)
            fprintf(stderr,"pthread_mutex_unlock %d",rtn), exit(-1);
        return 0;
    }

    tpool->queue_closed = 1;

    /* If the finish flag is set, wait for workers to drain queue */
    if (finish == 1) {
        while (tpool->cur_queue_size != 0) {
            if ((rtn = pthread_cond_wait(&(tpool->queue_empty),
                          &(tpool->queue_lock))) != 0)
                fprintf(stderr,"pthread_cond_wait %d",rtn), exit(-1);
        }
    }

    tpool->shutdown = 1;

    if ((rtn = pthread_mutex_unlock(&(tpool->queue_lock))) != 0)
        fprintf(stderr,"pthread_mutex_unlock %d",rtn), exit(-1);

    /* Wake up any workers so they recheck shutdown flag */
    if ((rtn = pthread_cond_broadcast(&(tpool->queue_not_empty))) != 0
```

Example 3-26: Deleting a Thread Pool (tpool.c) (continued)

```
        fprintf(stderr,"pthread_cond_broadcast %d",rtn), exit(-1);
    if ((rtn = pthread_cond_broadcast(&(tpool->queue_not_full))) != 0)
        fprintf(stderr,"pthread_cond_broadcast %d",rtn), exit(-1);

    /* Wait for workers to exit */
    for(i=0; i < tpool->num_threads; i++) {
        if ((rtn = pthread_join(tpool->threads[i],NULL)) != 0)
            fprintf(stderr,"pthread_join %d",rtn), exit(-1);
    }

    /* Now free pool structures */
    free(tpool->threads);
    while(tpool->queue_head != NULL) {
      cur_nodep = tpool->queue_head->next;
      tpool->queue_head = tpool->queue_head->next;
      free(cur_nodep);
    }
    free(tpool);
    return 0;
}
```

The *tpool_destroy* routine ensures that all threads are awake to see the *shutdown* flag by signaling both the *queue_not_empty* and *queue_not_full* conditions. Even still, some threads may be busy completing their current requests; it may still be some time before they learn that a shutdown has begun. To avoid interfering with in-progress requests, *tpool_destroy* waits for all worker threads to exit by calling *pthread_join* for each thread. When all workers have departed, *tpool_destroy* frees the pool's data structures.

The current edition of our *tpool_destroy* routine is not without its surprises. When it sets the *shutdown* flag, only those requests that are currently in progress are completed. Any requests that are still in the request queue are lost when the thread pool is deallocated. Instead, it could disallow additions to the queue and wait for the queue to empty before deactivating the thread pool. It could also speed performance by canceling workers rather than waiting for them to check the shutdown flag.

We'll leave the particulars of these enhancements to your imagination. In the meantime, we must move on to our next chapter, *Managing Pthreads*, in which we'll focus a bit more on some of the Pthreads features we've already introduced (such as attribute objects and keys) and add cancellation and scheduling capabilities to our multithreaded ATM server.

Adapting the atm_server_init and main routines

In Example 3-27, we'll make some quick changes to our *atm_server_init* so that it:

- Uses a new global thread pool structure (*tpool_t*) instead of our thread information structure (*thread_info_t*).

- Initializes the thread pool by supplying the maximum number of threads to *tpool_init*.

Example 3-27: Using the Thread Pool from the atm_server_init Routine (atm_svr_tpool.c)

```
#define ATM_MAX_THREADS 10
#define ATM_MAX_QUEUE 10

tpool_t atm_thread_pool;

void atm_server_init(int argc, char **argv)
{
  /* Process input arguments */
  .
  .
  .
  tpool_init(&atm_thread_pool, ATM_MAX_THREADS, ATM_MAX_QUEUE, 0);

  /*  Initialize database and communications */
  .
  .
  .
}
```

Now, we simply need to change the *main* routine of our ATM server so that it:

- Calls *tpool_add_work* for each new request instead of calling *pthread_create* directly to create a new thread.

- Calls *tpool_destroy* to synchronize shutdown of the threads and to release resources. There's no need for the thread exit notification we used in the previous examples.

Example 3-28 implements these changes.

Example 3-28: Using the Thread Pool from the main Routine (atm_svr_tpool.c)

```
extern int
main(int argc, char **argv)
{
  workorder_t *workorderp;
  int  trans_id;
  void *status;

  atm_server_init(argc, argv);

  for(;;) {
```

Example 3-28: Using the Thread Pool from the main Routine (atm_svr_tpool.c) (continued)

```
          /*** Wait for a request ***/
          server_comm_get_request(&workorderp->conn, workorderp->req_buf);

          /*** Is it a shutdown request? ***/
          sscanf(workorderp->req_buf, "%d", &trans_id);
          if (trans_id == SHUTDOWN) {
            char resp_buf[COMM_BUF_SIZE];

            tpool_destroy(atm_thread_pool, 1);

            /* process it here with main() thread */
            if (shutdown_req(workorderp->req_buf, resp_buf)) {
              server_comm_send_response(workorderp->conn, resp_buf);
              free(workorderp);
              break;
            }
          }

          /*** Use a thread to process this request ***/

      }

      server_comm_shutdown();
      return 0;
  }
```

4

Managing Pthreads

In previous chapters, we explored the advantages of multithreaded programs, examined various program design models, and experimented with simple and more complex synchronization mechanisms. Our ATM program is now a full-fledged, well-synchronized multithreaded server, designed after the boss/worker model and optimized to use a thread pool. On our way, we introduced many other Pthreads features in passing. It's now time to examine these features a little more closely and see how we can use them to enhance our ATM server.

Our agenda includes:

Thread attributes

A thread attribute allows you to create a thread in the detached state. On some systems you can also specify attributes that control a thread's stack configuration and its scheduling behavior.

The pthread_once mechanism

By using the *pthread_once* mechanism, you can ensure that an action is performed once—and only once—regardless of how many times the threads in your program attempt to perform it. This function is useful, for instance, when more than one thread shares a file or a procedure and you don't know which thread will execute first.

Keys

Threads use keys to maintain private copies of a shared data item. A single, globally defined key points to a different memory location, depending upon which thread is executing, thus allowing the thread to access its own copy of the data. Use a key, for example, when your threads make deeply nested procedure calls and you can't easily pass thread-specific information in procedure arguments.

Cancellation

Cancellation allows you to specify the conditions under which a thread allows itself to be terminated. You can also define a stack on which the terminating thread performs last-second cleanup before exiting. Use cancellation, for example, when threads are searching in parallel for an item in a database. The thread that started the search can terminate the other threads when one of the threads locates the item.

Scheduling

You use the Pthreads scheduling features to set up a policy that determines which thread the system first selects to run when CPU cycles become available, and how long each thread can run once it is given the CPU. Scheduling is often necessary in real-time applications in which some threads have more important work than others. For example, a thread that controls equipment on a factory floor could be given priority over other threads doing background processing. The Pthreads standard defines scheduling as an optional feature.

Mutex scheduling attributes

By using mutex attributes, you can avoid the phenomenon known as priority inversion. Priority inversion occurs when multiple threads of various scheduling priorities all compete for a common mutex. A higher priority thread may find that a lower priority thread holds a mutex it needs and may stop dead in its tracks until the mutex is released.

To some extent you might consider these features to be just bells and whistles. Each has a specialized purpose that may or may not apply to your program. Nevertheless, the situations in which they are useful are common enough that it's good that they're available to us in the portable Pthreads interface. We'll now look at some specific ways in which they can be used.

Setting Thread Attributes

Threads have certain properties, called *attributes*, that you can request through the Pthreads library. The Pthreads standard defines attributes that determine the following thread characteristics:

* Whether the thread is detached or joinable. All Pthreads implementations provide this attribute.

* Size of the thread's private stack. An implementation provides this attribute if the _POSIX_THREAD_ATTR_STACKSIZE compile-time constant is defined.

- Location of the thread's stack. An implementation provides this attribute if the _POSIX_THREAD_ATTR_STACKADDR compile-time constant is defined.

- A thread's scheduling policy (and other attributes that determine how it may be scheduled). An implementation provides these attributes if the _POSIX_THREAD_PRIORITY_SCHEDULING compile-time constant is defined.

Vendors often define custom attributes as a way of including extensions to the standard in their implementations.

As we've mentioned before, a thread is created with a set of default attributes. Because the threads we've been using in our examples thus far are threads of the gray flannel variety, we've accepted the defaults by passing NULL as an attribute parameter to the *pthread_create* call. To set a thread's attributes to something other than the default, we'd perform the following steps:

1. Define an attribute object of type *pthread_attr_t*.

2. Call *pthread_attr_init* to declare and initialize the attribute object.

3. Make calls to specific Pthreads functions to set individual attributes in the object.

4. Specify the fully initialized attribute object to the *pthread_create* call that creates the thread.

We'll walk through some specific examples of setting a thread's stack size, stack location, and detached state in the next few sections. We'll investigate the thread-scheduling attributes later in this chapter.

Setting a Thread's Stack Size

A thread uses its private stack to store local variables for each routine it has called (but not yet exited) up to its current point of execution. (It also leaves various pieces of procedure context information on the stack, like bread crumbs, so that it can find its way back to the previously executing routine when it exits the current one.) For instance, consider a worker thread in our ATM server. It calls *process_request*, does some processing, and pushes some of *process_request*'s local variables on the stack. It then calls *deposit*, pushing some information that allows it to return to the next instruction in *process_request* when it exits *deposit*. Now, it pushes *deposit*'s local variables on its stack. Suppose it then calls *retrieve_account*, and then some number-crunching routine, and then, and then . . . . We'd certainly like our thread to have ample stack space for all routines in its current call chain.

Two factors can affect whether a thread will have enough room on its stack:

- The size of the local variables to each routine
- The number of routines that may be in its call chain at any one time

If our worker thread begins to call routines that locally declare kilobyte-sized buffers, we might have a problem. If it makes nested procedure calls to some pretty hefty libraries (like a Kerberos security library or an X graphics library), we'd better start stretching its stack.

Even nonthreaded processes run out of stack space from time to time. However, an individual thread's stack is much smaller than that devoted to an entire process. The space for the stacks of all threads in a process is carved out of the memory previously allocated for the stack of the process as a whole. As shown in Figure 4-1, a process stack normally starts in high memory and works its way down in memory without anything in its way until it reaches 0. For a process with individual threads, one thread's stack is bounded by the start of the next thread's stack, even if the next thread isn't using all of its stack space.

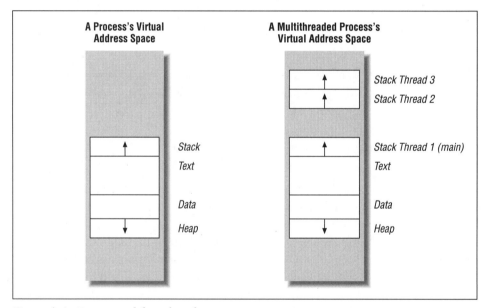

Figure 4-1: Process and thread stacks

To set a thread's stack size, we call *pthread_attr_init* to declare and initialize a custom thread attribute object (*pthread_attr_t*) in Example 4-1.

Example 4-1: Declaring a Custom Attribute (mattr.c)

```
#define MIN_REQ_SSIZE 81920
size_t default_stack_size;
pthread_attr_t stack_size_custom_attr;
    .
    .
    .
    pthread_attr_init(&stack_size_custom_attr);
    .
    .
    .
```

Now that we've created and initialized our attribute object, we can set and check the value of any attribute in it, using the appropriate Pthreads function. In Example 4-2, we'll read and adjust the thread's stack size by calling *pthread_attr_get-stacksize* and *pthread_attr_setstacksize*. The minimum stack size on the platform is always stored in PTHREAD_STACK_MIN and can be used to determine at run time if the default stack will be big enough.

Example 4-2: Checking and Setting Stack Size (mattr.c)

```
#ifdef _POSIX_THREAD_ATTR_STACKSIZE
pthread_attr_getstacksize(&stack_size_custom_attr,
              &default_stack_size);

if (default_stack_size < MIN_REQ_SSIZE) {
    .
    .
    .
    pthread_attr_setstacksize(&stack_size_custom_attr,
                (size_t)MIN_REQ_SSIZE);
}
#endif
```

In Example 4-3, we'll create a thread that has the desired attribute (a MIN_REQ_SSIZE stack) by specifying the attribute object in a *pthread_create* call.

Example 4-3: Using an Attribute Object in pthread_create (mattr.c)

```
pthread_create(&threads[num_threads],
              &stack_size_custom_attr,
              (void *) mult_worker,
              (void *) p);
```

Take special notice that fiddling with a thread's stack is inherently nonportable. Stack size and location are platform-dependent; the bytes and bounds of your threads' stacks on Platform A may not quite match those of the stacks on Platform B.

Specifying the Location of a Thread's Stack

The location of a thread's stack may be of some importance to an application that accesses memory areas with diverse properties, such as a programming language's run-time library or an embedded systems environment. An application of this sort can use its threads' attribute objects to situate thread stacks as it sees fit.

To check and adjust a thread's stack location, use *pthread_attr_getstackaddr* and *pthread_attr_setstackaddr*. Specify an address within the process's virtual address space to the *pthread_attr_setstackaddr* call. When managing thread stack locations in this way, you must take special care that the thread stacks are big enough and that they do not overlap. Dire consequences could result if you don't.

Setting a Thread's Detached State

Detaching from a thread informs the Pthreads library that no other thread will use the *pthread_join* mechanism to synchronize with the thread's exiting. Because the library doesn't preserve the exit status of a detached thread, it can operate more efficiently and make the library resources that were associated with a thread available for reuse more quickly. If no other thread cares when a particular thread in your program exits, consider detaching that thread.

Back in Chapter 2, *Designing Threaded Programs*, we discussed how to use the *pthread_detach* function to dynamically place a joinable thread into a detached state. In Example 4-4, we'll show you how to do it with an attribute object at thread creation.

Example 4-4: Setting the Detached State in an Attribute Object (mattr.c)

```
pthread_attr_t detached_attr;
 .
 .
 .
        pthread_attr_setdetachedstate(&detached_attr, PTHREAD_CREATE_DETACHED);
        .
        .
        .
        pthread_create(&thread, &detached_attr, ...);
        .
        .
        .
```

The *pthread_attr_setdetachedstate* function sets the detached state in an attribute object to either the PTHREAD_CREATE_DETACHED constant (detached) or the PTHREAD_CREATE_JOINABLE constant (joinable). The *pthread_attr_getdetached-state* function returns the current detached setting of a thread attribute object.

Setting Multiple Attributes

You can set multiple individual attributes within a single attribute object. In the next example, Example 4-5, we'll use calls to the *pthread_attr_setstacksize* function and the *pthread_attr_setdetachedstate* function to set a thread's stack size and detached state in the same object.

Example 4–5: Setting Multiple Attributes in an Attribute Object (mattr.c)

```
pthread_attr_t custom_attr;
        .
        pthread_attr_init(&custom_attr);
        .
        pthread_attr_setstacksize(&custom_attr, MIN_REQ_SSIZE);
        pthread_attr_setdetachedstate(&custom_attr, PTHREAD_CREATE_DETACHED);
        .
        .
        pthread_create(&thread, &custom_attr, ...);
        .
        .
        .
```

Destroying a Thread Attribute Object

Throughout this section, we've declared and initialized thread attribute objects using the *pthread_attr_init* call. When we're finished using a thread attribute object, we can call *pthread_attr_destroy* to destroy it. Note that existing threads that were created using this object are not affected when the object is destroyed.

The pthread_once Mechanism

When you create many threads that cooperate to accomplish a single task, you must sometimes perform a single operation up front so that all of these threads can proceed. For instance, you may need to open a file or initialize a mutex. Up to now, we've had our boss thread handle these chores, but that's not always feasible.

The *pthread_once* mechanism is the tool of choice for these situations. It, like mutexes and condition variables, is a synchronization tool, but its specialty is handling synchronization among threads at initialization time. If the *pthread_once* function didn't exist, we'd have to initialize all data, mutexes, and condition variables before we could create any thread that uses them. After our program has started and spawned its first thread, it would be very difficult for it to create new resources that require protection should some asynchronous event require that it do so.

If we're writing a library that can be called by a multithreaded application, this becomes more than just an annoyance. Perhaps we don't want (or can't have) a single function for our users to call that allows our library to initialize itself prior to its general use. Neither can we ask each of our library functions to first call an initialization routine. Remember, our library's multithreaded. How do we know whether or not another thread might be trying to initialize the same objects simultaneously?

Example: The ATM Server's Communication Module

Let's walk through an example that will help us illustrate the point. We'll use the communication module from our ATM server—that part of the server that receives requests from clients and unpacks them. The interface to the communication module is as shown in Example 4-6.

Example 4-6: Interface to the ATM Server Communication Module (atm_com_svr.c)

```
void server_comm_get_request(int *, char *);
void server_comm_send_response(int, char *);
void server_comm_close_conn(int);
void server_comm_shutdown(void);
```

Let's pretend that this is legacy code that we've been asked to incorporate into a multithreaded program. We'll also pretend that it contains an initialization routine and that we don't want to completely rewrite it to eliminate the routine.

The *server_comm_get_request* routine shown in Example 4-7 is typical of the interfaces in this module.

Example 4-7: Original server_comm_get_request Routine (atm_com_svr.c)

```
void server_comm_get_request(int *conn, char *req_buf)
{
  int i, nr, not_done = 1;
  fd_set read_selects;

  if (!srv_comm_inited) {
    server_comm_init();
    srv_comm_inited = TRUE;
  }
```

Example 4-7: Original server_comm_get_request Routine (atm_com_svr.c) (continued)

```
    /* loop, processing new connection requests until a client
       buffer is read in on an existing connection. */

    while (not_done) {
        .
        .
        .
    }
}
```

If the *server_comm_inited* flag is FALSE, the *server_comm_get_request* routine calls an initialization routine (*server_comm_init*) and sets the flag to TRUE. If we allow multiple threads to call *server_comm_init* concurrently, we introduce a race condition on the *srv_comm_inited* flag and on all of *server_comm_init*'s global variables and initializations. Consider: threads A and B enter the routine at the same time. Thread A checks the value of *srv_comm_inited* and finds FALSE. Thread B checks the value and also finds it FALSE. Then they both go forward and call *srv_comm_init*.

We'll consider two viable solutions:

- Adding a mutex to protect the *srv_comm_inited* flag and *server_comm_init* routine. Using PTHREAD_MUTEX_INITIALIZER, we'll statically initialize this mutex.

- Designating that the entire routine needs special synchronization handling by calling the *pthread_once* function.

Using a statically initialized mutex

If we choose to protect the *srv_comm_inited* flag and *server_comm_init* routine by a statically initialized mutex, our code would look like that in Example 4-8.

Example 4-8: The ATM with Static Initialization (atm_com_svr_init.c)

```
pthread_mutex_t init_mutex = PTHREAD_MUTEX_INITIALIZER;

void server_comm_get_request(int *conn, char *req_buf)
{
    int i, nr, not_done = 1;
    fd_set read_selects;

    pthread_mutex_lock(&init_mutex)
    if (!srv_comm_inited) {
        server_comm_init();

        srv_comm_inited = TRUE;
    }
    pthread_mutex_unlock(&init_mutex);
```

Example 4-8: The ATM with Static Initialization (atm_com_svr_init.c) (continued)

```
        /* loop, processing new connection requests until a client
           buffer is read in on an existing connection. */

    while (not_done) {
      .
      .
      .
    }
```

Using a statically defined mutex to protect the initialization flag and routine works
in this simple case but has its drawbacks as a module grows more complex:

- When the initialization routine introduces dynamically allocated mutexes, it
  must initialize them dynamically. This is not an insurmountable problem; as
  long as at least one mutex is statically defined, it can control the initialization
  of all the other mutexes.

- The mutex protecting the initialization flag routine will continue to act as a
  synchronization point long after it is needed. Each time any thread enters the
  library, it will lock and unlock the mutex to read the flag and learn the old
  news: initialization is complete. (Using the *pthread_once* function may also
  involve this type of overhead. However, because the purpose of the
  pthread_once call is known to the library, a clever library could optimize its
  use after initialization is complete.)

- You cannot define custom attributes for a statically initialized mutex. You can
  work around this problem, too; as long as at least one mutex is statically
  defined, it can control the initialization of all other mutexes that have custom
  attributes.

Using the pthread_once mechanism

If we use the *server_comm_init* routine only through the *pthread_once* mechanism, we can make the following synchronization guarantees:

- No matter how many times it is invoked by one or more threads, the routine
  will be executed only once by its first caller.

- No caller will exit from the *pthread_once* mechanism until the routine's first
  caller has returned.

To use the *pthread_once* mechanism, you must declare a variable known as a
once block (*pthread_once_t*), and you must statically initialize it to the value
PTHREAD_ONCE_INIT. The Pthreads library uses a once block to maintain the
state of *pthread_once* synchronization for a particular routine. Note that we are

statically initializing the once block to the PTHREAD_ONCE_INIT value. If the Pthreads standard allowed us to dynamically initialize it (that is, if the library defined a *pthread_once_init* call), we'd run into a race condition if multiple threads tried to initialize a given routine's once block at the same time.

In our ATM server, we'll call the once block *srv_comm_inited_once* and declare and initialize it globally:

```
pthread_once_t      srv_comm_inited_once = PTHREAD_ONCE_INIT;
```

Now that we've declared a once block, the *server_comm_get_request* routine no longer has to test a flag to determine whether to proceed with initialization. Instead, as shown in Example 4-9, it calls *pthread_once*, specifying the once block and the routine we've associated with it—*server_comm_init*.

Example 4-9: Using a Once Block in the ATM (atm_com_svr_once.c)

```
void server_comm_get_request(int *conn, char *req_buf)
{
  int i, nr, not_done = 1;
  fd_set read_selects;

  pthread_once(&srv_comm_inited_once, server_comm_init);

  /* loop, processing new connection requests until a client
     buffer is read in on an existing connection. */

  while (not_done) {
    .
    .
    .
  }
}
```

We'll change the other interface routines in our ATM server's communication module in the same manner. Any number of threads can call into the module. Each interface call will initially involve a call to *pthread_once*, but only the first thread will actually enter *server_comm_init* and execute our module's initialization routine.

You can declare multiple once blocks in a program, associating each with a different routine. Be careful, though. Once you associate a routine with the *pthread_once* mechanism, you must always call it through a *pthread_once* call, using the same once block. You cannot call the routine directly elsewhere in your program without subverting the synchronization the *pthread_once* mechanism is meant to provide

Notice that the *pthread_once* interface does not allow you to pass arguments to the routine that is protected by the once block. If you're trying to fit a predefined routine with arguments into the *pthread_once* mechanism, you'll have to fiddle a bit with global variables, wrapper routines, or environment variables to get it to work properly.

Keys: Using Thread-Specific Data

As a thread calls and returns from one routine or another, the local data on its stack comes and goes. To maintain long-lived data associated with a thread, we normally have two options:

- Pass the data as an argument to each call the thread makes.
- Store the data in a global variable associated with the thread.

These are perfectly good ways of preserving some types of data for the lifetime of a thread. However, in some instances, neither solution would work. Consider what might happen if you're rewriting a library of related routines to support multi-threading. Most likely you don't have the option of redefining the library's call arguments. Because you don't necessarily know at compile time how many threads will be making library calls, it's very difficult to define an adequate number of global variables with the right amount of storage. Fortunately, the Pthreads standard provides a clever way of maintaining thread-specific data in such cases.

Pthreads bases its implementation of thread-specific data on the concept of a key—a kind of pointer that associates data with a specific thread. Although all threads refer to the same key, each thread associates the key with different data. This magic is accomplished by the threads library, which stores the pointer to data on a per-thread basis and keeps track of which item of data is associated with each thread.

Suppose you were writing a communication module that allowed you to open a connection to another host name and read and write across it. A single-threaded version might look like Example 4-10.

Example 4-10: A Communications Module (specific.c)

```
static int cur_conn;

int open_connection(char *host)
{
        .
        .
        .
        cur_conn = ....
        .
        .
```

Example 4–10: A Communications Module (specific.c) (continued)

```
        .
}

int send_data(char *data)
{
        .
        .
        .
        write(cur_conn,...)
        .
        .
        .
}

int receive_data(char **data)
{
        .
        .
        .
        read(cur_conn,...)
        .
        .
        .
}
```

We've made the static variable *cur_conn* internal to this module. It stores the connection identifier between calls to send and receive data. When we add multiple threads to this module, we'll probably want them to communicate concurrently with the same or different hosts. As written, though, this module would have a rather surprising side effect for the thread that first opens a connection and starts to use it. Each subsequent *open_connection* call will reset the stored connection (*cur_conn*) in all threads!

If we couldn't use thread-specific data with keys, we'd still have a few ways of fixing this problem:

- Add the connection identifier as an output argument to the *open_connection* call and as an input argument to the *receive_data* and *send_data* calls.

  Although this would certainly work, it's a rather awkward solution for a couple of reasons. First, it forces each routine that currently uses the module to change as well. Any routine that makes calls to the module must store the connection identifier it receives from the *open_connection* call so it can use it in subsequent *receive_data* and *send_data* calls. Second, the connection variable is just an arbitrary value with meaning only within the module. As such, it should naturally be hidden within the module. If we did not force its use as a parameter to our module's interfaces, the caller would otherwise never reference it. It shouldn't even need to know about it.

- Add an array (*cur_conn*) that contains entries for multiple connections.

  This alone would not work, because the current version of our module has no way of returning to the caller of *open_connection* the index of the array entry at which it stored the connection identifier. We could proceed to add an argument to *open_connection, receive_data*, and *send_data* to pass back and forth an index into the *cur_conn* array, but that leads to the same disadvantages as our first solution. Furthermore, we don't know how much space to allocate for the array because the number of threads making connections can vary during the run of the program.

Now we can see more clearly the advantages of using thread-specific data. This way, our module can use a key to point to the connection identifier. We need no new arguments in the calls to the module. Each time a thread calls one of the routines in our module, our code uses the key to obtain its own particular connection identifier value.

Certain applications also use thread-specific data with keys to associate special properties with a thread in one routine and then retrieve them in another. Some examples include:

- A resource management module (such as a memory manager or a file manager) could use a key to point to a record of the resources that have been allocated for a given thread. When the thread makes a call to allocate more resources, the module uses the key to retrieve the thread's record and process its request.

- A performance statistics module for threads could use a key to point to a location where it saves the starting time for a calling thread.

- A debugging module that maintains mutex statistics could use a key to point to a per-thread count of mutex locks and unlocks.

- A thread-specific exception-handling module, when servicing a *try* call (which starts execution of the normal code path), could use a key to point to a location to which to jump in case the thread encounters an exception. The occurrence of an exception triggers a *catch* call to the module. The module checks the key to determine where to unwind the thread's execution.

- A random number generation module could use a key to point to a location where it maintains a unique seed value and number stream for each thread that calls it to obtain random numbers.

These examples share some common characteristics:

- They are libraries with internal state.

- They don't require their callers to provide context in interface arguments. They don't burden the caller with maintaining this type of context in the global environment.

- In a nonthreaded environment, the data to which the key refers would normally be stored as static data.

Note that thread-specific data is not a distinct data section like global, heap, and stack. It offers no special system protection or performance guarantees; it's as private or shared as other data in the same data section. There are no special advantages to using thread-specific data if you aren't writing a library and if you know exactly how many threads will be in your program at a given time. If this is the case, just allocate a global array with an element for each known thread and store each thread's data in a separate element.

Initializing a Key: pthread_key_create

Let's rewrite our ATM server's communication module so that it uses a key to point to the connection information for each thread. When a thread calls the *open_connection* routine, the routine will store the thread-specific connection identifier using a key. We'll initialize the key, as shown in Example 4-11.

Example 4-11: A Communication Module Using Keys (specific.c)

```
#include <pthread.h>

static pthread_key_t conn_key;

int init_comm(void)
{
        .
        .
        .
        pthread_key_create(&conn_key, (void *)free_conn);
        .
        .
        .
}

void free_conn(int *connp)
{
        free(connp);
}
```

We've defined *conn_key*, the key we're using to point to the thread-specific connection identifier, as a static variable within the module. We initialize it by calling *pthread_key_create* in the *init_comm* routine. The *pthread_key_create* call takes two arguments: the key and a destructor routine. The library uses the destructor routine to clean up the data stored in the key when a thread stores a new value in the key or exits. We'll discuss destructor routines some more in a moment.

When you're done with a key, call *pthread_key_delete* to allow the library to recover resources associated with the key itself.

Although the *pthread_key_create* function initializes a key that threads can use, it neither allocates memory for the data to be associated with the key, nor associates the data to the key. Next we'll show you how to handle the actual data.

Associating Data with a Key

The chief trick to using keys is that you must never assign a value directly to a key, nor can you use a key itself in an expression. You must always use *pthread_setspecific* and *pthread_getspecific* to refer to any data item that is being managed by a key. In Example 4-12, our communication module's *open_connection* routine calls *pthread_setspecific* to associate the *conn_key* key with a thread-specific pointer to an integer.

Example 4-12: Storing Data in a Key (specific.c)

```
int open_connection(char *host)
{
        int *connp;
        .
        .
        .
        connp = (int *)malloc(sizeof(int));
        *connp = ...
        pthread_setspecific(conn_key, (void *)connp);
        .
        .
        .
}
```

When a thread calls the *open_connection* routine, the routine calls *malloc* to allocate storage for an integer on the heap and sets the pointer *connp* to point at it. The routine then uses *connp* to set up a connection and store the connection identifier. Once the connection is complete, the *pthread_setspecific* call stores *connp* in a thread-specific location associated with *conn_key*.

The *pthread_setspecific* routine takes, as an argument, a pointer to the data to be associated with the key—not the data itself. Figure 4-2 shows what the *conn_key* key would look like after the first thread used it to store its thread-specific value.

The *open_connection* routine, executing in Thread 1's context, pushes the *connp* variable onto the thread's stack. After the call to *malloc*, *connp* points to storage

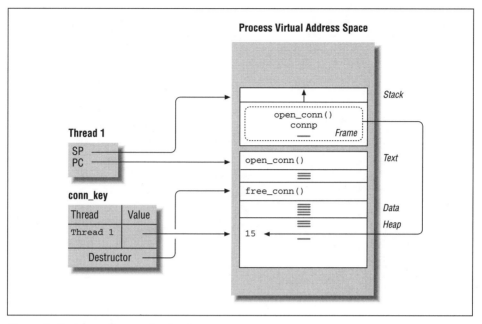

Figure 4–2: A key after a value is set

for an integer in the heap section of the process. The detailed communication code then uses the *connp* pointer to set the value of the connection identifier to 15. Once the connection is set up, the *pthread_setspecific* call stores the pointer to the allocated heap storage for this thread with the *conn_key* key. When Thread 1 returns from its *open_connection* procedure call, its stack frame for the procedure call is deallocated, including its *connp* pointer. The only place in which a pointer to Thread 1's connection identifier remains is within the key.

When another thread calls *open_connection*, as shown in Figure 4-3, the process is repeated.

Now Thread 2 has a stack frame for its *open_connection* procedure call. After the call to *malloc*, *connp* points to storage for an integer in a different area of the process's heap section. The detailed communications code comes up with a different connection identifier for Thread 2, but the *pthread_setspecific* call stores a pointer to this value, 22, in the very same key as it stored a pointer to Thread 1's connection identifier. When Thread 2 returns from its *open_connection* procedure call, its stack frame for the procedure call is deallocated, including its *connp* pointer. The only place in which a pointer to Thread 2's connection identifier remains is within the key.

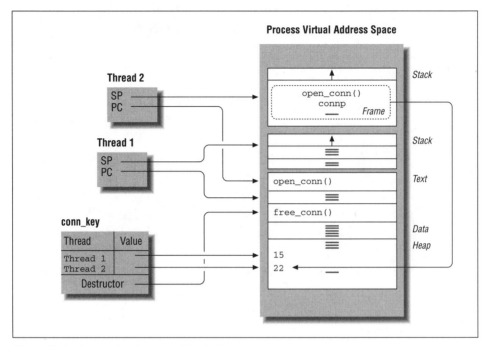

Figure 4–3: A second value stored in the key

Retrieving Data from a Key

The *send_data* and *receive_data* routines call *pthread_getspecific* to retrieve the connection identifier for the calling thread. Each routine uses a pointer, *saved_connp*, to point to the connection identifier, as shown in Example 4-13.

Example 4–13: Retrieving Data from a Key (specific.c)

```
int send_data(char *data)
{
      int *saved_connp;
      .
      .
      .
      pthread_getspecific(conn_key, (void **)&saved_connp);
      write(*saved_connp,...);
      .
      .
      .
}

int receive_data(char **data)

{
      int *saved_connp;
```

Example 4-13: Retrieving Data from a Key (specific.c) (continued)

```
       .
       .
       .
    saved_connp = pthread_getspecific(conn_key);
    read(*saved_connp,...)
       .
       .
       .
}
```

When Thread 1 calls the *send_data* or *receive_data* routine, as shown in Figure 4-4, the routine calls *pthread_getspecific* to return to *saved_connp* the thread-specific connection identifier associated with the *conn_key* key. It now has access to its connection identifier (15) and can write or read across the connection. When the second thread calls *send_data* or *receive_data*, it likewise retrieves its connection identifier (22) using the key.

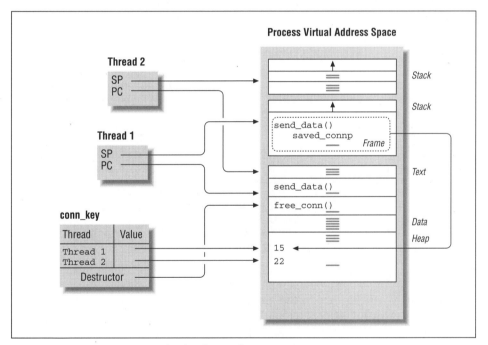

Figure 4-4: Retrieving a stored value from a key

The *pthread_getspecific* function returns NULL if no value has been associated with a key. If a thread received a NULL return value from its call to *receive_data* or *send_data*, it's likely that it neglected to make a prior call to *open_connection*.

Destructors

We've shown that keys often store pointers to thread-specific data that's been allocated on the heap. Memory leaks can occur when threads exit and leave their thread-specific data that was associated with keys. For this reason we must specify a destructor routine, or *destructor* for short, when we create a key. When a thread exits, the library invokes the destructor on the thread's behalf, passing to it the pointer to the thread-specific data currently associated with the key. In this manner, the destructor acts as a convenient plug for potential memory leaks, deallocating memory that would otherwise be forgotten and go to waste.

The destructor can be any routine you choose. In our *init_comm* routine shown in Example 4-11, we used a routine named *free_conn*. For the simple integer being stored, *free_conn* could have simply consisted of a *free* system call. If we were using more complex data, such as a linked list, the destructor would be a more complex routine that walked down the list, freeing each node. An even more complex example would be a data structure that includes handles on system resources, such as sockets and files, that the destructor would need to close.

Cancellation

Cancellation allows one thread to terminate another. One reason you may want to cancel a thread is to save system resources (such as CPU time) when your program determines that the thread's activity is no longer necessary. In an odd sense, you can consider cancellation to be a very rough synchronization mechanism: after you've canceled a thread, you know exactly where it is in its execution! A simple example of a thread you might want to cancel would be a thread performing a read-only data search. If one thread returns the results you are looking for, all other threads running the same routine could be canceled.

Okay, so you've decided that you'd like to cancel a thread. Now you must reckon whether the thread you've targeted can be canceled at all. The ability of a thread to go away or not go away when asked by another thread is known as its *cancelability state*. Let's assume that you can indeed cancel this thread. Now you must consider when it might go away—maybe immediately, maybe a bit later. The degree to which a thread persists after it has been asked to go away is known as its *cancelability type*. Finally, some threads are able to perform some special cleanup processing as part of being terminated (either through cancellation or through a *pthread_exit* call). These threads have an associated cleanup stack.

We'll get into cancelability states, cancelability types, and cleanup stacks a little bit later (probably not late enough for those of you who winced at the use of the term *cancelability*). Right now, remember that threads don't have a parent/child relationship as processes do. So, any thread can cancel any other thread, as long as the canceling thread has the thread handle of its victim. Because you want your application to be solidly structured, you'll cancel threads only from the thread that initially created them.

The Complication with Cancellation

Cancellation is not as convenient as you might think at first. Most tasks that make multithreading worthwhile involve taking thread-shared data through some intermediate states before bringing it to some final state. Any thread accessing this data must take and release locks, as appropriate, to maintain proper synchronization. If a thread is to be terminated in the middle of such a prolonged operation, you must first release its locks to prevent deadlock. Often, you must also reset the data to some correct or consistent state. A good example of this would be fixing forward or backward pointers that a thread may have left hanging in a linked list.

For this reason, you must use cancellation very carefully. The simplest approach is to restrict the use of cancellation to threads that execute only in simple routines that do not hold locks or ever put shared data in an inconsistent state. Another option is to restrict cancellation to certain points at which a thread is known to have neither locks nor resources. Lastly, you could create a cleanup stack for the thread that is to be canceled; it can then use the cleanup stack to release locks and reset the state of shared data.

These options are all well and good when you are in charge of all the code your threads might execute. What if your threads call library routines that you don't control? You may have no idea of the detailed operation of these interfaces. One solution to this problem is to create cancellation-safe library routines, a topic we'll defer to the next chapter along with other issues of integration into a UNIX environment.

Cancelability Types and States

Because canceling a thread that holds locks and manipulates shared data can be a tricky procedure, the Pthreads standard provides a mechanism by which you can set a given thread's cancelability (that is, its ability to allow itself to be canceled). In short, a thread can set its cancelability state and cancelability type to any of the combinations listed in Table 4-1, thereby ensuring that it can safely obtain locks or modify shared data when it needs to.

A thread can switch back and forth any number of times across the various permitted combinations of cancelability state and type. When a thread holds no locks and has no resources allocated, asynchronous cancellation is a valid option. When a thread must hold and release locks, it might temporarily disable cancellation altogether.

Note that the Pthreads standard gives you no attribute that would allow you to set a thread's cancelability state or type when you create it. A thread can set its own cancelability only at run time, dynamically, by calling into the Pthreads library.

Table 4-1: Cancelability of a Thread

Cancelability State	Cancelability Type	Description
PTHREAD_CANCEL_ DISABLE	Ignored	Disabled. The thread can never be canceled. Calls to *pthread_cancel* have no effect. The thread can safely acquire locks and resources.
PTHREAD_CANCEL_ ENABLE	PTHREAD_CANCEL_ ASYNCHRONOUS	Asynchronous cancellation. Cancellation takes effect immediately.[a]
PTHREAD_CANCEL_ ENABLE	PTHREAD_CANCEL_ DEFERRED	Deferred cancellation (the default). Cancellation takes effect only if and when the thread enters a cancellation point. The thread can hold and release locks but must keep data in some consistent state. If a pending cancellation exists at a cancellation point, the thread can terminate without leaving problems behind for the remaining threads.

a. The Pthreads standard states that cancellation will take place "at any time." We trust that most implementations interpret this phrase to mean "as soon as possible." The thread must avoid taking out locks and performing sensitive operations on shared data.

Cancellation Points: More on Deferred Cancellation

When a thread has enabled cancellation (that is, it has set its cancelability state to PTHREAD_CANCEL_ENABLE) and is using deferred cancellation (that is, it has set its cancelability type to PTHREAD_CANCEL_DEFERRED), time can elapse between the time it's asked to cancel itself and the time it's actually terminated.

These pending cancellations are delivered to a thread at defined locations in its code path. These locations are known as *cancellation points*, and they come in two flavors:

- Automatic cancellation points (*pthread_cond_wait, pthread_cond_timedwait,* and *pthread_join*). The Pthreads library defines these function calls as cancellation points because they can block the calling thread. Rather than maintain the overhead of a blocked routine that's destined to be canceled, the Pthreads library considers these calls to be a license to kill the thread. Note that, if the thread for which the cancellation is pending does not call any of these functions, it may never actually be terminated. This is one of the reasons you may need to consider using a programmer-defined cancellation point.

- Programmer-defined cancellation points (*pthread_testcancel*). To force a pending cancellation to be delivered at a particular point in a thread's code path, insert a call to *pthread_testcancel.* The *pthread_testcancel* function causes any pending cancellation to be delivered to the thread at the program location where it occurs. If no cancellation is pending on the thread, nothing happens. Thus, you can freely insert this call at those places in a thread's code path where it's safe for the thread to terminate. It's also prudent to call *pthread_testcancel* before a thread starts a time-consuming operation. If a cancellation is pending on the thread, it's better to terminate it as soon as possible, rather than have it continue and consume system resources needlessly.

The Pthreads standard also defines cancellation points at certain standard system and library calls. We'll address this topic in Chapter 5, *Pthreads and UNIX.*

A Simple Cancellation Example

Example 4-14 illustrates the basic mechanics of cancellation. The *main* routine creates three threads: *bullet_proof, ask_for_it,* and *sitting_duck.* Each thread selects a different cancellation policy: the *bullet_proof* routine disables cancellation, the *ask_for_it* routine selects deferred cancellation, and the *sitting_duck* routine enables asynchronous cancellation.

The *main* routine waits until all of the threads have started and entered an infinite loop. It then tries to cancel each thread with a *pthread_cancel* call. By issuing a *join* on each thread, it waits until all threads have terminated.

Example 4–14: The Simple Cancellation Example—main (cancel.c)

```
#include <stdlib.h>
#include <stdio.h>
#include <unistd.h>
#include <sys/types.h>
#include <pthread.h>
#define NUM_THREADS 3
int count = NUM_THREADS;
pthread_mutex_t lock=PTHREAD_MUTEX_INITIALIZER;
pthread_cond_t init_done=PTHREAD_COND_INITIALIZER;
int id_arg[NUM_THREADS] = {0,1,2};
```

Example 4-14: The Simple Cancellation Example—main (cancel.c) (continued)

```
extern int
main(void)
{
  int i;
  void *statusp;
  pthread_t threads[NUM_THREADS];

  /**** Create the threads ****/

  pthread_create(&(threads[0]), NULL, ask_for_it, (void *) &(id_arg[0]));
  pthread_create(&(threads[1]), NULL, sitting_duck, (void *) &(id_arg[1]));
  pthread_create(&(threads[2]), NULL, bullet_proof, (void *) &(id_arg[2]));

  printf("main(): %d threads created\n",count);

  /**** wait until all threads have initialized ****/

  pthread_mutex_lock(&lock);
  while (count != 0) {
    pthread_cond_wait(&init_done, &lock);
  }

  pthread_mutex_unlock(&lock);

  printf("main(): all threads have signaled that they're ready\n");

  /**** cancel each thread ****/

  for (i = 0; i < NUM_THREADS; i++) {
    pthread_cancel(threads[i]);
  }

  /**** wait until all threads have finished ****/

  for (i = 0; i < NUM_THREADS; i++) {
    pthread_join(threads[i], &statusp);
    if (statusp == PTHREAD_CANCELED) {
      printf("main(): joined to thread %d, statusp=PTHREAD_CANCELED\n", i);
    } else {
      printf("main(): joined to thread %d \n", i);
    }
  }
  printf("main(): all %d threads have finished. \n", NUM_THREADS);
  return 0;
}
```

The bullet_proof thread: no effect

When a thread, like *bullet_proof*, disables cancellation, it is impervious to *pthread_cancel* calls from other threads, as shown in Example 4-15.

Example 4-15: The Simple Cancellation Example—bullet_proof (cancel.c)

```
void *bullet_proof(int *my_id)
{
  int i=0, last_state;
  char *messagep;

  messagep = (char *)malloc(MESSAGE_MAX_LEN);
  sprintf(messagep, "bullet_proof, thread #%d: ", *my_id);

  printf("%s\tI'm alive, setting general cancelability OFF\n", messagep);

  /* We turn off general cancelability here */
  pthread_setcancelstate(PTHREAD_CANCEL_DISABLE, &last_state);

  pthread_mutex_lock(&lock);
  {
  printf("\n%s signaling main that my init is done\n", messagep);
  count -= 1;
  /* Signal to program that loop is being entered */
  pthread_cond_signal(&init_done);
  pthread_mutex_unlock(&lock);
  }

  /* Loop forever until picked off with a cancel */
  for(;;i++) {
    if (i%10000 == 0)
      print_count(messagep, *my_id, i);
    if (i%100000 == 0)
      printf("\n%s This is the thread that never ends... #%d\n", messagep, i);
  }

  /* Never get this far */
  return(NULL);
}
```

The *bullet_proof* thread calls *pthread_setcancelstate* to set its cancelability state to disabled (PTHREAD_CANCEL_DISABLE). After it enters its loop, it repeatedly taunts *main* until the program ends. Because the *main* thread has issued a *pthread_join* call to wait on the *bullet_proof* thread, we'll need to shoot the whole program with a CTRL-C to get *bullet_proof* to stop.

The ask_for_it thread: deferred cancellation

The *ask_for_it* thread calls *pthread_setcancelstate* to set its cancelability state to enabled (PTHREAD_CANCEL_ENABLE) and *pthread_setcanceltype* to set its cancelability type to deferred (PTHREAD_CANCEL_DEFERRED). (It actually didn't need to explicitly do so, as deferred cancellation is the default for all threads.) After *main* has issued a *pthread_cancel* for it, the *ask_for_it* thread terminates when it enters the next cancellation point, as shown in Example 4-16.

Example 4-16: The Simple Cancellation Example—ask_for_it (cancel.c)

```
void *ask_for_it(int *my_id)
{
   int i=0, last_state, last_type;
   char *messagep;

   messagep = (char *)malloc(MESSAGE_MAX_LEN);
   sprintf(messagep, "ask_for_it, thread #%d: ", *my_id);

   /* We can turn on general cancelability here and disable async cancellation. */
   printf("%s\tI'm alive, setting deferred cancellation ON\n", messagep);
   pthread_setcancelstate(PTHREAD_CANCEL_ENABLE, &last_state);
   pthread_setcanceltype(PTHREAD_CANCEL_DEFERRED, &last_type);


   pthread_mutex_lock(&lock);
   {
   printf("\n%s signaling main that my init is done\n", messagep);
   count -= 1;
   /* Signal to program that loop is being entered */
   pthread_cond_signal(&init_done);
   pthread_mutex_unlock(&lock);
   }

   /* Loop forever until picked off with a cancel */
   for(;;i++) {
     if (i%1000 == 0)
       print_count(messagep, *my_id, i);
     if (i%10000 == 0)
       printf("\n%s\tLook, I'll tell you when you can cancel me.%d\n", messagep, i);
       pthread_testcancel();
   }

   /* Never get this far */
   return(NULL);
}
```

We'll force the delivery of *main*'s cancellation request by adding a *pthread_testcancel* call to its loop. After *main* calls *pthread_cancel*, *ask_for_it* will terminate when it encounters *pthread_testcancel* in the next iteration of the loop.

The sitting_duck thread: asynchronous cancellation

The *sitting_duck* thread calls *pthread_setcancelstate* to set its cancelability state to enabled (PTHREAD_CANCEL_ENABLE) and *pthread_setcanceltype* to set its cancelability type to asynchronous (PTHREAD_CANCEL_ASYNCHRONOUS). When *main* issues a *pthread_cancel* for it, the *sitting_duck* thread terminates immediately, regardless of what it is doing.

If we leave our thread in this state, it can be canceled during library and system calls as well. However, unless these calls are documented as "asynchronous cancellation-safe," we should guard against this. (The Pthreads standard requires that only three routines be asynchronous cancellation-safe: *pthread_cancel*, *pthread_setcanceltype*, and *pthread_setcancelstate*.) If we don't, our thread could be canceled in the middle of such a call, leaving its call state in disarray and potentially messing up things for the other threads in the process. In Example 4-17, we'll protect the *printf* call against asynchronous cancellation by setting cancellation to deferred for the duration of the call. Note that the *print_count* routine called by the *sitting_duck* thread would also need to take this precaution before it makes library or system calls.

Example 4-17: The Simple Cancellation Example—sitting_duck (cancel.c)

```
void *sitting_duck(int *my_id)
{
  int i=0, last_state, last_type, last_tmp;
  char messagep;

  messagep = (char *)malloc(MESSAGE_MAX_LEN);
  sprintf(messagep, "sitting_duck, thread #%d: ", *my_id);

  pthread_mutex_lock(&lock);
  {
    printf("\n%s signaling main that my init is done\n", messagep);
    count -= 1;
    /* Signal to program that loop is being entered */
    pthread_cond_signal(&init_done);
    pthread_mutex_unlock(&lock);
  }

  /* Now, we're safe to turn on async cancelability */
  printf("%s\tI'm alive, setting async cancellation ON\n", messagep);
  pthread_setcanceltype(PTHREAD_CANCEL_ASYNCHRONOUS, &last_type);
  pthread_setcancelstate(PTHREAD_CANCEL_ENABLE, &last_state);

  /* Loop forever until picked off with a cancel */
  for(;;i++) {
    if (i%1000) == 0)
      print_count(messagep, *my_id, i);
    if (i%10000 == 0) {
      pthread_setcanceltype(PTHREAD_CANCEL_DEFERRED, &last_tmp);
      printf("\n%s\tHum, nobody here but us chickens. %d\n", messagep, i);
      pthread_setcanceltype(PTHREAD_CANCEL_ASYNCHRONOUS, &last_tmp);
      }
  }

  /* Never get this far */
  return(NULL);
}
```

When the *sitting_duck* thread has asynchronous cancellation enabled, it is canceled when *main* requests its cancellation—whether it's blocked by the scheduler or in the middle of its *print_count* loop.

Cleanup Stacks

Pthreads associates a cleanup stack with each thread. The stack allows a thread to do some final processing before it terminates. Although we're discussing cleanup stacks as a way to facilitate a thread's cancellation, you can also use cleanup stacks in threads that call *pthread_exit* to terminate themselves.

A cleanup stack contains pointers to routines to be executed just before the thread terminates. By default the stack is empty; you use *pthread_cleanup_push* to add routines to the stack, and *pthread_cleanup_pop* to remove them. When the library processes a thread's termination, the thread executes routines from the cleanup stack in last-in first-out order.

We'll adjust Example 4-17 to show how cleanup stacks work. We'll keep the *main* routine the same but have it start all the threads it creates in the *sitting_duck* routine. We'll change *sitting_duck* so that it uses the cleanup stack of the thread in which it is executing. Finally, we'll create a new routine, *last_breath*, so that our threads have something they can push on the stack. The *sitting_duck* routine calls *pthread_cleanup_push* to put the *last_breath* routine on top of the thread's cleanup stack. At its end, it calls *pthread_cleanup_pop* to remove the routine from the stack, as shown in Example 4-18.

Example 4-18: Cleanup Stacks—last_breath and sitting_duck (cancel.c)

```
/*
 * Cleanup routine: last_breath
 */

void last_breath(char *messagep)
{
  printf("\n\n%s last_breath cleanup routine: freeing 0x%x\n\n", messagep,
          messagep);
  free(messagep);
}

/*
 * sitting_duck routine
 */

void *sitting_duck(int *my_id)
{
  int i=0, last_state, last_type, last_tmp;
  char *messagep;

  messagep = (char *)malloc(MESSAGE_MAX_LEN);
```

Example 4-18: Cleanup Stacks—last_breath and sitting_duck (cancel.c) (continued)

```
    sprintf(messagep, "sitting_duck, thread #%d: ", *my_id);

    /* Push last_breath routine onto stack */
    pthread_cleanup_push((void *)last_breath, (void *)messagep);

    pthread_mutex_lock(&lock);
    {
    printf("\n%s signaling main that my init is done\n", messagep);
    count -= 1;
    /* Signal program that loop is being entered */
    pthread_cond_signal(&init_done);
    pthread_mutex_unlock(&lock);
    }

  printf("%s\tI'm alive, setting general cancelability ON, async cancellation
    ON\n", messagep);

    /* Now we're safe to turn on async cancelability */
    pthread_setcancelstate(PTHREAD_CANCEL_ENABLE, &last_state);
    pthread_setcanceltype(PTHREAD_CANCEL_ASYNCHRONOUS, &last_type);

  /* Loop forever until picked off with a cancel */
    for(;;i++) {
      if (i%1000) == 0)
        print_count(messagep, *my_id, i);
      if (i%10000 == 0) {
        pthread_setcanceltype(PTHREAD_CANCEL_DEFERRED, &last_tmp);
        printf("\n%s\tHum, nobody here but us chickens. %d\n", messagep, i);
        pthread_setcanceltype(PTHREAD_CANCEL_ASYNCHRONOUS, &last_tmp);
      }
    }

    /* Never get this far */
    return(NULL);

    /* This pop is required by the standard, every push must
       have a pop in the same lexical block. */

    pthread_cleanup_pop(0);
  }
```

Other cleanup routines might perform additional tasks, such as resetting shared resources to some consistent state, freeing resources the thread still has allocated, and releasing the locks the thread still holds. We can design our own cleanup routines or simply use standard library calls like *pthread_mutex_unlock* or *free* if they would suffice.

There are a few more things about the *pthread_cleanup_pop* function you should know. First, *pthread_cleanup_pop* takes a single argument—an integer that can have either of two values:

- If the value of this argument is 1, the thread that called *pthread_cleanup_pop* executes the cleanup routine whose pointer is being removed from the cleanup stack. Afterwards, the thread resumes at the line following its *pthread_cleanup_pop* call. This allows a thread to execute a cleanup routine whether or not it is actually being terminated.

- If the value of this argument is 0, as it is in Example 4-18, the pointer to the routine is popped off the cleanup stack, but the routine itself does not execute.

Second, the Pthreads standard requires that there be one *pthread_cleanup_pop* for each *pthread_cleanup_push* within a given lexical scope of code. (*Lexical scope* refers to the code within a basic block of a C program—that set of instructions bounded by the curly braces { and }.) Why is this required? After all, the *pthread_cleanup_pop* function call we planted in *sitting_duck* occurs after an infinite loop and is never called. The reason is that this requirement makes it easier for Pthreads library vendors to implement cleanup routines. The *pthread_cleanup_push* and *pthread_cleanup_pop* function calls are easily and commonly implemented as macros that define the start and end of a block. Picture the *pthread_cleanup_push* routine as a macro that ends with an open curly brace ({) and the *pthread_cleanup_pop* routine as a macro that begins with a close curly brace (}). It's not hard to see why a C compiler would complain if we omitted the *pthread_cleanup_pop* call.

Cancellation in the ATM Server

The worker threads in our ATM server are likely candidates for cancellation. There are a couple of reasons why we might want to terminate a worker that is processing an account request:

- To allow a customer to abort a transaction that is in progress

- To allow the system to abort a transaction for security reasons or when it is shutting down

Remember that our worker threads do hold locks and do manipulate shared data—accounts in the bank's database. Dealing with the possibility of cancellation in our worker threads will have some interesting challenges.

In the remainder of this discussion, we'll focus on those changes to the server required to make its worker threads cancelable, without worrying about how the cancellation requests are generated. As a general model for a thread performing any type of request, we'll look at how a worker thread processes a deposit request.

Aborting a deposit

The basic steps a worker thread performs in processing a deposit request are shown in the following pseudocode:

```
1  process_request
2          switch based on transaction type to deposit()
3          deposit()
4                  parse request arguments
5                  check arguments
6                  lock account mutex
7                  retrieve account from database
8                  check password
9                  modify account to add deposit amount
10                 store modified account with database
11                 unlock account mutex
12         send response to client
13         free request buffer
14 return and implicit termination
```

Up to Step 5, the thread would have little difficulty accommodating a cancellation request and terminating. After Step 5, it performs some tasks that make us consider ways in which it must respond to cancellation:

- At Step 6, the thread obtains a lock on an account. At this moment, it must ensure somehow that, if it is the victim of cancellation, it can release the lock so that other threads can use the account after its demise. We can handle this from a cleanup routine that we'll push onto the cleanup stack.

- At Step 10, the thread commits a change to the account but has yet to send an acknowledgment to the client. Let's assume that, after we commit a change to an account, we want to make every effort to send a "transaction completed" response to the client. We'll give the thread a chance to do this by having it turn off cancellation before it writes a new balance. From that point to its termination at the end of *process_request*, it cannot be canceled.

- At Step 13, the thread frees the request buffer. The buffer was originally allocated by the boss thread, which passed it to the worker as an argument to the *process_request* routine. Because the boss does not save its pointer to this buffer, the worker is the only thread that knows where in the heap the buffer resides. If the worker doesn't free the buffer, nothing will. This is another chore we'll assign to the cleanup routine.

We'll rewrite our *process_request* and *deposit* routines to illustrate these changes in Example 4-19. We'll tackle *process_request* first. Note that, by default, threads starting in *process_request* will have deferred cancellation enabled.

Example 4-19: Changes to process_request for Cancellation (atm_svr_cancel.c)

```
void process_request(workorder_t *workorderp)
{
    char resp_buf[COMM_BUF_SIZE];
    int  trans_id;

    /**** Deferred cancellation is enabled by default ****/
    pthread_cleanup_push((void *)free, (void *)workorderp);
    sscanf(workorderp->req_buf, "%d", &trans_id);
    pthread_testcancel();
    switch(trans_id) {

    case CREATE_ACCT_TRANS:
        create_account(resp_buf);
        break;

    case DEPOSIT_TRANS:
        deposit(workorderp->req_buf, resp_buf);
        break;

    case WITHDRAW_TRANS:
        withdraw(workorderp->req_buf, resp_buf);
        break;

    case BALANCE_TRANS:
        balance(workorderp->req_buf, resp_buf);
        break;

    default:
        handle_bad_trans_id(workorderp->req_buf, resp_buf);
        break;
    }

    /* Cancellation may be disabled by the time we get here, but this
       won't hurt either way. */
    pthread_testcancel();
    server_comm_send_response(workorderp->conn, resp_buf);
    pthread_cleanup_pop(1);
}
```

This version of *process_request* starts by calling *pthread_cleanup_push* to place a
pointer to the *free* system routine at the top of the thread's cleanup stack. It passes
a single parameter to *free*—the address of its request buffer. We've placed a
matching call to *pthread_cleanup_pop* at the end of *process_request*. We pass
pthread_cleanup_pop an argument of 1 so that *free* will run and deallocate the
buffer regardless of whether or not the thread is actually canceled. If the thread is
canceled, the buffer will be freed before it terminates; if not, the buffer will be
freed at the *pthread_cleanup_pop* call.

We'll now look at the changes to *deposit* in Example 4-20.

Example 4-20: A Cancelable ATM Deposit Routine (atm_svr_cancel.c)

```
void deposit(char *req_buf, char *resp_buf)
{
   int rtn;
   int temp, id, password, amount, last_state;
   account_t *accountp;

   /* Parse input string */
   sscanf(req_buf, "%d %d %d %d ", &temp, &id, &password, &amount);
   .
   .
   .


   pthread_testcancel();
   pthread_cleanup_push((void *)pthread_mutex_unlock, (void *)&account_mutex[id]);
   pthread_mutex_lock(&account_mutex[id]);

   /* Retrieve account from database */
   rtn = retrieve_account( id, &accountp);
   .
   .
   .
   pthread_testcancel();
   pthread_setcancelstate(PTHREAD_CANCEL_DISABLE, &last_state);

   /* Store back to database */
   if ((rtn = store_account(accountp)) < 0) {
   .
   .
   .
   pthread_cleanup_pop(1);
}
```

This version of the *deposit* routine pushes the address of the *pthread_mutex_unlock* function onto the thread's cleanup stack before calling *pthread_mutex_lock* to obtain the mutex. As we did in the *process_request* routine, we've placed a matching call to *pthread_cleanup_pop* at the end of *deposit*. We pass *pthread_cleanup_pop* an argument of 1 so that *pthread_mutex_unlock* will be run at the *pthread_cleanup_pop* call, if the thread is not previously terminated and the mutex unlocked, as the result of a cancellation request.

Because deferred cancellation is enabled for the thread, we can be sure that it can be cancelled only at a cancellation point. However, if there were a cancellation point between the calls to *pthread_cleanup_push* and *pthread_mutex_lock* we could get into trouble. If our thread were cancelled at that time, the cleanup would try to unlock a mutex that hasn't yet been locked! The consequences of such extravagance are undefined by the Pthreads standard, so we most surely want to avoid them. Our code is safe because there's no such cancellation point between the calls. For the same reason, the order in which we make the calls is immaterial.

Let's see what this means for our *process_request* routine. Remember that the request buffer was allocated by the boss thread and passed to the worker thread in the *pthread_create* call. Even though the new thread executing *process_request* immediately pushes the address of *free* onto its cleanup stack, its push inarguably happens sometime after the boss performed the initial *malloc*. Is this a case of too little too late?

Not necessarily. In our example of cancellation, the boss thread implicitly hands off responsibility for the request buffer to the worker thread that's executing *process_request*. The boss thread knows for certain that *process_request* is the first routine any newly created worker thread will run. By default, all threads are created with deferred cancellation enabled, and this is the cancelability type of the thread at the time it pushes the address of *free* onto the stack. If it doesn't encounter a cancellation point before we push *free* on the cleanup stack, there's no exposure. However, because some system and library calls contain cancellation points, a thread is best off when it expects to be canceled at any time. If any of your code relies on a particular thread not having any cancellation points, be sure to include a comment to that effect.

Just before the *deposit* routine writes the new balance to the account database, it disables cancellation by calling *pthread_setcancelstate*. Subsequently, the thread can complete the *deposit* routine without fear of cancellation. In fact, when the thread exits the *deposit* and returns to *process_request*, cancellation is still disabled.

We've made a lot of changes to our *process_request* and *deposit* routines to allow other threads to cancel a worker thread in the middle of a deposit request. Each change adds overhead to the real work of our ATM server. These safeguards against unexpected cancellation are charged against the performance of a thread each time it executes *process_request* or *deposit*, not just when it's destined to be canceled. Consequently, we should carefully consider whether making our threads cancelable is worth the extra performance cost. If the threads in question run for only a short period of time before exiting, the complexity is hardly worthwhile. However, if the threads run for a long period of time and consume many system resources, the performance gains of a cancellation policy may certainly outweigh its inevitable overhead.

Following this line of reasoning, the Pthreads standard defines most blocking system calls, plus many others that can take a long time to execute, as cancellation points. Some implementations may include other library and system calls. See your platform's documentation for information on exactly which calls it defines as cancellation points.

Scheduling Pthreads

The operating system continuously selects a single thread to run from a systemwide collection of all threads that are not waiting for the completion of an I/O request or are not blocked by some other activity. Many threaded programs have no reason to interfere with the default behavior of the system's scheduler. Nevertheless, the Pthreads standard defines a thread-scheduling interface that allows programs with real-time tasks to get involved in the process.

Using the Pthreads scheduling feature, you can designate how threads share the available processing power. You may decide that all threads should have equal access to all available CPUs, or you can give some threads preferential treatment. In some applications, it's beneficial to give those threads that perform important tasks an advantage over those that perform background work. For instance, in a process-control application, a thread that responds to input for special devices could be given priority over a thread that simply maintains the log. Used in conjunction with POSIX real-time extensions, such as memory locking and real-time clocks, the Pthreads scheduling feature lets you create real-time applications in which the threads with important tasks can be guaranteed to complete their tasks in a predictable, finite amount of time.[*]

Note that, even though the Pthreads standard specifies a scheduling interface, it allows vendors to support or not support its programming interface at their option. If your system supports the scheduling programming interface, the compile-time constant _POSIX_THREAD_PRIORITY_SCHEDULING will be TRUE.[†]

Scheduling Priority and Policy

The eligibility of any given thread for special scheduling treatment is determined by the settings of two thread-specific attributes:

---

[*] See the book *POSIX.4: Programming for the Real World* by Bill O. Gallmeister, from O'Reilly & Associates, for in-depth discussion of the POSIX real-time extensions.

[†] If your implementation supports the POSIX real-time extensions, you can use the *sched_yield* call to force some broad form of scheduling. A *sched_yield* call places the calling thread at the end of its scheduling priority queue and lets another thread of the same priority take its place.

- Scheduling priority

  A thread's scheduling priority, in relation to that of other threads, determines which thread gets preferential access to the available CPUs at any given time.

- Scheduling policy

  A thread's scheduling policy is a way of expressing how threads of the same priority run and share the available CPUs.

We'll be using these terms throughout the discussions that follow. Once we've set the stage with some background information about scheduling scope, we'll consider the scheduling priority and policy thread attributes in much greater detail.

Scheduling Scope and Allocation Domains

The concept of *scheduling scope* refers to the inclusiveness of the scheduling activity in which a thread participates. In other words, scope determines how many threads—and which threads—a given thread must compete against when it's time for the scheduler to select one of them to run on a free CPU.

Because some operating system kernels know little about threads, the scope of thread scheduling depends upon the abilities of an implementation.* A given implementation may allow you to schedule threads either in process scope or in system scope. When scheduling occurs in *process scope*, threads are scheduled against only other threads in the same program. When scheduling occurs in *system scope*, threads are scheduled against all other active threads systemwide. Implementations may also provide a thread attribute that allows you to set the scheduling scope on a per-thread basis. Here, too, you can choose that a thread participate in scheduling in either process or system scope.

The discussion of scheduling scope is complicated when multiprocessing systems are involved. Many operating systems allow collections of CPUs to be treated as separate units for scheduling purposes. In Digital UNIX, for example, such a grouping is called a *processor set* and can be created by system calls or administrative commands. The Pthreads standard does recognize that such groupings may exist and refers to them as scheduling *allocation domains*. However, to avoid forcing all vendors to implement specific allocation domain sizes, the standard leaves all policies and interfaces relating to them undefined. As a result, there's a wide range of standard-compliant implementations out there. Some vendors, such as Digital, provide rich functionality, and others provide very little, even placing all CPUs in a single allocation domain.

---

* As we'll discuss in Chapter 6, *Practical Considerations*, some systems provide the abstraction of a thread within the container of the process without any help from the kernel. On these systems the lower-level operating system kernel schedules processes to run, not threads.

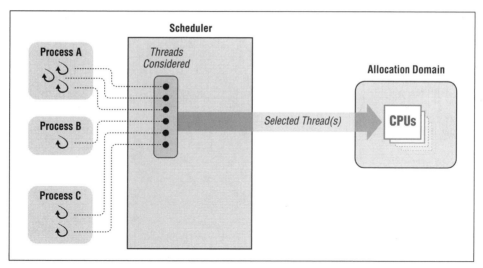

Figure 4–5: Scheduling with system scope and one allocation domain

Figure 4-5 shows a system using only system scheduling scope and a single alloca-tion domain. On one side of the scheduler we have processes containing one or more threads that need to be scheduled. On the other side the scheduler has the available CPU processing power of the system combined into the one allocation domain. The scheduler compares the priorities of all runnable threads of all pro-cesses systemwide when selecting a thread to run on an available CPU. It gives the thread with the highest priority first preference, regardless of which process it belongs to.

Figure 4-6 shows a system with only process scope and a single allocation domain.

The standard requires a scheduler that supports process scope to compare the scheduling priority of a thread only to the priorities of other threads of the same process. How the scheduler makes the comparison is also undefined. As a result, the priorities set by the Pthreads library on a system that provides this type of scheduling may not necessarily have any systemwide meaning.

For instance, consider such a scheduler on a multiprocessing system on which the threads of a given process (Process A) are competing for CPUs. Process A has three threads, one with very high priority and two with medium priority. The scheduler can place the high priority thread on one of the CPUs and thus meet the standard's requirements for process-scope scheduling. It need do no more—even if other CPUs in the allocation domain have lower priority threads from other pro-cesses running on them. The scheduler can leave Process A's remaining runnable medium priority threads waiting for its high priority thread to finish running. Thus,

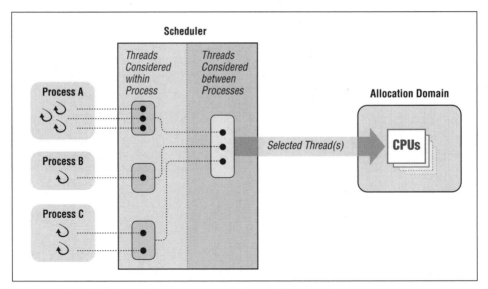

Figure 4–6: Scheduling with process scope and one allocation domain

this type of scheduling can deny a multithreaded application the benefit of multiple CPUs within the allocation domain.

An implementation that uses system-scope scheduling with a single allocation domain, such as the one we showed in Figure 4-5, behaves quite differently. If the threads of a process in system scope have high enough priorities, they will be scheduled on multiple CPUs at the same time. System-scope scheduling is thereby much more useful than process-scope scheduling for real-time or parallel processing applications when only a single allocation domain is available.

Figure 4-7 shows a system with multiple allocation domains supporting both process and system scope. The threads of Process A all have process scheduling scope and exclusive access to an allocation domain. Process B's threads have system scope and their own allocation domain as well. The threads of all other processes have system scope and are assigned to the remaining allocation domain.

Because the threads of Process A and Process B don't share an allocation domain with those of other processes, they will execute more predictably. Their threads will never wait for a higher priority thread of another process to finish or preempt another process's lower priority thread. Because Process B's threads use system scope, they will always be able to simultaneously access the multiple CPUs within its domain. However, because Process A's threads use process scope, they may not always be able to do so. It depends on the implementation on which they run.

You should take into account one potential pitfall of using multiple scheduler allocation domains if your implementation allows you to define them. ·When none of

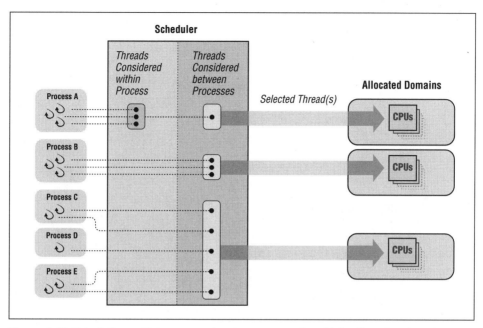

Figure 4–7: Scheduling with process and system scope and multiple allocation domains

the threads in Process A or B are running on the CPUs in their allocation domains, the CPUs are idle, regardless of the load on other CPUs in other domains. You may in fact obtain higher overall CPU utilization by limiting the number of allocation domains. Be certain that you understand the characteristics of your application and its threads before you set scheduling policies that affect its performance and behavior.

If an implementation allows you to select the scheduling scope of a thread using a per-thread attribute, you'll probably set up the thread's attribute object, as shown in Example 4-21.

Example 4–21: Setting Scheduling Scope in an Attribute Object (sched.c)

```
pthread_attr_t custom_sched_attr;
    .
    .
    .
    pthread_attr_init(&custom_sched_attr);
    pthread_attr_setscope(&custom_sched_attr, PTHREAD_SCOPE_SYSTEM);
    pthread_create(&thread, &custom_sched_attr, ...);
    .
    .
    .
```

The *pthread_attr_setscope* function sets the scheduling-scope attribute in a thread attribute object to either system-scope scheduling (PTHREAD_SCOPE_SYSTEM), as in Example 4-21, or process-scope scheduling (PTHREAD_SCOPE_PROCESS). Conversely, you'd use *pthread_attr_getscope* to obtain the current scope setting of an attribute object.

For the remainder of our discussion, we'll try to ignore scope. We can't avoid using terms that have different meanings depending upon what type of scheduling scope is active. As a cheat sheet for those occasions when these terms appear, refer to the following:

- When we say *pool of threads*, we mean:

   - In process scope: all other threads in the same process

   - In system scope: all threads of all processes in the same allocation domain

- When we say *scheduler*, we mean:

   - In process scope: the Pthreads library and/or the scheduler in the operating system's kernel

   - In system scope: the scheduler in the operating system's kernel

- When we say *processing slot*, we mean:

   - In process scope: the portion of CPU time allocated to the process as a whole within its allocation domain

   - In system scope: the portion of CPU time allocated to a specific thread within its allocation domain

Runnable and Blocked Threads

In selecting a thread for a processing slot, the scheduler first considers whether it is runnable or blocked. A blocked thread must wait for some particular event, such as I/O completion, a mutex, or a signal on a condition variable, before it can continue its execution. By contrast, a runnable thread can resume execution as soon as it's given a processing slot.

After it has weeded out the blocked threads, the scheduler must select one of the remaining runnable threads to which it will give the processing slot. If there are enough slots for all runnable threads (for instance, there are four CPUs and four threads), the scheduler doesn't need to apply its scheduling algorithm at all, and all runnable threads will get a chance to run simultaneously.

Scheduling Priority

The selection algorithm that the scheduler uses is affected by each runnable thread's scheduling priority and scheduling policy. As we mentioned before, these are per-thread attributes; we'll show you how to set them in a few pages.

The scheduler begins by looking at an array of priority queues, as shown in Figure 4-8. There is a queue for each scheduling priority and, at any given priority level, the threads that are assigned that priority reside. When looking for a thread to run in a processing slot, the scheduler starts with the highest priority queue and works its way down to the lower priority queues until it finds the first thread.

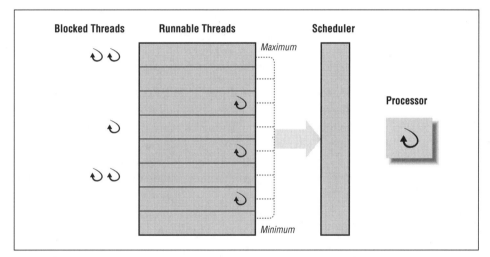

Figure 4–8: Priority queues

In this illustration only three of the priority queues hold runnable threads. When running threads either involuntarily give up their processing slot (more on this later) or go from blocked to runnable, they are placed at the end of the queue for their priority. Over time, the population of the priority queues will grow and decline.

Whenever a thread with a higher priority than the current running thread becomes runnable, it interrupts the running thread and replaces it in the processing slot. From the standpoint of the thread that's been replaced, this is known as an *involuntary context switch*.

Scheduling Policy

A thread's scheduling policy determines how long it runs when it moves from the head of its priority queue to a processing slot. The two main scheduling policies are SCHED_FIFO and SCHED-RR:

- SCHED_FIFO

  This policy (first-in first-out) lets a thread run until it either exits or blocks. As soon as it becomes unblocked, a blocked thread that has given up its processing slot is placed at the end of its priority queue.

- SCHED_RR

  This policy (round robin) allows a thread to run for only a fixed amount of time before it must yield its processing slot to another thread of the same priority. This fixed amount of time is usually referred to as a *quantum*. When a thread is interrupted, it is placed at the end of its priority queue.

The Pthreads standard defines an additional policy, SCHED_OTHER, and leaves its behavior up to the implementors. On most systems, selecting SCHED_OTHER will give a thread a policy that uses some sort of time sharing with priority adjustment. By default, all threads start life with the SCHED_OTHER policy. After all, time sharing with priority adjustment is the typical UNIX scheduling algorithm for processes. It works like SCHED_RR, giving threads a quantum of time in which to run. Unlike SCHED_FIFO and SCHED_RR, however, it causes the scheduler to occasionally adjust a thread's priority without any input from the programmer. This priority adjustment favors threads that don't use all their quantum before blocking, increasing their priority. The idea behind this policy is that it gives interactive I/O-bound threads preferential treatment over CPU-bound threads that consume all their quantum.

The definitions of SCHED_FIFO, SCHED_RR, and SCHED_OTHER actually come from the POSIX real-time extensions (POSIX.1b). Any Pthreads implementation that uses the compile-time constant _POSIX_THREAD_PRIORITY_SCHEDULING will also recognize them. As we'll continue our discussion, we'll find other POSIX.1b features that are useful in manipulating priorities.

Using Priorities and Policies

Although you can set different scheduling priorities and policies for each thread in an application, and even dynamically change them in a running thread, most applications don't need this complexity.

A real-time application designer would typically first make a broad division between those tasks that must be completed in a finite amount of time and those that are less time critical. Those threads with real-time tasks would be given a SCHED_FIFO policy and high priority. The remaining threads would be given a SCHED_RR policy and a lower priority. The scheduling priority of all of these threads would be set to be higher than those of any other threads on the system. Ideally the host would be capable of system-scope scheduling.

As shown in Figure 4-9, the real-time threads of the real-time application will always get access to the CPU when they are runnable, because they have higher priority than any other thread on the system. When a real-time thread gets the CPU it will complete its task without interruption (unless, of course, it blocks—but that would be a result of poor design). No other thread can preempt it; no quantum stands in its way. These threads behave like event (or interrupt) handlers; they wait for something to happen and then process it to completion within the shortest time possible.

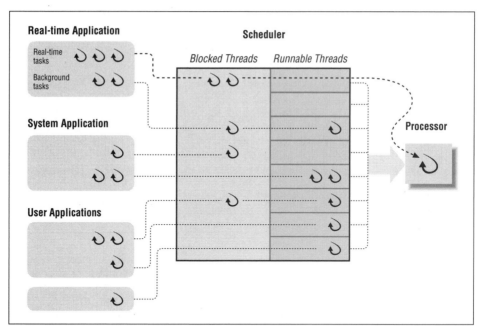

Figure 4-9: Using policies and priorities in an application

Because of their high priority, the non-real-time threads in the application also get preferential treatment, but they must share the CPU with each other as their quantums expire. These threads usually perform the background processing for the application.

An example of this kind of real-time application would be a program that runs chemical processing equipment. The threads that deploy hardware control algorithms—periodically reading sensors, computing new control values, and sending signals to actuators—would run with the SCHED_FIFO policy and a high priority. Other threads that performed the less critical tasks—updating accounting records for chemicals used and recording the hours for employees running the equipment—would run with the SCHED_RR policy and at a lower priority.

Setting Scheduling Policy and Priority

You can set a thread's scheduling policy and priority in the thread attribute object you specify in the *pthread_create* call that creates the thread. Assume that we have a thread attribute object named *custom_sched_attr*. We've initialized it with a call to *pthread_attr_init*. We specify it in calls to *pthread_attr_setschedpolicy* to set the scheduling policy and *pthread_attr_setschedparam* to set the scheduling priority, as shown in Example 4-22.

Example 4-22: Setting a Thread's Scheduling Attributes (sched.c)

```
pthread_attr_t custom_sched_attr;
int fifo_max_prio, fifo_min_prio;
struct sched_param fifo_param;
.
.
.

  pthread_attr_init(&custom_sched_attr);
  pthread_attr_setinheritsched(&custom_sched_attr, PTHREAD_EXPLICIT_SCHED);
  pthread_attr_setschedpolicy(&custom_sched_attr, SCHED_FIFO);

  fifo_max_prio = sched_get_priority_max(SCHED_FIFO);
  fifo_min_prio = sched_get_priority_min(SCHED_FIFO);
  fifo_mid_prio = (fifo_min_prio + fifo_max_prio)/2;
  fifo_param.sched_priority = fifo_mid_prio;

  pthread_attr_setschedparam(&custom_sched_attr, &fifo_param);
  pthread_create(&(threads[i]), &custom_sched_attr, ....);
```

The way in which *pthread_attr_setschedparam* is used demands a little more explanation.

When you use *pthread_attr_setschedpolicy* to set a thread's policy to SCHED_FIFO or SCHED_RR, you can also call *pthread_attr_setschedparam* to set its parameters. The *pthread_attr_setschedparam* function takes two arguments: the first is a thread attribute object, the second is a curious thing defined in the POSIX.1b standard and known as a*struct sched_param*. It looks like this:

```
struct sched_param {
        int sched_priority;
}
```

That's it. The *struct sched_param* has only a single required member and specifies a single attribute—a scheduling priority. (Some Pthreads implementations may store other information in this structure.) Let's see how we stick a priority into this thing.

The POSIX.1b standard specifies that there must be at least 32 unique priority values apiece for the SCHED_RR and SCHED_FIFO priorities. (The standard does not require that there be defined priorities for SCHED_OTHER.) The absolute values and actual range of the priorities depend upon the implementation, but one thing's for certain—you can use *sched_get_priority_max* and *sched_get_priority_min* to get a handle on them.

In our example, we call *sched_get_priority_max* and *sched_get_priority_min* to obtain the maximum and minimum priority values for the SCHED_FIFO policy. We add the two together and divide by two, coming up with a priority level that's happily in the middle of the SCHED_FIFO priority range. It's this priority value that we insert in the *priority* member of our *struct sched_param*. A call to *pthread_attr_setschedparam* and, voila!—our thread has a nice middling priority with which to work.

Before we leave our discussion of setting a thread's scheduling attributes statically when the thread is created, we'll make one final point. If you must retrieve the scheduling attribute settings from a thread attribute object, you can use the functions *pthread_attr_getschedpolicy* and *pthread_attr_getschedparam*. They work in the same way as the corresponding functions for other thread attributes.

Now we'll look at a way to set the scheduling policy and priority of a selected thread while it's running. In Example 4-23, we set a target thread's policy to SCHED_FIFO and its priority to the priority level stored in the variable *fifo_min_prio*.

Example 4-23: Setting Policy and Priority Dynamically (sched.c)

```
fifo_sched_param.sched_priority = fifo_min_prio;
pthread_setschedparam(threads[i], SCHED_FIFO, &fifo_min_prio);
```

As you can see, the *pthread_setschedparam* call sets both policy and priority at the same time. Conversely, the *pthread_getschedparam* function returns the current policy and priority for a specified thread. Be careful when you use the *pthread_setschedparam* function to dynamically adjust another thread's priority. If you raise a thread's priority higher than your own and it is runnable, it will preempt you when you make the call.

Inheritance

If you decide to use scheduling, you don't need to individually set the scheduling attributes of each thread you create. Instead, you can specify that each thread should inherit its scheduling characteristics from the thread that created it. Like other per-thread scheduling attributes, the inheritance attribute is specified in the attribute object used at thread creation, as shown in Example 4-24.

Example 4-24: Setting Scheduling Inheritance in an Attribute Object (sched.c)

```
pthread_attr_t custom_sched_attr;
    .
    .
    .
    pthread_attr_init(&custom_sched_attr);
    pthread_attr_setinheritsched(&custom_sched_attr, PTHREAD_INHERIT_SCHED)
    .
    .
    .
    pthread_create(&thread, &custom_sched_attr, ...);
```

The *pthread_attr_setinheritsched* function takes a thread attribute object as its first argument and as its second argument either the PTHREAD_INHERIT_SCHED flag or the PTHREAD_EXPLICIT_SCHED flag. You can obtain the current inheritance attribute from an attribute object by calling *pthread_attr_getinheritsched*.

Scheduling in the ATM Server

We're now ready to assign different scheduling priorities to the worker threads in our ATM server, based on the type of transaction they are processing. To illustrate how our server might use scheduling attributes, we'll give highest priority to the threads that service deposit requests. After all, time is money and the sooner the bank has your money the sooner they can start making money with it. Specifically, we'll add code to our server so that deposit threads run at a high priority with a SCHED_FIFO scheduling policy and the other threads run at a lower priority using a SCHED_RR scheduling policy.

We don't need to change worker thread code; only the boss thread concerns itself with setting scheduling attributes. We'll globally declare some additional thread attribute objects (*pthread_attr_t*) in our *atm_server_init* routine in Example 4-25 and prepare them to be used by the boss thread when it creates worker threads.

Example 4-25: Creating Attribute Objects for Worker Threads (sched.c)

```
/* global variables */
    .
    .
    .
pthread_attr_t custom_attr_fifo, custom_attr_rr;
```

Example 4-25: Creating Attribute Objects for Worker Threads (sched.c) (continued)

```
int fifo_max_prio, rr_min_prio;
struct sched_param fifo_param, rr_param;

atm_server_init()
{
    .
    .
    .
    pthread_attr_init(&custom_attr_fifo);
    pthread_attr_setschedpolicy(&custom_attr_fifo, SCHED_FIFO);
    fifo_param.sched_priority = sched_get_priority_max(SCHED_FIFO);
    pthread_attr_setschedparam(&custom_attr_fifo, &fifo_param);

    pthread_attr_init(&custom_attr_rr);
    pthread_attr_setschedpolicy(&custom_attr_rr, SCHED_RR);
    rr_param.sched_priority = sched_get_priority_min(SCHED_RR);
    pthread_attr_setschedparam(&custom_attr_rr, &rr_param);
    .
    .
    .
}
```

The boss thread will use the *custom_attr_fifo* attribute object when creating deposit threads. The *atm_server_init* routine sets this attribute object to use the SCHED_FIFO scheduling policy and the maximum priority defined for the policy. The boss thread will use the *custom_attr_rr* attribute object for all other worker threads. It is set with the SCHED_RR scheduling policy and the minimum priority defined for the policy. The boss thread uses these attribute objects in the server's *main* routine:

Example 4-26: Creating threads with custom scheduling attributes (sched.c)

```
extern int
main(void)
    .
    .
    .
    atm_server_init(argc, argv);
    for(;;) {

        /*** Wait for a request ***/
        workorderp = (workorder_t *)malloc(sizeof(workorder_t));
        server_comm_get_request(&workorderp->conn, workorderp->req_buf);
        sscanf(workorderp->req_buf, "%d", &trans_id);
        .
        .
        .
        switch(trans_id) {
        case DEPOSIT_TRANS:
            pthread_create(worker_threadp, &custom_attr_fifo, process_request,
                        (void *)workorderp);
            break;
```

Example 4-26: Creating threads with custom scheduling attributes (sched.c) (continued)

```
        default:
            pthread_create(worker_threadp, &custom_attr_rr, process_request,
                           (void *)workorderp);
            break;
    }


    pthread_detach(*worker_threadp);

}

server_comm_shutdown();
return 0;
}
```

In our server's *main* routine, the boss thread checks the request type before creating a thread to process it. If the request is a deposit, the boss specifies the *custom_attr_fifo* attribute object in the *pthread_create* call. Otherwise, it uses the *custom_attr_rr* attribute object.

Mutex Scheduling Attributes

We may take great pains to apply scheduling to the threads in our program, designating those threads that should be given preferential access to the CPU when they're ready to run. However, what if our high priority threads must contend for the same resources as our lower priority threads? It's likely that at times a high priority thread will stall waiting for a mutex lock held by a lower priority thread. This is the priority inversion phenomenon of which we spoke earlier. The mutex plainly doesn't recognize that some threads that ask for it are more important than others.

Consider a real-time multithreaded application that controls the operation of a power plant. One controls fuel intake and must react quickly and predictably to changes in flow rate and line pressure; this thread has high priority. Another thread collects statistics on plant operations for monthly reports and collects information on the state of the plant once an hour; this thread is assigned a lower priority. An additional thread, of medium priority in the application, perhaps, faxes sandwich orders at lunch time.

Both the fuel-control and statistic-gathering threads must control a mechanical arm to position a temperature sensor at various locations within the plant to take temperature readings. Each contends for a single mutex that synchronizes access to the arm.

We'll start with a situation in which all threads are blocked and the mutex is unlocked. Suppose that the sequence of events listed in the left column of Table 4-2 occurs. The statistics-gathering thread runs first, grabs the mutex, and ends up by blocking the fuel-control thread that is ready to run.

Table 4–2: Priority Inversion in a Power Plant Application (1)

Event	Fuel-Control Thread	Medium Priority Thread	Statistics-Gathering Thread	Arm Mutex
Start	Blocked	Blocked	Blocked	Unlocked
The statistics-gathering thread must take a temperature.	Blocked	Blocked	Running	Unlocked
The statistics-gathering thread acquires the mutex.	Blocked	Blocked	Running	Locked by statistics-gathering thread
An event occurs, waking the fuel-control thread. It preempts the statistics thread.	Running	Blocked	Runnable	Locked by statistics-gathering thread
The fuel-control thread tries to get the mutex and blocks. The statistics thread regains the CPU.	Blocked on mutex	Blocked	Running	Locked by statistics-gathering thread

The situation can actually get worse when, as shown in Table 4-3, the medium priority thread awakens. It has a higher priority than the statistics-gathering thread and does not need to wait for the mutex the medium thread currently holds. It's runnable and will preempt the statistics-gathering thread. Now the fuel-control thread must wait for the medium priority thread, too—and this thread doesn't even need to use the arm!

Table 4–3: Priority Inversion in a Power Plant Application (2)

Event	Fuel-Control Thread	Medium Priority Thread	Statistics-Gathering Thread	Arm Mutex
An event occurs, waking the medium priority thread. It preempts the statistics-gathering thread.	Blocked on mutex	Running	Runnable	Locked by statistics-gathering thread

If the sirens and flashing lights weren't so distracting, we'd redesign the application so that the fuel-control and statistics-gathering threads no longer use a common resource. But we need to introduce a new Pthreads feature, and besides, we have only so much time before we have to evacuate the plant.

The Pthreads standard allows (but does not require) implementations to design mutexes that can give a priority boost to low priority threads that hold them. We can associate a mutex with either of two priority protocols that provide this feature: priority ceiling or priority inheritance. We'll start with a discussion of priority ceiling, the simpler of the two protocols.

Priority Ceiling

The priority ceiling protocol associates a scheduling priority with a mutex. Thus equipped, a mutex can assign its holder an effective priority equal to its own, if the mutex holder has a lower priority to begin with.

Let's apply this feature to our power plant example and see what happens. We'll associate a high priority with the mutex that controls access to the arm and revisit the earlier sequence of events. Table 4-4 illustrates the results.

Table 4–4: Priority Inversion in a Power Plant Application

Event	Fuel-Control Thread	Medium Priority Thread	Statistics-Gathering Thread	Arm Mutex (High Priority)
Start	Blocked	Blocked	Blocked	Unlocked
The statistics-gathering thread must take a temperature.	Blocked	Blocked	Running	Unlocked
The statistics-gathering thread acquires the mutex. It gets an effective priority of high.	Blocked	Blocked	Running	Locked by statistics-gathering thread
An event occurs, waking the fuel-control thread. It does not preempt the statistics-gathering thread, which is also at high priority.	Runnable	Blocked	Running	Locked by statistics-gathering thread
An event occurs, waking the medium priority thread. It does not preempt the statistics-gathering thread, which is also at high priority.	Runnable	Runnable	Running	Locked by statistics-gathering thread

At this point, the statistics-gathering thread will complete its operation at the highest priority and in the shortest period of time. Table 4-5 shows the sequence of events that occurs when it releases the mutex.

Table 4-5: Priority Inversion in a Power Plant Application

Event	Fuel-Control Thread	Medium Priority Thread	Statistics-Gathering Thread	Arm Mutex (High Priority)
The statistics-gathering thread unlocks the mutex. It reverts to low priority and is preempted by the highest priority runnable thread. This is the fuel-control thread.	Running	Runnable	Runnable	Unlocked
The fuel-control thread tries to get the mutex and succeeds.	Running	Runnable	Running	Locked by fuel thread

Now the fuel-control thread can do its work, having to wait only for the statistics-gathering thread—not for the medium priority thread as well. Although the fuel-control thread must wait, it waits for a shorter period of time and in a more predictable manner.

If your platform supports the priority ceiling protocol, the compile-time constant _POSIX_THREAD_PRIO_PROTECT will be defined. Example 4-27 shows how to create a mutex that uses the priority ceiling protocol.

Example 4-27: Setting a Priority Ceiling on a Mutex (mutex_ceiling.c)

```
pthread_mutex_t m1;
pthread_mutexattr_t mutexattr_prioceiling;
int mutex_protocol, high_prio;
.
high_prio = sched_get_priority_max(SCHED_FIFO);
.
pthread_mutexattr_init(&mutexattr_prioceiling);
pthread_mutexattr_getprotocol(&mutexattr_prioceiling, &mutex_protocol);
pthread_mutexattr_setprotocol(&mutexattr_prioceiling, PTHREAD_PRIO_PROTECT);
pthread_mutexattr_setprioceiling(&mutexattr_prioceiling, high_prio);
pthread_mutex_init(&m1, &mutexattr_prioceiling);
```

We first declare a mutex attribute object (*pthread_mutex_attr_t*) and initialize it by calling *pthread_mutexattr_init*. Our call to *pthread_mutexattr_getprotocol* returns the priority protocol that is associated with our mutex by default. The priority protocol attribute can have one of three values:

- PTHREAD_PRIO_NONE

  The mutex uses no priority protocol.

- PTHREAD_PRIO_PROTECT

  The mutex uses the priority ceiling protocol.

- PTHREAD_PRIO_INHERIT

  The mutex uses the priority inheritance protocol.

If the *pthread_mutexattr_getprotocol* call does not show that the mutex is using the priority ceiling protocol, we call the *pthread_mutexattr_setprotocol* function to set this protocol in the mutex's attribute object. After we've done so, we call *pthread_mutexattr_setprioceiling* to set the fixed priority ceiling attribute in the mutex object. (Conversely, a call to *pthread_mutexattr_getprioceiling* would return the current value of this attribute.) The priority passed is an integer argument set up in the same manner as a thread's priority value. Finally, we initialize the mutex by specifying the mutex attribute object to *pthread_mutex_init*.

Priority Inheritance

The priority inheritance protocol lets a mutex elevate the priority of its holder to that of the waiting thread with the highest priority. If we applied the priority inheritance protocol to the arm mutex in our power plant example, the result would be that the statistics-gathering thread wouldn't unconditionally receive a priority boost as soon as it won the mutex lock; it would be elevated to high priority only when the fuel-control thread starts to wait on the mutex. Because the priority inheritance protocol awards a priority boost to a mutex holder only when it's absolutely needed, it can be more efficient than the priority ceiling protocol.

If your platform supports the priority inheritance feature, the compile-time constant _POSIX_THREAD_PRIO_INHERIT will be TRUE. Example 4-28 shows how to create a mutex with the priority inheritance attribute. The process is nearly identical to the one we used to set up the priority ceiling protocol for the mutex in Example 4-27.

Example 4-28: Setting Priority Inheritance on a Mutex (mutex_priority.c)

```
pthread_mutex_t m1;
pthread_mutexattr_t mutexattr_prioinherit;
int mutex_procotol;
    .
    .
    .
pthread_mutexattr_init(&mutexattr_prioinherit);
pthread_mutexattr_getprotocol(&mutexattr_prioinherit, &mutex_protocol);
if (mutex_protocol != PTHREAD_PRIO_INHERIT) {
    pthread_mutexattr_setprotocol(&mutexattr_prioinherit, PTHREAD_PRIO_INHERIT);
```

Example 4-28: Setting Priority Inheritance on a Mutex (mutex_priority.c) (continued)

```
}
pthread_mutex_init(&m1, &mutexattr_prioinherit);
```

The ATM Example and Priority Inversion

Let's return to our ATM server example. In its most recent version, we introduced a scheduling framework and started to assign different priorities to different threads. Having done so, we've introduced a risk that our threads may encounter priority inversion situations. A high priority thread could attempt to perform a deposit transaction on the same account for which a low priority thread is already processing a different transaction. When it does so, the high priority thread will very likely need to wait on the mutex that the low priority thread currently holds. We can help out our high priority threads by assigning this mutex a scheduling attribute of some sort.

Which protocol should we use—priority ceiling or priority inheritance? If we use the priority ceiling protocol, we would have to associate a very high priority ceiling with the mutexes that guard the accounts. Overall, this would have a rather negative effect on our server's behavior and the performance of deposit transactions in particular. Low priority threads would always be given a priority boost whenever they obtained a mutex, regardless of whether a deposit thread needs to lock the same mutex. Because each worker thread holds the mutex for an account for a significant length of time, the scheduler's priority queues would fill with runnable, high priority threads. A deposit thread would just be another high priority thread in the queue and would not get any special treatment. This is not what we want.

For a program like our ATM server, it makes much more sense to use the priority inheritance protocol. If we assign the priority inheritance attribute to each of our account mutexes, each mutex would boost the priority of its owner only when a high priority thread is waiting. This would give our high priority deposit threads a better chance to access accounts. The scheduler continues to favor the deposit threads, and when a deposit thread is blocked by a low priority thread that is holding a required mutex, the mutex's priority inheritance policy ensures that the low priority thread gets a needed boost. As a result, the low priority thread can get its business done quickly, release the mutex, and get out of the way of our important deposit threads. The worst case would be when the deposit thread must wait for one in-progress operation on the account before it can start its transaction.

To associate the priority inheritance protocol with our mutexes, we'll change our server's initialization routine as shown in Example 4-29.

Example 4-29: Initializing Priority-Savvy Mutex in the ATM (mutex_priority.c)

```
    .
    .
    .

pthread_mutex_attr_t mutexattr_prioinherit;
    .
    .
    .

void atm_server_init(int argc, char **argv)
{
    .
    .
    .

    pthread_mutexattr_setprotocol(&mutexattr_prioinherit, PTHREAD_PRIO_INHERIT);
      for (i = 0; i < MAX_NUM_ACCOUNTS; i++)
              pthread_mutex_init(&account_mutex[i], &mutexattr_prioinherit);
    .
    .
    .

}
```

5

Pthreads and UNIX

Because operating systems are inherently designed to accommodate processes, not threads, system implementors must often bend tradition to introduce thread support. It's as if we were to discover one day that the sun did not orbit the earth, but that, in reality, the earth revolves around the sun. The process is no longer central to our operating system world. Whereas it used to schedule processes, our system now schedules threads—no minor feat because, to do so, it must rototill its internal data structures and reinvent some of its most basic notions. What's more, whereas it used to deliver signals to processes, it now must deliver signals to threads. How it selects the thread to which it delivers a given signal is yet another added complexity.

Further, the operating system has always allowed us to perform certain operations on processes that become riddles in the world of threads. If we now consider a process to be a sort of container for threads, and we recognize that all threads share their process's address space, what happens when one of these threads launches an operation that has processwide ramifications? Does a *fork* result in a copy of the entire process, including all existing threads? Does an *exec* wipe them out?

Finally, it's a rare, and probably not very useful, program that does not make a single library call. In the world of threads, what happens when a batch of threads in the same process call the same library function concurrently? If this is the same library that existed in the pre-threaded implementation, there's a great chance that the library's static data will be overwritten at each successive call. Thus, operating system vendors must address the behavior of libraries and system calls on top of everything else.

If a multithreaded program is to work correctly, it must rely on some well-defined, consistent behavior from the operating system. A little knowledge about the areas in which Pthreads and the operating system cross is well advised. In this chapter, we'll examine some ways in which Pthreads implementors attempt to make an operating system "thread friendly." We'll discuss:

- Signals

  Every program must respond to signal delivery in some way. Often a program must provide a routine that handles signals of various kinds. The Pthreads standard defines a method for threads to participate in signal handling that is compatible with the traditional method in which processes handle signals.

- Threadsafe libraries

  Most system libraries maintain internal data for the currently executing process in internal data. To allow multiple threads from the same process to execute library routines simultaneously, library implementors must somehow protect this data from unsynchronized accesses by otherwise cooperative threads. Libraries that eliminate such race conditions are known as *threadsafe libraries*.

- Cancellation-safe library functions

  If a thread is canceled while in the middle of a library call that is modifying a library's internal data, it may exit, leaving the data in an inconsistent or corrupted state. A library function in which a thread can be canceled safely is known as a *cancellation-safe library routine*.

- Blocking functions

  One of the greatest benefits of threads programming relies on the expectation that, if one thread blocks while calling a library function, others may continue. The Pthreads standard defines exactly which library functions can block and when.

- Process management

  Operating system support for threads complicates the standard operations that create and destroy processes (such as *fork*, *exec*, and *exit*). The Pthreads standard specifies the behavior of these operations in a multithreaded environment and requires backward compatibility for nonthreaded applications.

- Multiprocessor memory synchronization

  Although more of an issue for platform machine architectures than for the operating system, threads must be assured that their views of shared data (including the states of mutexes and condition variables) are identical. This guarantee, as enforced by the Pthreads standard, must hold true whether the threads are running on a uniprocessor or on a multiprocessor.

Threads and Signals

The odd thing about signals in UNIX is that, although they're everywhere, their arrival—by its very nature—is always a bit of surprise. (Well, that's a bit of an exaggeration. When we're told that the furniture delivery person will be at our house between 9 a.m. and noon on Tuesday, we're prepared for a knock on the door—maybe at 9:15, maybe at 11:45, maybe even at 1:00, perhaps never. When the knock comes, we're ready with well-rehearsed instructions for the paths the delivery person must follow through our house to the place where the sofa will ultimately be placed. Some types of signals are like that; others are more like our smoke alarm before the furniture delivery person knocked it down.)

Nevertheless, our program may be interrupted at any time by a signal, and that signal may have been sent from any of a number of places. The system may send us a signal to report a hardware condition (a divide-by-zero or some other fault) or a software error. We can use various facilities so that the system sends us a signal when a particular event occurs, such as the expiration of a timer or the completion of an I/O operation. Other processes can send us a signal (and we can send one back) as a sort of low-level IPC mechanism. Even human beings can send us a signal by hitting CTRL-Z at the keyboard to suspend our program.

Most programs that accomplish serious work must have a built-in way of dealing with all of these signals flying around the system for all of these various purposes. This presented the Pthreads standard committee with three chief challenges:

- A thread should be able to send and receive signals, yet, to allow this, a Pthreads implementation cannot subvert a single-threaded process's ability to process signals in the way it always has.

- When a signal is delivered to a multithreaded process, a Pthreads implementation must select one of the threads to perform the required action.

- What can a thread do, while in a signal handler, that won't interfere with its mainline execution?

The committee met the first of these challenges by not changing the semantics of signal delivery to processes. In a Pthreads implementation, signals continue to be delivered to processes, not threads. The table that lists the process's reaction to specific signals (the *sigaction*) is shared by all threads. It dealt with the second by defining per-thread signal masks that you can manipulate to direct a signal to (or away from) particular threads.

Unfortunately, the committee seriously limited the work that a signal handler can perform in a thread's context. In fact, it left the behavior of the Pthreads tools themselves (mutex variables, condition variables, keys, and the like) undefined when they're used in a handler. Thus hampered, the signal handler cannot use Pthreads calls to communicate or synchronize with other threads in the program.

We'll see how you can work around this problem a little later. Right now, let's quickly review some basic signal-handling concepts and explore how signals work with threads.

Traditional Signal Processing

A special signal action structure (*sigaction*) allows a process to associate an action with each type of signal that may be delivered to it. A process may choose to:

- Ignore the signal (SIG_IGN)

- Use the default action (SIG_DFL)

  The default signal action depends on which signal is being received. Most signals terminate the process, but a few are ignored by default. SIGSTOP and SIGTSTP suspend the process, while SIGCONT resumes it.

- Catch the signal, and execute a user-specified handler routine

When it's created, a process is given the default action for each signal. You can change the action for most signals by using the *sigaction* call. Some signals (such as SIGKILL and SIGSTOP), however, cannot be ignored or caught.

The arrival of a signal interrupts a process at its current point of execution and transfers execution to a signal-handling routine. When the signal handler returns, the process resumes at its prior execution point.

Sending signals and waiting for signals

Signals can be generated in a number of ways—a process can do something that causes the system to deliver a signal to it, or some other process can send a signal to it by using the *kill* system call. (The *kill* system call is poorly named; you can use it to send a variety of signals, not just the termination signal, SIGKILL.) A process can also send a signal to itself, by using either the *kill* or *raise* system call.

Normally the arrival of a signal interrupts process execution. However, some signals resume a process that was suspended by a call to *wait*, *sigsuspend*, *sleep*, or *pause*.

Using a signal mask to block signals

A process can block certain types of signal for an indefinite period of time. If a process is blocking a given type of signal and that type of signal happens to be sent to it, the signal is marked as pending. The process may unblock the signal type later, at which time the pending signal will be delivered.

A process specifies the signals it wants to block in its signal mask. By default, no signals are blocked. The signals to be blocked are designated in a process's signal mask. The program can use *sigaction* and *sigsuspend* to set and reset the blocking status for each signal.

Signal Processing in a Multithreaded World

If multiple threads are executing within a process when a signal is delivered to it, the system must select a thread to process it. At the highest level, the selection of the thread is dictated by how the signal was generated, what action caused the signal, and what the effective target of the signal is. The three possibilities are shown in Table 5-1.

Table 5–1: System Selection of a Thread to Handle a Signal

How signal was generated	What generated the signal	Effective target of the signal	How the signal-processing thread is selected
Synchronously	The system, because of an exception	A specific thread	Always the offending thread
Synchronously	An internal thread using *pthread_kill*	A specific thread	Always the targeted thread
Asynchronously	An external process using *kill*	The process as a whole	Per-thread signal masks of all threads in the process

Let's examine the information in this table a little more closely.

Synchronously generated signals

Certain signals are synchronously generated in the sense that they are sent to a process as the direct result of an operation within a particular thread. The system is sending the process a signal because one of its threads tried to divide by zero (SIGFPE), touch forbidden memory in the wrong way (SIGSEGV), use a broken pipe (SIGPIPE), or do something else that triggered an exception. These signals are closely bound to the activities of a given thread, and it will be that thread, in its own context, that will handle the signal on behalf of the process as a whole.

The other type of synchronously generated signal results from one thread in a process calling *pthread_kill* to send a signal to another thread in the same process. The calling thread explicitly names the target thread by specifying its thread handle, as well as the signal to be delivered to it. You cannot use *pthread_kill* to send signals to threads in other processes.

Note that you shouldn't use *pthread_kill* in place of cancellation or condition variables. Because the Pthreads standard doesn't define any new signals with a thread-specific semantic, the *pthread_kill* function is limited to sending POSIX.1 and POSIX.1b signals. Trying to terminate (or direct the behavior of) a single thread using a traditional signal is like trying to comb your hair with a rake. It'll be difficult and you won't exactly get what you want.

Asynchronously generated signals

Other signals are asynchronously generated in the sense that they cannot be easily pinned to a particular thread. The arrival of these signals is asynchronous to the activities of any and all threads within the process. They are typically job control signals—SIGALRM, SIGHUP, SIGINT, and SIGKILL—or the user-defined signals— SIGUSR1 and SIGUSR2. They are sent to the process by a *kill* call and can be handled by almost any of its threads. (Because thread handles are unique only within a process, there's no way that a *kill* call—or a *pthread_kill* call, for that matter—can send a signal from one process to a thread in another process. As a result, all *kill* calls result in an asynchronously generated signal.)

Per-thread signal masks

Like a traditional process, a thread has a signal mask that indicates which asynchronous signals it's willing to handle (these are considered unblocked) and which ones it's not (these are considered blocked). By default, the first thread in a child process inherits its signal mask from the thread in its parent that called *fork*. Additional threads inherit the signal mask of the thread that issued the *pthread_create* that created them. Use the *pthread_sigmask* call to block and unblock signals in the mask.

When an asynchronously generated signal arrives at a process, it is handled once by exactly one thread in the process. The system selects this thread by referring to the collection of per-thread signal masks of all the threads. If more than one thread has the signal unblocked, the system arbitrarily selects one of them. Although you can manipulate the masks to influence the selection process, you cannot explicitly assign a specific thread to handle a particular signal. Nevertheless, it's not hard to control the delivery of signals. Here are some guidelines:

- If any thread can handle the signal, rest easy. The signal is, by default, unblocked for all threads.

- If only certain threads can handle the signal, mask the signal in all but those threads. The system will choose one of them to process the signal.

- If only one thread can handle the signal, mask the signal in all other threads.

Suppose you want your program to perform some special processing when data arrives or some other event occurs. If you associate a signal with this event, you can arrange it so that the signal is blocked in all but one thread. No matter what is happening in any thread in the program, it will be that thread that executes the handler when the signal arrives.

If all threads have a certain signal blocked and one of these signals arrives, it becomes pending for the entire process. Sometime later any thread can unblock the signal and accept its delivery. Using this type of signal delivery policy, you can design a thread that polls for a signal by setting and clearing the appropriate bit in its signal mask until the signal is delivered.

Note that a fatal signal will terminate the whole process, regardless of which thread it's delivered to. As a result, you don't need to do anything special to manage these signals or others that you allow to kill the process.

Per-process signal actions

Although each thread has its own signal mask, all threads in a process must share the process's own signal action (*sigaction*) structure. Consequently, if a process specifies that a given signal should be ignored, it will be ignored, regardless of to which thread in the process the system delivers it. Similarly, if a process's *sigaction* structure deems that a certain signal should be subjected to the default action (whatever that might be for the signal) or processed by a signal handler, the specified action will be carried out when the signal is delivered to any of the process's threads.

Any thread can make a *sigaction* call to set the action for a signal. If a thread calls *sigaction* to set the SIG_IGN action for the SIGTERM signal, any other thread in the same process that does not block this signal is prepared to ignore a SIGTERM should one be delivered to it. If a thread assigns the *ei-e-io* signal handler to the SIGIO signal, any thread selected to handle SIGIO will call *ei-e-io*.

Putting it all together

Before investing a lot of complexity in your code by using these features, remember that, by default, your multithreaded program will have the same response to signals as a nonthreaded one. If you want to ignore signals, all you need to do is to use *sigaction* as usual to set the signals' action to SIG_IGN. A standard *sigaction* call will also serve you well if there are signals you want to handle and it doesn't matter which of your threads process them. Even if you do want a specific thread to handle a particular signal, you may not need to invent special code. For instance, if one thread in your program handles all I/O operations, you might have that thread handle any SIGIO signal that may arrive (or wait for the signal at times using *sigwait*).

A word to the wise: after you've set up particular threads to handle particular signals, it's simplest to keep them that way. If you try to reassign signal-handling responsibilities in the middle of your program, you'll likely encounter all the synchronization difficulties that usually result from any change to a process state.

Threads in Signal Handlers

POSIX labels calls that can be made safely from a signal handler as *asynchronous signal-safe functions*. These functions have a special property known as *reentrancy* that allows a process to have multiple calls to these functions in progress at the same time. Because a signal handler doesn't inherently know what calls were in progress at the time it is placed in execution, it must restrict itself to calling only those functions that are advertised as asynchronous signal-safe. In fact, many, many base POSIX calls can be made from a handler:

access	*alarm*	*cfgetispeed*	*cfgetospeed*	*cfsetispeed*	*cfsetospeed*
chdir	*chmod*	*chown*	*close*	*creat*	*dup*
dup2	*execle*	*execve*	*_exit*	*fcntl*	*fork*
fstat	*getgroups*	*getpgrp*	*getpid*	*getppid*	*getuid*
kill	*link*	*lseek*	*mkdir*	*mkfifo*	*open*
pathconf	*pause*	*pipe*	*read*	*rename*	*rmdir*
setgid	*setpgid*	*setsid*	*setuid*	*sigaction*	*sigaddset*
sigdelset	*sigemptyset*	*sigfillset*	*sigismember*	*sigpending*	*sigprocmask*
sigsuspend	*sleep*	*stat*	*sysconf*	*tcdrain*	*tcflow*

tcflush	*tcgetattr*	*tcgetpgrp*	*tcsendbreak*	*tcsetattr*
tcsetgrp	*time*	*times*	*umask*	*uname*
unlink	*utime*	*wait*	*waitpid*	*write*

If your system supports the POSIX real-time extensions, you can also make any of the following calls:

aio_error	*aio_return*	*aio_suspend*
clock_gettime	*fdatasync*	*fsync*
getegid	*geteuid*	*sem_post*
sigqueue	*timer_getoverrun*	
timer_gettime	*timer_settime*	

But where are the Pthreads calls? They're not in either of these lists! In fact, the Pthreads standard specifies that the behavior of all Pthreads functions is undefined when the function is called from a signal handler. If your handler needs to manipulate data that is shared with other threads—buffers, flags, or state variables—it's out of luck. The Pthreads mutex and condition variable synchronization calls are off limits.[*]

Fine. We've explained very carefully how you can set up a particular thread in your program so that it gets placed in a signal handler, and now you learn that, once it's there, your thread can't make any Pthreads calls! Rest easy. If your thread must manipulate shared data or communicate with other threads while it's executing its signal handler, it has a number of options. If the POSIX real-time extensions are available to it, it can use the *sem_post* call to communicate with other threads of the same process using a semaphore. A better solution would be to forgo the idea of using the handler in the first place and, instead, call *sigwait* to wait synchronously for the arrival of the signal. The *sigwait* call either returns immediately to the calling thread because a signal is already pending to the process but blocked or suspends the thread until a signal becomes pending.

To make our program take an action when a signal arrives we can use *sigwait* as follows:

• Mask the interesting signals in all threads so that their arrival is made pending. The *sigwait* call will detect these signals.

---

[*] Even if the data you intend to manipulate is private to a thread and you don't think you need any Pthreads calls, you still need to be careful. Just as you would in a non-threaded program, you must synchronize access to the data between the normal context of the thread and its handler context. This synchronization is accomplished by masking the arrival of the signal in the normal flow of the thread whenever it accesses the data it shares with the handler.

- Create a dedicated thread that waits specifically for interesting signals to arrive.

- Insert a simple loop in the dedicated thread's code that calls *sigwait,* indicating the signals that it will handle. Add the action routine that executes when the *sigwait* call returns.

A Simple Example

Let's look at a program that processes an input stream and provides a statistics report, upon request, to its users. Users ask the program for a report by sending the asynchronous signal SIGUSR1 to the process. When it catches this signal, the program should be able to generate and deliver the report without interrupting its computations on the data stream. To allow this to happen, we'll set up a separate thread that waits for the signal and responds accordingly.

In Example 5-1, we'll block the SIGUSR1 signal from delivery in all threads, including the one that will ultimately handle it.

Example 5-1: Blocking the Signal (stat_sigwait.c)

```
pthread_t stats_thread;
pthread_mutex_t stats_lock = PTHREAD_MUTEX_INITIALIZER;
extern int
main(void)
{
 .
 .
 .
sigset_t sigs_to_block;
 .
 .
 .
/* Set main thread's signal mask to block SIGUSR1.

All other threads will inherit mask and have it blocked too
 */
sigemptyset(&sigs_to_block);
sigaddset(&sigs_to_block, SIGUSR1);
pthread_sigmask(SIG_BLOCK, &sigs_to_block, NULL);
 .
 .
 .
pthread_create(&stats_thread, NULL, report_stats, NULL);
 .
 .
}
```

In Example 5-2, we'll create the statistics-reporting thread (*report_stats*) and have it wait for SIGUSR1. When it calls *sigwait,* it must have SIGUSR1 blocked; here it does because it inherited its signal mask from the main thread. While *report_stats* is processing one SIGUSR1 signal, any other SIGUSR1 signals sent to the process will be held pending, because all threads, including this one, have it blocked. The signal will be delivered the next time the *report_stats* thread reenters *sigwait*.

Example 5–2: Waiting for and Handling the Signal (stat_sigwait.c)

```
void * report_stats(void *p)
{
sigset_t sigs_to_catch;
int caught;

sigemptyset(&sigs_to_catch);
sigaddset(&sigs_to_catch, SIGUSR1);
for (;;) {
      sigwait(&sigs_to_catch, &caught);

      /* Proceed to lock mutex and display statistics */
      pthread_mutex_lock(&stats_lock);
      display_stats();
      pthread_mutex_unlock(&stats_lock);
      }
return NULL;
}
```

Now, if we chose to process this signal in a signal handler instead of trapping it in a *sigwait* call, we'd have a major problem. The *display_stats* routine references data modified by other threads in the program. The routine would need to lock this data with a mutex before printing it. However, it can't do this because it executes in a signal handler's context, and the Pthreads mutex-locking routines are not asynchronous signal-safe.

Some Signal Issues

Some POSIX.1 functions return EINTR if they are interrupted by a signal. If a thread that has called one of these functions receives this return value, it may have to reissue the call. No Pthreads functions behave this way.

In addition, certain real-time extensions to the signal interface (specified by POSIX.1b) have special adaptations that support threads. Most notably, the *signotify* structure can be set to indicate that a new thread should be created and run in a start routine when a timer event occurs.

Handling Signals in the ATM Example

We'll revise our ATM server to show how a more complex multithreaded program can deal with signals. Let's fix it so that a remote client can send the SIGUSR1 signal to the server to cause it to gracefully shut down. We added the shutdown capability at the end of our discussion of synchronization in Chapter 3, *Synchronizing Pthreads*.

When the server process receives a shutdown request, it must allow existing workers to complete their current requests and prevent the boss from creating any more. To implement this we'll create an additional thread—a shutdown thread. We'll create the shutdown thread at server startup and have it call *sigwait* to wait for the signal to arrive. When this happens, the shutdown thread is released from the *sigwait*. It sets a global flag that indicates to the boss and active workers that a shutdown should occur.

Before it creates the shutdown thread, the boss thread's server initialization routine must make sure that the boss and all other threads have the SIGUSR1 signal blocked from the get-go. (If it did not, a SIGUSR1 signal might be delivered before the threads themselves could issue a *pthread_sigmask* call to block it.) We'll rely on the way a thread inherits its signal mask from the thread that creates it and arrange it so that the boss blocks the SIGUSR1 signal in its signal mask just before it creates the shutdown and worker threads. As a result, at each of the boss *pthread_create* calls, a thread is created with a signal mask that blocks SIGUSR1.

The other change we'll make to the server initialization routine involves the creation of the shutdown thread itself and its start routine *shutdown_thread*, shown in Example 5-3.

Example 5-3: Creating a Signal Handling Thread in the ATM (atm_svr_signals.c)

```
int received_shutdown_req = FALSE;
pthread_mutex_t shutdown_lock = PTHREAD_MUTEX_INITIALIZER;
pthread_t shutdown_thread_id;

void atm_server_init(...)
{
sigset_t signals_to_block;
    :
    :

/* set signal mask to mask out SIGUSR1 in this thread
and all the threads we'll create */
sigemptyset(&signals_to_block);
sigaddset(&signals_to_block, SIGUSR1);
pthread_sigmask(SIG_BLOCK, &sigs_to_block, NULL);

/* create thread to catch shutdown signal */
pthread_create(&shutdown_thread_id,
    NULL,
    shutdown_thread,
    NULL);
```

Example 5-3: Creating a Signal Handling Thread in the ATM (atm_svr_signals.c) (continued)

```
    ⋮

}
```

The shutdown thread is pretty simple. It sets up a signal set to pass to *sigwait* to indicate it's interested in SIGUSR1. Then it calls *sigwait*. If the signal has already been received and is pending, the call returns immediately. Otherwise, it blocks until the signal is sent. When the *sigwait* call returns, the shutdown thread does the following:

- Sets a global flag to indicate to the boss thread that the time to shut down has arrived. This causes the boss to stop creating new worker threads.

- Checks the current count of worker threads and waits if necessary for it to reach zero.

- When all worker threads have completed, terminates the program by calling *exit*.

Example 5-4 illustrates the actions of the shutdown thread.

Example 5-4: Waiting for a Shutdown Signal in the ATM (atm_svr_signals.c)

```c
void shutdown_thread(void *arg)
{
  sigset_t signals_to_catch;
  int caught;

  /* Wait for SIGUSR1 */
  sigemptyset(&signals_to_catch);
  sigaddset(&signals_to_catch, SIGUSR1);

  sigwait(&signals_to_catch, &caught);

  /* got SIGUSR1—start shutdown */
  pthread_mutex_lock(&pthread_info.mutex);

  pthread_info.received_shutdown_req = TRUE;

  /* Wait for in-progress requests threads to finish */
  while (pthread_info.num_active > 0) {
    pthread_cond_wait(&pthread_info.thread_exit_cv, &pthread_info.mutex);
  }
  pthread_mutex_unlock(&pthread_info.mutex);
  exit(0);
  return (NULL);
}
```

Threadsafe Library Functions and System Calls

Up to this point we've spent a lot of effort to ensure that multiple threads can execute cleanly and efficiently in our own code. However, it's easy to forget that our applications spend a lot of time in system-supplied libraries (and third-party-supplied libraries), running code over which we have no control whatsoever. If the library fails to recognize potential race conditions when its data is shared among threads and neglects to enforce appropriate synchronization, our program will fail—just as if it ignored these issues itself!

This problem isn't an issue just for threaded programs. Race conditions can also occur in traditional, single-threaded programs that use signal handlers or that call routines recursively. A single-threaded program of this kind may have the same routine in progress in various call frames on its process stack.

Threadsafe and Reentrant Functions

The degree to which a library function or routine allows itself to have multiple instances of itself in progress at the same time is known as its *reentrancy*. The behavior of a reentrant function doesn't vary whether one call or multiple calls to it are in progress. For multiple, simultaneous function calls to work properly, a function cannot write to static data. If it does, it creates a race condition with regard to the data, and its callers risk obtaining bad results.

The Pthreads standard not only requires that almost all system-supplied library functions be reentrant but also requires them to be *threadsafe*. A threadsafe function has been designed to allow multiple, simultaneous calls specifically from threads. Whereas the normal mechanism for making a function reentrant is to remove all references to global data, a threadsafe function can employ thread synchronization primitives (such as mutexes and condition variables) to protect the global data.

Example of Thread-Unsafe and Threadsafe Versions of the Same Function

We'll show the behavior of a function that disregards the basic rules of thread safety in Example 5-5. Although the example is contrived and oversimplified, it does illustrate how certain functions were designed on many systems before Pthreads support was added. Although it may be obvious to you that using a fixed-length global buffer in a callable library is bad programming style, there are a couple of important lessons to be learned here:

- What may be bad programming style in a library called by different processes will be deadly to threads calling the library from the same process.

- It's a big, wonderful, and sometimes dangerous world out there! Know the types of libraries your threads hang around in!

In Example 5-5, our thread-unsafe function is called *reverse_string*. It uses a static buffer (*my_buffer*) as a temporary workspace while it reverses the order of the characters in an input string.

Example 5-5: A Thread-Unsafe String Reversing Routine (reverse_string.c)

```
static char work_buffer[100];
void reverse_string(in_str)
char *in_str;
{
int size = 0, i = 0, j = 0;
/* Find the end of the in_str */
while ( (in_str[size] != '\0') && (size != 100)) {
        size++;
  }

/* Copy from in_str into buffer, reversing it */
for (i = size-1; i > -1; i--) {
        work_buffer[j++] = in_str[i];
  }
work_buffer[j] = '\0';
/* Copy back from buffer to in_str */
for (i = 0; i < size+1; i++)
        in_str[i] = work_buffer[i];
}
```

Here's how a race condition develops when two threads call *reverse_string* at the same time:

1. Thread A calls the *reverse_string* function with the input string "the cat". The scheduler preempts the thread at the point at which the function has copied "tac e" into *work_buffer*.

2. Thread B now calls *reverse_string* with the input string "dog house". The function writes "esuoh god" into *work_buffer* and returns.

3. When Thread A continues, *reverse_string* continues copying "the cat" into *work_buffer*. When it completes, it returns the string "esuohht" instead of the correct string "tac eht".

The problem with *reverse_string* does not lie with the indexes it uses; the indexes are automatic data that is maintained by each individual thread. The problem is in the static array *work_buffer*.

We can easily make *reverse_string* threadsafe by the few keystrokes it takes to move the *my_buffer* array from the static variable area to the automatic variable area in Example 5-6.

Example 5-6: A Threadsafe String Reversing Routine (reverse_string.c)

```
void reverse_string(in_str)
char *in_str;
{
int size = 0, i = 0, j = 0;
char my_buffer[100];

/* Find the end of the in_str */
while ( (in_str[size] != '\0') && (size != 100)) {
        size++;
  }

/* Copy from in_str into buffer, reversing it */
for (i = size-1; i > -1; i--) {
        my_buffer[j++] = in_str[i];
  }
  .
  .
  .
}
```

When calling this version of *reverse_string*, each thread gets its own copy of *my_buffer* on its own per-thread stack. The danger of corruption is removed because no other thread can access the buffer.

Functions That Return Pointers to Static Data

Notice how transparent our solution is to the race condition in *reverse_string*. Because we didn't add or change any parameters, its callers, Thread A and Thread B, don't need to change—unless they depended on the previously incorrect results! Unfortunately, for other thread-unsafe functions, there isn't such a simple and tidy solution. What if the function call's interface includes in its argument list a return pointer to static data? Its callers are bound to this interface (and, for many of them—the single-threaded callers—it works fine). Moreover, this type of interface is not uncommon. You often find it in functions that cache information (such as directory listings, host names, or times). It's often easier and quicker to return a pointer to the static results than to copy information into a caller-specified buffer.

The only way to produce a threadsafe version of this type of function is to change its argument list. Regrettably, the threadsafe version will no longer be compatible with the previous version, thus causing some amount of inconvenience to its callers.

Library Use of errno

In Chapter 1, *Why Threads?*, we pointed out that Pthreads library functions do not use **errno**. However, traditional UNIX and POSIX.1 system calls (such as *read* and *write*) do use **errno**, and this could be a big problem for multithreaded programs that call these functions.

When a program makes an unsuccessful call to one of these functions, the system sets the value of the global *int* variable **errno** to an error number. The programmer first tests the function's return value to see if an error has occurred and then reads *errno* to determine why. Typically, the *libc* function *perror* is used to decode the error and print an explanatory string to standard error.

The following snippets of code show two threads making an unsuccessful system call at the same time.

```
Thread 1                              Thread 2
amt=read(...);                        rtn=ioctl(...);
if (amt<0) {                          if (rtn<0) {
   fprintf(stderr, "error read() %d",    fprintf(stderr, "error ioctl() %d",
        errno)                                errno);
exit(-1);                             exit(-1);
}                                     }
```

Because there is only one **errno** global variable for the entire process, the failing *read* call and the failing *ioctl* call encounter a race condition when they write to it. Consequently, when Thread 1 reads and prints out the value of **errno**, it can't tell whether the error value is the result of its *read* call or Thread 2's *ioctl* call.

The Pthreads standard recognizes this problem and dictates that each thread must perceive **errno** as having a thread-private value, independent of the **errno** values seen by other threads. To achieve this, Pthreads library implementations define the string "errno" as a macro. When expanded, this macro returns a thread-specific errno value. Thus, existing error-checking code doesn't need to change to work within a thread. In fact, our examples would work, too.

The Pthreads Standard Specifies Which Functions Must Be Threadsafe

One of the most time-consuming aspects of deploying Pthreads for many system vendors is the effort required to make their libraries and system calls threadsafe. The Pthreads standard dictates that almost all POSIX.1 calls must be threadsafe. (Note that the POSIX.1 calls include not only library functions but also system calls such as *dup, chmod, getpid*, and *open*, and C language bindings such as *atoi, malloc, printf*, and *scanf*.)

The small number of exceptions allowed by the standard include:

*   Calls whose argument lists include static data

*   Calls for which performance is a concern

*   Calls that involve file locking

Additionally, a vendor may make certain of its non-POSIX calls threadsafe. Before using any non-POSIX interface in a multithreaded application, ensure that it is threadsafe by checking your system's documentation.

Alternative interfaces for functions that return static data

The POSIX.1 *readdir* and *localtime* functions are good examples of the sort of function that returns to its caller a pointer to static data (either a structure or string). Each time you call one of these functions, it overwrites its static data area. In nonthreaded applications, this means you need to use the returned pointer to copy the data somewhere else; this may be annoying, but it does not prevent the call from returning correct results. However, when you call one of these routines from multiple threads at the same time, it will return corrupt results.

We've already mentioned that this type of function can be made threadsafe only by some visible change to its call interface. The major drawback to this is that we'd break a lot of programs if we change the existing interface of a call like *readdir* or *localtime*.

The solution the Pthreads standard adopts for functions like these is to leave the existing functions alone and create new, alternative versions of the functions that are threadsafe. In the new threadsafe functions (whose names end in _*r* for reen-trant), the caller provides a pointer to a buffer to which the function copies its results. Each time a thread calls the threadsafe version of one of these functions, it maintains the data unique to its call in its own buffer.

The Pthreads standard defines the following threadsafe versions of existing POSIX.1 functions:

asctime_r	*ctime_r*
getgrgid_r	*getgrnam_r*
getlogin_r	*getpwnam_r*
getpwuid_r	*gmtime_r*
localtime_r	*rand_r*
readdir_r	*strtok_r*
ttyname_r	

Additional routines for performance considerations

The *getc, getchar, putc,* and *putchar* functions are commonly used POSIX.1 functions that perform I/O to standard input and output. Because of the frequency with which certain applications call them, the Pthreads standard committee determined that making these functions threadsafe would result in serious performance hits for some single-threaded applications (which don't need the extra thread-specific synchronization). As a result, it decreed that, while vendors should make the existing functions threadsafe, they should also offer new versions of the functions that provide better performance.

The new, thread-unsafe, better-performing versions of the *getc, getchar, putc,* and *putchar* functions are *getc_unlocked, getchar_unlocked, putc_unlocked,* and *putchar_unlocked.*

File-locking functions for threads

It's fairly common for a thread to read and write to a shared file. Although POSIX.1 defines calls (such as *flock*) that allow a thread to synchronize access to a file shared with another process, it did not define calls that allowed multiple threads within the same process to synchronize similar activity. A thread that calls *flock* effectively locks a file against access by threads from other processes but leaves it wide open to other threads in its own process.

To synchronize access to a file shared with threads from the same process as well as those of other processes, a thread could use a mutex in conjunction with its *flock* calls. However, the Pthreads standard defines functions, listed in Table 5-2, that give you this degree of synchronization with a lot less effort.

Table 5–2: New Routines for Thread-Specific File Locking

Function	Description
flockfile	Locks a file on a per-thread basis
ftrylockfile	Tries to lock a file on a per-thread basis (returns immediately)
funlockfile	Unlocks a file on a per-thread basis

Where are the threadsafe functions?

The Pthreads standard specifies that the threadsafe versions of most POSIX.1 functions must be available on your platform, but where?

Here, too, you should consult your operating system's documentation. Some systems may support the new threadsafe versions of standard functions in one library while continuing to support the thread-unsafe versions in another.[*] These systems may keep the original functions in a standard library (named lib*xxx*.a) and the threadsafe functions in a new library, lib*xxx*_r.a.

Using Thread-Unsafe Functions in a Multithreaded Program

Speaking of safety, if you are intent on walking on the sea wall during high tide, make sure you do so only when the wind has stopped and you're wearing your good sneakers—and stay away from those rocks! Similarly, if you are determined that your multithreaded program needs the unique functionality of a system library or toolkit that is thread-unsafe, you can still use it in your multithreaded application. However, if you do, you must treat the entire function call as if it were a shared resource and use appropriate synchronization.

The simplest synchronization scheme is to allow only one thread in your program to make calls using the thread-unsafe interface. A little more complex solution would be to associate a mutex or a condition variable with some or all of the interface calls. Any thread in your program must lock the appropriate mutex before calling the thread-unsafe function it protects.

For example, assume that we failed to make *reverse_string* unsafe. In Example 5-7, we'll insert some code in a multithreaded program that calls it, surrounding the *reverse_string* call with calls to lock and unlock a *reverse_string_mutex* lock and defining a macro that will invoke this whole block of code. Now any thread in our program can use the *safe_reverse_string* macro to launch a thread-safe call to the thread-unsafe *reverse_string* function.

Example 5-7: Using a Mutex with a Thread-Unsafe Interface (reverse_string.c)

```
pthread_mutex_t reverse_string_mutex
#define safe_reverse_string(x) \
pthread_mutex_lock(&reverse_string_mutex); \
reverse_string(x); \
pthread_mutex_unlock(&reverse_string_mutex);
```

---

[*] There are a number of reasons the thread-unsafe libraries may still be available, including performance (the traditional functions may be faster than the threadsafe ones) and quality (the threadsafe functions may not have been tested as much as the traditional ones).

Cancellation-Safe Library Functions and System Calls

Using thread cancellation can have a number of pitfalls, not the least of which is the accidental cancellation of a thread that holds a lock or that has just allocated some memory. We helped you safeguard your code against such disasters in Chapter 4, *Managing Pthreads*. Now we'll take some time to acquaint you with what Pthreads vendors do to ensure that their libraries continue to work as expected when confronted with cancellation in a multithreaded environment.

When you call library functions from a program that uses thread cancellation, you must consider two important questions:

- Can the thread be safely canceled while it's executing in these functions?

- Do any of these functions act as cancellation points for a deferred cancellation?

Asynchronous Cancellation-Safe Functions

Remember that, when asynchronous cancellation is enabled for a thread, any *pthread_cancel* call aimed at it will terminate the thread immediately, no matter what it's doing. It's up to you to ensure that a routine running under the threat of thread cancellation doesn't hold locks or have resources allocated. When a routine is designed in this way, it's known as an *asynchronous cancellation-safe function.*

As we've seen, system libraries were originally written without consideration of threads. Although the Pthreads standard requires vendors to make most POSIX.1 function calls threadsafe (and defines various workarounds for the others), it doesn't force them to make POSIX.1 libraries (or ANSI C or vendor-specific libraries) asynchronous cancellation-safe. This means if a thread is canceled in the middle of a library call, it may terminate while library data is in an inconsistent state or while the library holds memory allocated on the thread's behalf. As a result, when using asynchronous cancellation in a multithreaded program, you should call only those library functions that are documented as being asynchronous cancellation-safe. Very few are.

Nevertheless, if your program truly needs the functionality that these asynchronous cancellation-unsafe functions provide, you can dodge potential problems by resetting the thread's cancelability type to deferred for the duration of the function call. Defining a wrapper macro, as shown in Example 5-8, should do the trick.

Example 5-8: An Asynchronous Cancellation Wrapper Macro (async_safe.c)

```
#define async_cancel_safe_read(fd, buf, amt) \
    {\
int oldtype; \
pthread_setcanceltype(PTHREAD_CANCEL_DEFERRED, &oldtype); \
if (read(fd, buf, amt) < 0) \
perror("read"), exit(-1); \
pthread_setcanceltype(oldtype, NULL); \
pthread_testcancel(); \
    }
```

A thread invokes the *async_cancel_safe_read* macro instead of calling *read* directly. The macro first enables deferred cancellation with a *pthread_setcanceltype* call, which sets things up so that while the thread is in the *read* call any cancellations delivered to it will be made pending. When the read call returns, the macro makes a *pthread_testcancel* call, forcing any pending cancellations to be delivered. If this is not the case, the macro proceeds to the next line, a *pthread_setcanceltype* call that sets the thread's cancelability type back to asynchronous.

Cancellation Points in System and Library Calls

Let's review what we know about cancellation points.

When deferred cancellation is enabled for a thread, it can be terminated only at defined cancellation points. Thus far, we know of four Pthreads function calls that act as cancellation points: they are *pthread_testcancel, pthread_cond_wait, pthread_cond_timedwait,* and *pthread_join.* The *pthread_testcancel* function allows you to insert an explicit cancellation point in a thread. Because the other functions can cause a calling thread to block for a long time, they force a thread's termination if its cancellation is pending at the time of the call.

It would be useful if other system and library calls that impose long waits on their callers could also act as cancellation points. In fact, the Pthreads standard lists over fifty POSIX.1 and ANSI C routines that vendors may define as cancellation points:

closedir	*ctermid*	*fclose*	*fcntl*	*fflush*
fgetc	*fgets*	*fopen*	*fprintf*	*fputc*
fputs	*fread*	*freopen*	*fscanf*	*fseek*
ftell	*fwrite*	*getc*	*getchar*	*getchar_unlocked*
getc_unlocked	*getcwd*	*getgrgid*	*getgrgid_r*	*getgrnam*
getgrnam_r	*getlogin*	*getlogin_r*	*getpwnam*	*getpwnam_r*
getpwuid	*getpwuid_r*	*gets*	*lseek*	*opendir*
perror	*printf*	*putc*	*putchar*	*putchar_unlocked*

putc_unlocked	*puts*	*readdir*	*remove*	*rename*
rewind	*rewinddir*	*scanf*	*tmpfile*	*tmpname*
ttyname	*ttyname_r*	*ungetc*	*unlink*	

The following routines must be defined as cancellation points on all implementations:

aio_suspend	*close*	*creat*	*fcntl*	*fsync*	*mg_receive*
mg_send	*msync*	*nanosleep*	*open*	*pause*	*read*
sem_wait	*sigsuspend*	*sigtimedwait*	*sigwait*	*sigwaitinfo*	*sleep*
system	*tcdrain*	*wait*	*waitpid*	*write*	

Thread-Blocking Library Functions and System Calls

The key reason for using threads lies in the convenience and efficiency of letting one thread block on an I/O operation or synchronization call while others continue performing the useful work of your program. With this in mind, we've assumed from the start of the book that each time a thread makes a system call that blocks, only the thread itself is stalled, not the entire process. We haven't been entirely up front with you. Our assumption's a bit presumptuous.

In a nonthreaded program, system calls that perform file I/O (like *open*, *read*, and *write*) or synchronize processes (*wait*) block their callers until the requested operation completes. You can avoid some blocking on a file operation by passing the POSIX O_NONBLOCK flag or the BSD O_NDELAY flag to the file's *open* call, or the FIONBIO flag to an *ioctl* call to the file. When a process issues a subsequent *read* or *write* call on that file, it would receive notification of I/O completion through a SIGIO signal.

Process blocking is fine when a process has a single execution state, but it subverts the whole purpose of threads. A system call that blocks a process would block all of our threads, and we'd lose all of the advantages of concurrency until the system call completes. If we used nonblocking calls as described previously, we'd need to add synchronization code to our threads to wait for the completion signal.

Fortunately, the Pthreads standard requires that vendors implement many blocking POSIX.1 calls so that they suspend only the calling thread and not the entire process. (The nonblocking behavior of the I/O calls remains the same.) They include:

fcntl   *open*
pause   *read*
sigsuspend   *sleep*
wait   *waitpid*
write

What if a blocking call supplied by your system is not listed here? If you must use the call, you have a few options:

- You may get lucky and discover your implementation has implemented the code as nonblocking. So much for portability!

- Let your entire application stall while the call blocks. (Think of it as a rock-climbing expedition in which your more athletically adept friends stop to wait for you as you haul yourself up behind them.)

- Fork another process to do the call. (It works, but using threads was supposed to eliminate the need for you to do this.)

- Use any available nonblocking alternative. Here, you avoid blocking the process, but you'll need to add explicit synchronization to your thread so it can retrieve the results of the call.

Threads and Process Management

On a Pthreads-compliant system, calls that manipulate processes, like *fork* and *exec*, still behave in the way they always have for nonthreaded programs. Let's see what happens when we make these calls from a multithreaded process.

Calling fork from a Thread

A process creates another process by issuing a *fork* call. The newly created child process has a new process ID but starts with the same memory image and state as its parent. At its birth it's an exact clone of its parent, starting execution at the point of its parent's *fork* call in the same program. Often, the new process immediately calls *exec* to replace its parent's program with a new program. It then sets out on its own business.

In a Pthreads-compliant implementation, the *fork* call always creates a new child process with a single thread, regardless of how many threads its parent may have had at the time of the call. Furthermore, the child's thread is a replica of the thread in the parent that called *fork*—including a process address space shared by *all* of its parent's threads and its parent thread's per-thread stack.

Consider the headaches:

- The new single-threaded child process could inherit held locks from threads in the parent that don't exist in the child. It may have no idea what these locks mean, let alone realize that it holds one of them. Confusion and deadlock are in the forecast.

- The child process could inherit heap areas that were allocated by threads in the parent that don't exist in the child. Here we see memory leaks, data loss, and bug reports.

The Pthreads standard defines the *pthread_atfork* call to help you manage these problems. The *pthread_atfork* function allows a parent process to specify preparation and cleanup routines that parent and child processes run as part of the *fork* operation. Using these routines a parent or child process can manage the release and reacquisition of locks and resources before and after the *fork*.

This is pretty complex stuff, so please bear with us.

Fork-handling stacks

To perform its magic, the *pthread_atfork* call pushes addresses of preparation and cleanup routines on any of three fork-handling stacks:

- Routines placed on the *prepare stack* are run in the parent before the *fork*.

- Routines placed on the *parent stack* are run in the parent after the *fork*.

- Routines placed on the *child stack* are run in the child after the *fork*.

A single call to *pthread_atfork* places a routine on one or more of these stacks. With multiple calls you can place routines on any given stack in a first-in last-out order. Because the fork-handling stacks are a processwide resource, any thread— not just the one that will call *fork*—can push routines on them.

In those carefree times when we throw caution to the winds and decide to *fork* from the middle of a multithread program, we typically use *pthread_atfork* to push mutex-locking calls on the prepare fork-handling stack and mutex-unlocking calls on the parent and child stacks. We might also place routines that release resources and reset variables on the child stack.

Let's demonstrate what would happen if we did not use *pthread_atfork*'s capabilities in one of those *fork*-crazy programs of ours. In Figure 5-1, we have two threads: a mutex (Lock L) and the data the mutex protects. Thread A acquires Lock L and starts to modify the data. Meanwhile, Thread B decides to *fork*. Now, the *fork* creates a child process that's a clone of its parent process, and this child shows a locked Lock L. The child process has a single thread, a replica of Thread B (the thread in the parent process that called *fork*). The assortment of clones and replicas that result from the *fork* has little effect on the threads in the parent process. However, things are not okay in the child. The locked Lock L is an utter mystery to the new Thread B in the child. If it tries to acquire Lock L, it will deadlock. (There's no Thread A in the child that will ever release Lock L in the child process's context.) If it tries to access the data without first obtaining Lock L, it may see the data in an inconsistent form. Life's never easy for our kids.

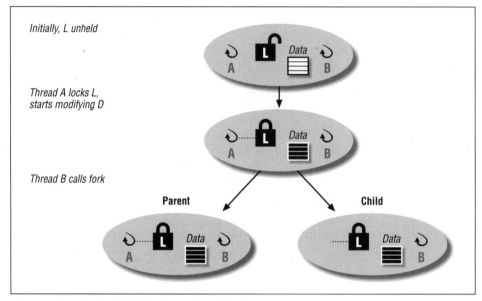

Figure 5-1: Results of a fork when pthread_atfork is not used

Now, let's use *pthread_atfork* to control Lock L's state at the time of the *fork*. The program we show in Figure 5-2 also has Threads A and B, Lock L, and scrupulously guarded data. However, we've added an initialization routine that pushes a routine that locks L on the prepare fork-handling stack, and a routine that unlocks L on the child and parent fork-handling stacks. We've taken care to do this in a routine that executes before any thread actually uses the lock.

Sometime later, Thread A acquires the lock and starts to modify the data. When Thread B calls *fork*, the routine on the prepare stack runs in Thread B's context. This routine tries to obtain Lock L and will block; Lock L is still held by Thread A. Ultimately, the *fork* is delayed until Thread A releases Lock L. When this happens, the prepare routine succeeds, Thread B will become the owner of the lock, and the *fork* proceeds. As expected, a child process is created that's a replica of its par-

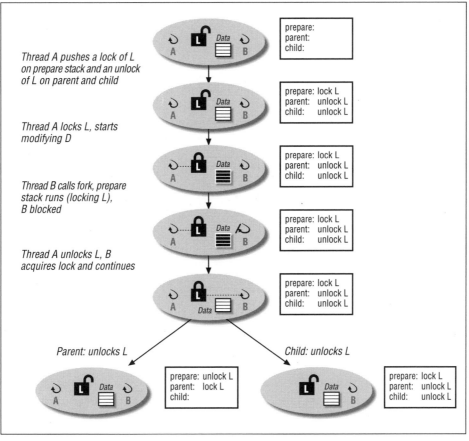

Figure 5–2: Results of a fork when pthread_atfork is used

ent. However, in this case, the newly cloned Thread B in the child knows about the locked lock it finds in the child's context. At this point, the routine we placed on the child fork-handling stack runs and releases Lock L. The same routine runs from the parent fork-handling stack and releases the lock in the parent process. When the dust settles, the lock is unowned in both parent and child, and the data it protects is in a consistent state. Who could ask for more?

Even given the capabilities of *pthread_atfork*, forking from a multithreaded program is no picnic. We kept our example simple. Imagine having to track every lock and every resource that may be held by every thread in your program and in every library call it makes! Before pursuing this course, you should consider a less complex alternative:

- If possible, fork before you've created any threads.

  Instead of forking, create a new thread. If you are forking to *exec* a binary image, can you convert the image to a callable shared library to which you could simply link?

- Consider the surrogate parent model.

  In the surrogate parent model, a program forks a child process at initialization time. The sole purpose of the child is to serve as a sort of "surrogate parent" for the original process should it ever need to fork another child. After initialization, the original parent can proceed to create its additional threads. When it wants to *exec* an image, it communicates this to its child (which has remained single-threaded). The child then performs the *fork* and *exec* on behalf of the original process.

Calling exec from a Thread

An *exec* call changes the program image of a process. For instance, using an *exec*, a process running the shell program can switch to the *vi* editor program. After the *exec* the identity of the process remains the same (that is, it has the same process ID, user ID, etc.), but its virtual memory image is completely new and based on the program it has been asked to run.

If a thread in a multithreaded process issues an *exec*, we'd expect that thread to start in the *main* routine of the new image. And this is essentially what happens. But what of the other threads? It wouldn't be of much use if the system loader picked some random routine entry points for them to start in. With this in mind, the Pthreads standard specifies that an *exec* call from any thread must terminate all threads in the process and start a single new thread at *main* in the new image.

Process Exit and Threads

Regardless of whether or not a process contains multiple threads, it can be terminated when:

- Any thread in it makes an *exit* system call.

- The thread running the *main* routine completes its execution.

- A fatal signal is delivered.

When a process exits, all threads in it die immediately, and their resources are released. (If you call _*exit* directly, the system doesn't guarantee the cleanup.)

Multiprocessor Memory Synchronization

The Pthreads standard requires library implementors to synchronize memory writes (with respect to reads and other writes) for a subset of Pthreads and POSIX.1 functions. For example, if a thread calls *pthread_mutex_lock*, the function not only protects access to the shared data but also ensures that prior modifications to that data are committed to memory at the point of the call. The way in which this is done is implementation-specific, but typically involves some memory-barrier machine instruction that synchronizes cache and memory contents across the CPUs in a multiprocessing system. The end result is that any thread's view of memory is the same as that of any other thread in the same process, regardless of which CPUs the threads are running on.

The functions that must synchronize memory operations include:

pthread_cond_broadcast	*pthread_mutex_unlock*
pthread_cond_signal	*sem_post*
pthread_cond_timedwait	*sem_trywait*
pthread_cond_wait	*sem_wait*
pthread_create	*fork*
pthread_join	*wait*
pthread_mutex_trylock	*waitpid*
pthread_mutex_lock	

6

Practical Considerations

Writing a multithreaded program is a lot like being a bebop jazz musician in the late Forties. It's great to know what notes to play and the order in which to play them, but if the object is to play "Cherokee" as fast as possible, technique doesn't matter all that much. You need to fit as many notes in as short a space of time as possible and be done it with before the audience can catch its breath. It's performance, performance, performance!

So it is with you, the writer of threaded applications. Portable library calls that provide task concurrency within a process are fine, but only if they deliver on the promised performance. So in this chapter, we move from the abstract to the practical, from the world of standards and reference pages to the world in which things often go wrong or don't go as well as we'd like. With this in mind, our discussions will focus on:

Pthreads implementations

Pthreads implementations differ to the degree to which they're based in user space or kernel space. The way in which a thread library is designed on a given platform determines how your threads are scheduled, whether they can actually run in parallel, and, ultimately, how well they perform. Knowing a little bit about how your platform supports Pthreads can help you design your program to take advantage of the implementation's strong points

Debugging

Debugging a multithreaded program is something else. (We encourage you to write yours without bugs.) A multithreaded program can encounter errors, such as race conditions and deadlocks, that aren't found in a traditional program, and these types of errors are not easy to debug. Moreover, the command set of conventional debuggers allows you to direct only process execution; some may provide a similar command set to allow you to control the execution of threads. Armed with a suitable tool, how do we proceed to uncover and eradicate the bugs in our threads?

Performance

We added threads to our program to obtain performance we couldn't achieve in a single-threaded version. How do we measure this performance? How can we tune it?

Understanding Pthreads Implementation

Pthreads implementations fall into three basic categories:

- Based on pure user space.

- Based on pure kernel thread.

- Implementations somewhere between the two. These hybrid implementations are referred to variously as *two-level schedulers, lightweight processes* (LWPs), or *activations.*

All implementations in these categories conform to the Pthreads standard and provide concurrency (the basic goal of threads). However, your platform's choice of implementation has a radical effect on the scheduling and performance of the threads in your program. Just look for a moment at the extremes! Pure user-space thread implementations don't provide global scheduling scope and don't actually allow multiple threads from the same process to execute in parallel on different CPUs. At the other extreme, pure kernel-thread implementations don't scale well when a process has 10, 20, 30, or more threads.

Because Pthreads implementations are varied and complex and because implementations are evolving and improving at a swift rate, we can't do justice to them in the brief space we have in this book. The goal of this section is to introduce you to those differences in architectures that impact the way your program performs on various implementations.

We'll set the stage for later discussions by reviewing some basic vocabulary.

Two Worlds

User mode commonly refers to the times when a process (or, by extension, a thread) is executing the instructions in its program or a library (to which the program is linked). The program or library knows about the various objects upon which it operates (such as code, data, and other abstractions) because they are defined in *user space* and not in the underlying operating system kernel.

Kernel mode refers to a process's (or a thread's) operational mode when it's executing within the operating system's kernel—usually as a result of a system call or an exception. In kernel mode, a process runs the instructions of the core operating system to access resources and services on a program's behalf. While it's running in kernel mode, the process can access objects that are defined in *kernel space* and, thereby, known only to the kernel.

Two Kinds of Threads

The threads we've discussed in this book are *user threads*. They are programming abstractions that exist to be accessed by calls from within your program. In fact, the Pthreads standard doesn't require the operating system kernel to know anything at all about them. Whether a Pthread has any meaning inside the kernel or within kernel mode is up to the implementation.

A *kernel thread** can be something quite different. It's an abstraction for an operating system execution point within a process. To support the Pthreads standard, an implementor doesn't need to use kernel threads. As we'll see, the standard allows for great flexibility in the underlying implementation.

Some platforms have native, nonstandard user-space thread implementations that predate the Pthreads standard. (The proliferation of these nonstandard interfaces was actually the motivating force behind the effort to define the Pthreads standard.) These native thread interfaces often have very similar semantics to those of the Pthreads interfaces, but they don't fully comply with the syntax and functionality the standard requires. On these platforms, an additional layer—sometimes only an include file—exists to turn the native user-space threads into Pthreads that conform to the portable Pthread interface.

Who's Providing the Thread?

A Pthreads implementation supports user threads by a Pthreads-compliant library and, optionally, by changes to the operating system kernel. So, when we issue a *pthread_create* call on a given implementation, what is involved in creating the thread—the Pthreads library alone, the kernel itself, or some combination of the two? We'll look at the various possibilities.

---

* The various UNIX operating systems use different terms for kernel thread. Digital UNIX, which was derived from Mach 2.5, uses the term *kernel thread*; Sun's Solaris uses the term *lightweight process (LWP)*; others use the term *activation* or *two-level scheduler.*

User-space Pthreads implementations

In pure user-space implementations, the kernel isn't involved at all in providing a user thread. As shown in Figure 6-1, the Pthreads library itself schedules threads, multiplexing all of a process's threads onto its single execution context. The kernel has no notion of threads; it continues to schedule processes as it usually does.

This design is known as an *all-to-one mapping.* Out of all of a process's threads that are able to run at a given time, the Pthreads library selects just one to run in its process's context when that process is next scheduled by the kernel.

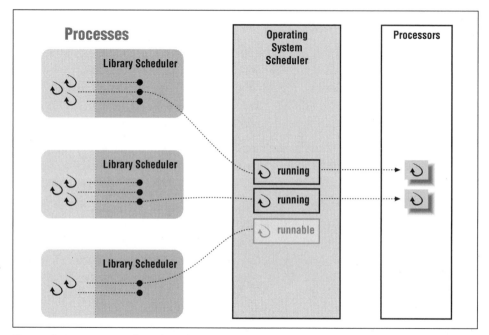

Figure 6-1: User-space thread implementations

A pure user-space implementation can be based quite simply on tools that *UNIX* programmers have traditionally used to manage multiple contexts within a single process: namely, *setjmp, longjmp,* and signals. The Pthreads library may define a user thread as a data structure that stores an execution point in the form of a *jmp_buf* structure saved by a *setjmp* call. When the current thread is rescheduled, it resumes the new thread that has been selected to run by performing a *longjmp* to the new thread's stored *jmp_buf* execution point.

There are several advantages to a pure user-space implementation:

- Because it doesn't require changes to the operating system itself, it allows many UNIX vendors, and vendors of other operating systems, to quickly provide a Pthreads-compliant library without having to invent kernel threads. For instance, Digital implemented its Pthreads library in this way on versions of OpenVMS prior to Version 7.0. (Version 7.0 uses kernel threads.) Additionally, DCE includes a user-space implementation, thus encouraging its vendors to provide support for DCE threads by relieving them of wholescale changes to their operating systems.

- Because user-space implementation doesn't use expensive system calls to create threads and doesn't require the operating system to perform a context switch between threads, certain types of multithreaded applications can run faster than they would in a kernel-thread implementation. Among these applications are those that run exclusively on uniprocessing systems and those that don't have enough CPU-bound work to effectively use multiple CPUs.

- Because user-space threads aren't known to the operating system, they can be created quickly and without impact to the kernel. This scales well: you can create more and more threads without overloading the system. Each thread is just another timeslice from the set of resources originally assigned to your process.

There are also two considerable disadvantages:

- The Pthreads library manages the scheduling of user threads using an all-to-one mapping of threads to a single process's execution context. As a result, threads within the same process compete against each other for CPU cycles. The operating system never sees an individual thread, only the process. If you raise the priority of a thread, it'll run more often and longer than other threads of lower priority in the same process. If it was your intention to give it a scheduling advantage over threads from other processes on the system, you'll be disappointed. To get the responsiveness you expect for a real-time thread from this type of implementation, you must either throw everybody else off the system or always run your entire process and all of its threads at a higher priority than everyone else. Either approach is likely to bring a system administrator to your office.

- Because the Pthreads library's thread-scheduling ability is limited to threads within a process, it restricts your multithreaded program from taking advantage of multiple CPUs. Because the operating system is utterly unaware that many streams of processing are beneath a given process, it allocates available CPUs to processes, not threads. All threads in a process must share the CPU on which the process was scheduled (and do so in the timeslice given to the process). The threads can never run in parallel across the available CPUs, even if another CPU happens to be idle!

Kernel thread–based Pthreads implementations

In pure kernel thread–based implementations, the Pthreads library creates a kernel thread for each user thread. Because each kernel thread represents the execution context of a single user thread, this design is known as a *one-to-one mapping*. As we show in Figure 6-2, when a CPU becomes available, the kernel chooses a kernel thread to run from among all the kernel threads available on the system, regardless of which processes they represent.

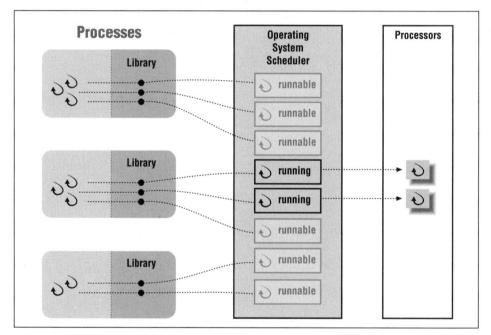

Figure 6–2: Kernel thread–based implementations

A pure kernel thread–based implementation depends upon the operating system to define, store, and reload the execution states of individual threads. The operating system must now manage on a per-thread basis some of the information it's traditionally maintained for an individual process. For instance, each thread must have its own scheduling priority, its own set of saved registers, and its own CPU assignment. Other types of information, such as the file table, remain associated with the process.

A good example of a pure kernel thread–based implementation is the pre-Version 4.0 Digital UNIX, which was known as DEC OSF/1 at the time. Digital UNIX, based in part on the Mach operating system developed at Carnegie-Mellon University (CMU), adopted Mach's kernel thread design. Mach threads operate at a much lower level than Pthreads and provide minimal functionality. Prior to Version 4.0, the Digital UNIX Pthreads library requested a new Mach kernel thread from the system for each *pthread_create* call. Because the Mach kernel thread design provides few synchronization primitives, it's the role of the Pthreads library to implement such features as mutexes and thread joins atop the Mach kernel thread functionality.

The advantages of a pure kernel thread–based implementation set to right the disadvantages of the pure user-space implementation:

- The Pthreads library schedules user threads on a one-to-one basis to kernel threads. As a result, threads compete against all other threads on the system for CPU cycles, not just against other threads in the same process. The kernel is aware of threads. If you raise the priority of a thread, it'll run more often and longer than other threads of lower priority throughout the system.

- Because the kernel schedules threads globally across the entire system, multiple threads in your program can run on different CPUs simultaneously, as long as their relative priorities are higher than those of other threads on the system. Unlike a pure user-space implementation, a pure kernel thread–based implementation doesn't limit your program to a single executing thread.

The disadvantages of a kernel thread–based implementation are as follows:

- Although less expensive than creating a new process, the creation of a new kernel thread does require some kernel overhead—the processing of a system call and the maintenance of kernel data structures. If your application will never run on a multiprocessor, or if its threads are not CPU bound, this overhead is unnecessary. A user-space implementation would probably provide better performance.

- Because some cost is associated with creating and maintaining kernel threads, applications that use a lot of threads ("a lot" meaning 10 or more on some systems, hundreds on others) can significantly load a system and degrade its overall performance, thus affecting all running applications.

Two-level scheduler Pthreads implementations: the best of both worlds

In a two-level scheduler implementation, the Pthreads library and the operating system kernel cooperate to schedule user threads. Like a pure kernel thread–based implementation, a two-level scheduler implementation maps user threads to kernel threads, but instead of mapping each user thread to a kernel thread, it may map many user threads to any of a pool of kernel threads (see Figure 6-3). This is known as a *some-to-one-mapping*. A user thread may not have a unique relationship to a specific kernel thread; rather, it may be mapped to different kernel threads at different times.

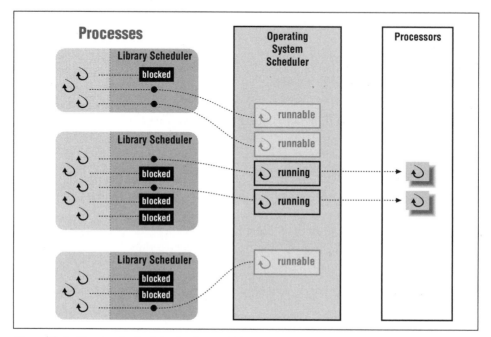

Figure 6–3: Two-level scheduler implementations

Both the Pthreads library and the kernel maintain data structures that represent threads (user threads and kernel threads, respectively). The Pthreads library assigns user threads to run in a process's available kernel threads;[*] the kernel schedules kernel threads from the collection of all processes' runnable kernel threads. The two levels of scheduling allow better customized fits of actual execution contexts (kernel threads) to user-specified concurrency (user threads).

For example, if a program's user threads frequently sleep on timers, events, or I/O completion, it makes little sense to dedicate a kernel thread to each of them. The kernel threads will see little CPU activity. It's much more efficient to allow the Pthreads library in a two-level scheduler implementation to accommodate some of

---

[*] The Solaris Pthreads library maps user threads to LWPs. Digital UNIX Version 4.0 and OpenVMS Version 7.0 map user threads to kernel threads.

its user threads' spare and sporadic execution behavior by allotting them a single kernel thread altogether. For this type of program, the two-level scheduler effectively provides the benefits of a pure user-space implementation—less kernel overhead and better performance.

At the other extreme, another program's user threads might be completely CPU-bound and runnable. Here, the two-level scheduler might assign a kernel thread to each user thread up to the number of CPUs on the system, acting like a pure kernel thread–based implementation. Whenever a CPU becomes available, the kernel may thereby select any of these user threads for scheduling.[*]

Of course, most multithreaded programs are at neither extreme. In fact, a single program may encounter periods of high I/O activity and intense CPU use over time as it executes. Its resource demands may change based on the input assigned to it on a given run. It may be subject to different constraints, such as processor speed and I/O responsiveness, depending upon the platform on which it's run. The ability to tailor its kernel thread allocation policies to an individual program is the greatest advantage of a two-level scheduler implementation. It can adapt automatically (or respond to customizations) to be more responsive to different programs, or maintain an optimal execution environment as a program's execution behavior changes.

Unlike a pure user-space implementation, a two-level scheduler implementation doesn't bind all user threads in a process to a single kernel execution context. Instead, it allows multiple threads in a process to run in parallel on multiple CPUs. Unlike a pure kernel thread–based implementation, a two-level scheduler implementation doesn't create a kernel thread for every user thread. By not doing so, it avoids needless overhead if a kernel thread is not used enough to justify its creation. All in all, when you design tasks for a multithreaded program that will run under a two-level scheduler, you can be less finicky about segregating CPU-bound from I/O-bound work. The two-level scheduler will adopt user-to-kernel thread mappings that are suitable to the program's actual execution behavior.

---

[*] The policies by which two-level scheduler implementations apportion their kernel threads to deserving user-space threads vary considerably. Some sophisticated implementations, such as Digital UNIX, may actually detect a change in a thread's execution behavior (for instance, as it becomes more or less CPU-bound) and adjust their kernel-thread assignments accordingly. Discussing the full range of implementation possibilities is beyond the scope of this book. However, if you are interested in reading more about two-level scheduler designs, we encourage you to look at the following publications:

UNIX Internals: The New Frontiers by Uresh Vahala, Prentice Hall, 1996. Discusses recent technological developments in UNIX operating systems, including Solaris, SVR4, Digital UNIX, and Mach.

"Scheduler Activations: Effective Kernel Support for the User-Level Management of Parallelism" by Anderson, Bershad, Lazowaska, and Levy, Department of Computer Science and Engineering, University of Washington, Seattle. Describes activations in their research operating system. This technology bears some resemblance to the Digital UNIX Version 4.0 two-level scheduler implementation.

"SunOS Multi-Threaded Architecture," *USENIX Winter Conference Proceedings*, Dallas, Texas, 1991. Describes Solaris's lightweight process implementation.

Perhaps the only disadvantage of a two-level scheduler is in its level of internal complexity and the effort a system developer must muster to implement one. That, fortunately, is not a problem for you, the application developer. Nevertheless, you may share in some of this complexity when you attempt to debug a multithreaded program on a two-level scheduler implementation and discover that it's difficult to keep track of how your user threads relate to the kernel threads that get placed into execution.

What a great way to get into our next topic!

Debugging

Well, you probably have an independent streak and, against our earlier advice, will write some multithreaded programs with bugs. Debugging multithreaded programs will provide you with some interesting new challenges. First of all, you'll investigate types of programming errors that result from thread synchronization problems, namely deadlocks and race conditions. Second, once you've seen a problem (for instance, some data corruption or a hang), you'll discover you may have a hard time duplicating it. Because the alignment of events among threads that run concurrently is largely left up to chance, errors, once found, may be unrepeatable. Finally, because threads are a new technology, many vendors have yet to upgrade their debuggers to operate well on threaded programs.

All of this is to say, quite simply, that you'll need your wits about you when debugging a multithreaded application! Sound like fun? Read on!

Deadlock

When one or more threads are spinning or have stopped permanently, chances are that you've encountered a deadlock. You'll have a good idea that you've run into a deadlock, because your program . . . will . . . just . . . , er, stop.

The most common reason for a deadlock—and the easiest to solve—is forgetting to unlock a mutex. Deadlocks can also result from problems in the order in which threads obtain locks. You may need to perform a bit of detective work to resolve these. The rule is that all threads in your program must always pursue locks in the same order. If, en route to obtaining Lock B, a lock must first obtain Lock A, then no thread should try to obtain Lock B without first obtaining Lock A.

You may also encounter another form of deadlock. A thread may suspend itself to wait on a condition variable that is never signaled by any other thread, thus falling into some sort of deep, undisturbed sleep. If you see a deadlock of this sort, you'd do well to look for an inconsistency in the way in which your thread interprets the condition. For instance, does one thread sleep on *count* = = *0* and another thread signal the condition when *count* < *0*? A condition is usually signaled when a variable reaches a certain value. If the variable can never reach that value, you can anticipate trouble. If you expect a flag to be set, double check to ensure that it actually is; if you expect a counter to reach zero, make sure that it actually does.

Fortunately, the Pthreads library knows all about the mutexes and condition variables in use. If you are armed with a good thread-knowledgeable debugger, you can list which thread is waiting for which mutex or condition variable and make great strides toward pinpointing the culprits of the deadlock. Even without such a debugger, you can periodically tap into the Pthreads library's statistics by adding simple wrapper routines around the Pthreads calls in your program.

Race Conditions

A friend once told us the story of the time she and her husband set out to purchase a new car. On her way home from work one Friday, she stopped at a Dodge dealer in New Hampshire, saw the ideal minivan, and arranged a trade-in. On his way home from work the same day, her husband stopped at a Dodge dealer in Massachusetts, found the perfect vehicle, and also arranged a trade-in. We were at first surprised that they took a multithreaded approach to buying an automobile (where we would have chosen a more traditional monolithic approach) but that evening began to think about their predicament—proud owners of three Dodge Caravans. Then again, it might be just two Caravans—they did in fact trade one in. But they actually traded in the same minivan twice—to two different dealers in two different states. The pettiest of crimes (inadvertent fraud would surely qualify) becomes grossly magnified when state lines are crossed; maybe they would somehow wind up with no Caravans if the dealers claimed a breach of contract. At length, they did work things out (probably by using a *pthread_join* or something) and ended up with a single minivan—a brand new one!

In our imagination, the behavior of our threaded friends may have had several possible outcomes, some more inconvenient than others. At the end, they "got the right answer." We wonder if they would get the right answer each time they set out to buy a new car in this way.

This is a type of race condition. A race condition occurs when multiple threads share data and at least one of the threads accesses the data without going through a defined synchronization mechanism. (You'd think our friends would have used a mutex or, better, a telephone call, to synchronize their car hunting.) As a result, a thread that reads the data at the same time as the first thread may get a corrupted value—or not, depending upon the timing between the two threads.

A race condition may be difficult to detect. It may lie around in your code like an accident waiting to happen. It may not surface consistently; it might occur once in every hundred (or thousand) executions. Even if does arise, you may miss it if you're not looking very closely at your program's output. If you're lucky, a race condition will make a bad memory reference, cause a fatal signal, and crash your program. At least then you can begin the process of isolating the problem and identifying its cause.

Unlike deadlocks, race conditions involve resources (such as files, buffers, and counters) that aren't managed by the Pthreads library. Often, a race condition involves a resource that you didn't realize was shared among your threads. For example, perhaps two threads called a nonreentrant routine from a system library, or executed some initialization code that you intended to be run only once. A subtler problem arises if a thread passes a pointer to its stack data as a parameter in a *pthread_create* call. Even though a thread's automatic data is supposed to be private, nothing prevents another thread from accessing it if you pass it its address! In other cases, you may be aware that a particular resource is shared by multiple threads, but you didn't get its synchronization right. For example, a thread might reference shared data after it has yielded the mutex that protects the data.

Event Ordering

Because problems like deadlocks and race conditions can be intermittent, rearing up only once every hundred or so program runs, debugging a multithreaded program requires keener detective skills and more patience than you'd bring to a more traditional debugging session.

The ordering of the events performed collectively by a program's threads at run time becomes supremely important in debugging a multithreaded program. Unsynchronized access to shared data often works if events on that data don't collide. For instance, if Thread A performs an unsynchronized access of a resource it shares with Thread B before Thread B accesses the resource, there's no chance for a race condition to develop. However, if Thread B happens to access the resource while Thread A is still busy with it, a race condition will result. Now, the race condition may not cause an error every time it occurs. Sometimes your threads may, almost accidentally, come out of the race condition with the right answers.

To make matters worse, various things in your program's run-time environment, unrelated to the program itself, can impact the ordering of the program's events.

Introducing a debugger, for instance, can cause the events to occur in an order that's different from the sequence they'd follow when the program is run in a production environment. Similarly, you may discover bugs as you move your program from one platform to another. The new platform's scheduling policy, performance, and system load could be different enough so that some tasks complete faster than others, thus disrupting the usual ordering of events that had up to that point concealed the bug.

Less Is Better

Remember, the roots of your program's race conditions and deadlocks are in its threads' use of shared data. If your threads share little data, you'll have little opportunity to create bugs that cause either of these problems. Moreover, because there is less synchronization overhead, your threads will run faster. The reduction in a program's complexity, as well as potential improvements in its performance, may make it worth your while to look at ways of localizing data access to specific threads and minimizing the program's overall synchronization needs.

Trace Statements

Regardless of the capabilities of your debugger, you can insert trace statements in your code to monitor your program's activities. A trace statement usually takes the form of a *printf* or a *write* to a log file.

If your debugger does not have built-in thread support, trace statements may be your only means of monitoring what your threads are doing at the time of a deadlock.

It's handy to define trace statements as macros that can be conditionally compiled based on the definition of a DEBUG symbol, as shown in Example 6-1.

Example 6-1: Trace Statement (trace.c)

```
#if DEBUG
#define DPRINTF(x)     printf x
#else
#define DPRINTF(x)
#end
```

In our definition of DPRINTF, we allow a variable-sized argument list, as long as you surround the list with double parentheses:

```
DPRINTF(("module com: start. %count, %size", count, size));
```

Where should you place trace statements? Trace statements are most useful when they are inserted at those places where deadlocks and race conditions usually occur. For the best payback, place them before and after each call to these functions: *pthread_mutex_lock*, *pthread_mutex_unlock*, *pthread_cond_wait*, and *pthread_cond_signal*. You can also use a trace statement at other points to track the ongoing status of your program: for instance, which modules have been executed and what the values of counters and key variables are.

What sort of information should a trace statement print? You should include the name of the current routine at the very least, plus other information that is useful in that module's context. If the routine is called by only one thread, the routine name may suffice to identify the message. However, if the routine can be called by multiple threads, you must also include some sort of thread identification, particularly if you're logging to the monitor or a common log file. You may not be able to do this as neatly as you'd like. The Pthreads library doesn't provide thread IDs, only thread handles. You could, however, pull something together that works fairly well. You could print out the thread handle address, which does uniquely identify each thread, and cope with a bit of awkward reading in the trace output. Better yet, you could assign a meaningful string to each thread handle address, storing them in keys or in a global array of pointers to *char*.

There is one last problem to solve here. You may remember that the thread handle is returned in an output argument to the caller of *pthread_create*. This means that the created thread doesn't know the address in which its creator stored its handle. You'll need to provide some way for a thread to obtain this address so that it can include it in its trace messages. One approach might be to have each creating thread store the handles of the threads it creates in a global table. A thread that needs to find out the address of its own thread handle calls *pthread_self* to obtain a copy of its handle. It then indexes through this table to determine its unique handle address.

Beware of synchronization issues when using trace statements, particularly if they write information to a common log file. If threads don't synchronize their writes, trace messages in the log file may be garbled or out of order. Moreover, if they do synchronize their writes by locking a mutex on the file, their execution will become linked at each trace, possibly masking race conditions that could occur during normal program execution. Furthermore, if you deploy the application with logging enabled, its performance will be abysmal!

Debugger Support for Threads

Not surprisingly, the Pthreads standard does not address debugging support for threads. Consequently, any thread-debugging capability you find in a debugger will be vendor-specific. Nevertheless, a good system will extend its standard system debugger to help thread programmers.

In some cases a system's debugger will not work, or become hopelessly confused, when it's used with a multithreaded program. Some of the issues for a debugger are formidable. When we set a breakpoint somewhere in a program, does it cause just the thread that hits it to stop, or all threads of the process? It should probably stop all threads. When we step through code, which thread runs?

As an example, the *ladebug* debugger on Digital UNIX has features to support the debugging of multithreaded programs. The *ladebug* debugger has built-in features for identifying individual threads within a process and printing out their state. For instance, the *where* command allows you to specify which threads' call stacks you want to examine. The *thread* command allows you to set a particular thread as being a "current" thread, to which subsequent commands will apply. If we were to use *ladebug* to debug our ATM server, the session might look like this:

```
% ladebug atm_svr
Welcome to the Ladebug Debugger Version 4.0-19
------------------
object file name: atm_svr
Reading symbolic information ...done
(ladebug) stop in main[#1: stop in int main(int, char**) ]
(ladebug) run
```

Here, we didn't specify that any particular thread take the breakpoint. Consequently, when we run the program, the entire process is stopped when any thread reaches *main*:

```
[1] stopped at [main:127 0x1200022bc]

   127     atm_server_init(argc, argv);
(ladebug) show thread
Thread State       Substate        Policy      Priority Name
------ ---------- --------------- ---------- -------- ------------
>    1 running                    throughput 11       default thread
    -1 blocked    kernel          fifo       32       manager thread
    -2 ready                      idle       0        null thread for VP 0x0

(ladebug) where
>0  0x1200022bc in main(argc=1, argv=0x11ffff308) atm_svr.c:127
(ladebug) p $curthread
1
```

The *show thread* command tells us that three threads are running. Surprise! The Pthreads library is itself a threaded program and creates its own daemon threads. (Digital's implementation uses negative numbers to identify threads that are put there by the system.) Thread 1 is the only thread that is created by our application. This makes sense because we've only just gotten into *main*! The *where* command confirms that we're in the first line of *main*.

Next, we ask the debugger to stop in *process_request.* This breakpoint will apply to all threads—including those we're about to create. And so we continue:

```
(ladebug) stop in process_request
[#2: stop in void* process_request(void*) ]
(ladebug) c
```

After a client issues a request, the server program hits the new breakpoint:

```
[2] stopped at [process_request:210 0x120002518]
   210   workorder_t *workorderp = (workorder_t *)input_orderp;
```

```
(ladebug) show thread
```

Thread State	Substate	Policy	Priority	Name
1 blocked	kernel	throughput	11	default thread
-1 blocked	kernel	fifo	32	manager thread
-2 ready		idle	0	null thread for VP 0x0
> 2 running		throughput	11	<anonymous>

```
(ladebug) where
>0  0x120002518 in process_request(input_orderp=0x140011000) atm_svr.c:210
#1  0x3ff80823e94 in thdBase(0x0, 0x0, 0x0, 0x1, 0x45586732, 0x3)
DebugInformationStrippedFromFile101:???
```

Now, we can see the new thread our server just created to process the incoming request. The > in the output of *show thread* tells us that this is our current thread. When we subsequently issue the *where* command, this thread's start function, *process_request,* appears on the stack above the thread "base."

You don't need to change the current thread in *ladebug* just to look at a thread's stack, but, just for illustration purposes, that's what we'll do here:

```
(ladebug) thread 1
```

Thread State	Substate	Policy	Priority	Name
1 blocked	kernel	throughput	11	default thread

```
(ladebug) p $curthread
1
(ladebug) where
>0  0x3ff82050f28 in /usr/shlib/libc.so
#1  0x120003a38 in server_comm_get_request(conn=0x140011100,
                         req_buf=0x140011104="") atm_com_svr.c:187
#2  0x120002308 in main(argc=1, argv=0x11fffff308) atm_svr.c:135
```

We use the *thread* command to change the current thread, and then we show its stack with the *where* command. The *main* thread is hanging out in a Standard C library (*libc*) routine (*select,* to be exact) in *server_comm_get_request.*

As long as we don't send it another request, Thread 1 isn't going to do much. Let's step through some of the processing of the request in Thread 2. Here we'll step to the beginning of the *open_account* procedure:

```
(ladebug) thread 2
Thread State      Substate        Policy     Priority Name
------ ----------  --------------- ---------- -------- -------------
     2 running                     throughput 11        <anonymous>
(ladebug) s
stopped at [process_request:216 0x12000251c]

    216   sscanf(workorderp->req_buf, "%d", &trans_id);
(ladebug) s
stopped at [process_request:220 0x12000253c]

    220   switch(trans_id) {
(ladebug) s
stopped at [process_request:223 0x1200025dc]
    223   open_account(resp_buf);(ladebug) s
stopped at [open_account:327 0x120002a20]

    327 void open_account(char *resp_buf)
(ladebug) c
 .
 .
 .
Process has exited with status 0
(ladebug) quit

%
```

Digital UNIX has integrated many Pthreads features into its *ladebug* debugger. The *ladebug* debugger allows you to access even more detailed information by using the *pthread* command. The *pthread* command allows you to issue a subclass of thread-display commands that can show you the detailed states of mutexes, condition variables, and threads, plus various other types of information that can help you debug a threaded application. For example, you'd use the *pthread* command to see threads' cancellation states and types, which threads have which signals blocked, or what the last exception a thread handled was.

The *pthread help* command shows us a full listing of available commands.

Example: Debugging the ATM Server

Let's pretend we made some mistakes when writing our ATM server, and we've encountered deadlocks during some of our test runs. In this section, we'll illustrate how we'd investigate the problem using a thread-smart debugger. We'll use the Digital UNIX *ladebug* debugger just because it has good thread support. Reading this section will help you learn how to troubleshoot a deadlock or a race condition, even if you don't have this debugger.

Debugging a deadlock caused by a missing unlock

A deadlock would occur if a worker thread's service routine failed to unlock the mutex after it modified an account, as shown in Example 6-2.

Example 6–2: A Broken Deposit Routine (atm_svr_broken.c)

```
void deposit(char *req_buf, char *resp_buf)
{
  int rtn;
  int temp, id, password, amount;
  account_t *accountp;

  /* Parse input string */
  sscanf(req_buf, "%d %d %d %d ", &temp, &id, &password, &amount);

  /* Check inputs */
  if ((id < 0) || (id >= MAX_NUM_ACCOUNTS)) {
    sprintf(resp_buf, "%d %s", TRANS_FAILURE, ERR_MSG_BAD_ACCOUNT);
    return;
  }

  pthread_mutex_lock(&global_data_mutex);

  /* Retrieve account from database */
  if ((rtn = retrieve_account( id, &accountp)) < 0) {
    sprintf(resp_buf, "%d %s", TRANS_FAILURE, atm_err_tbl[-rtn]);
  }
      .
      .
      .
  /* Finish processing deposit */
  /* pthread_mutex_unlock(&global_data_mutex); */
}
```

Consider the following series of transactions on our account database:

1. Read balance in account 3.

2. Deposit $100 in account 3.

3. Read balance in account 4.

4. Deposit $25 in account 3.

Although the mutex unlock is missing, we can run the first three transactions without a problem. Because the read service routine's locking behavior is correct, its read of account 3 does not prevent the subsequent deposit to the same account. Remember too that each account has its own lock, so the read to account 4 does not reveal a problem. It's only when we again access account 3 that we stumble.

The worker thread that handles our fourth transaction suspends in its *pthread_mutex_lock* call, waiting forever for the thread that performed the second transaction to unlock account 3. Because of the flaw in the deposit routine, this will never happen. Over time, the server will launch its maximum number of worker threads. Each will eventually be drawn into the black hole of account 3 (and any other account to which a previous thread has made a deposit).

We could easily identify the problem by inspecting our sources, but let's use the strange behavior we've noticed in our server as a good reason to summon the debugger.

```
% ladebug atm_svr_broken
Welcome to the Ladebug Debugger Version 4.0-19
------------------
object file name: atm_svr_broken
Reading symbolic information ...done
(ladebug)
```

First, we'll need to choose a useful breakpoint. This is often the most difficult part of troubleshooting. When in doubt, you should place breakpoints at the beginning and end of the thread start routine, if your program contains one. In the ATM server, this would be the *process_request* routine:

```
(ladebug) stop at process_request
[#1: stop in void* process_request(void*) ]
(ladebug) stop at "atm_svr_broken.c":257
[#2: stop at "atm_svr_broken.c":257  ]
(ladebug) run
```

We'll get our debugging session moving by issuing some client requests. Our first request, a deposit, would cause the debugger to stop the program at the breakpoint we placed at the beginning of *process_request*. Here, we'll take a look at the locked mutexes using the *show mutex* command:

```
[1] stopped at [process_request:213 0x120002518]

    213    workorder_t *workorderp = (workorder_t *)input_orderp;
(ladebug) where
>0  0x120002518 in process_request(input_orderp=0x140011100) atm_svr_broken.c:213
#1  0x3ff80823e94 in thdBase(0x0, 0x0, 0x0, 0x1, 0x45586732, 0x3)
                              DebugInformationStrippedFromFile101:???
(ladebug) show mutex with state == locked
(ladebug)
```

The *show mutex* command shows that no mutex locks are being held by any thread at this point. Let's continue the program so that we reach the breakpoint at the end of *process_request*:

```
(ladebug) c
[2] stopped at [process_request:257 0x120002678]

    257    return(NULL);
(ladebug) show mutex with state == locked
Mutex 49 (normal) "mutex at 0x140001760" is locked
(ladebug)
```

Now we've hit the end of our *process_request* routine. This time, *show mutex* is telling us there's a mutex still locked. At this point, the error is evident. There are no other transactions in progress, so we know our thread has failed to unlock the mutex.

If we disable the breakpoints and continue (or even if we step through the program), we find that subsequent commands to the same account hang. While one is hung, we can get the debugger's attention with CTRL-C, and see what's happening (see Example 6-3).

Example 6-3: Watching Threads Hang in the ladebug Debugger

```
(ladebug) c
Thread received signal INT
stopped at [msg_receive_trap: ??? 0x3ff8100ea44]

(ladebug) show thread
Thread State      Substate          Policy      Priority Name
------ ---------- ----------------- ----------  -------- -------------
     1 blocked    kernel            throughput  11       default thread
>   -1 blocked    kernel            fifo        32       manager thread
    -2 running                      idle        0        null thread for VP 0x0
     4 blocked    mutex wait        throughput  11       <anonymous>
(ladebug) where thread 1
Stack trace for thread 1
#0  0x3ff82050f28 in /usr/shlib/libc.so
#1  0x120003a08 in server_comm_get_request(conn=0x140011000,
                       req_buf=0x140011004="") atm_com_svr.c:187
#2  0x120002308 in main(argc=1, argv=0x140008030) atm_svr_broken.c:138
(ladebug) where thread 4
Stack trace for thread 4
#0  0x3ff8082bbf4 in /usr/shlib/libpthread.so
#1  0x3ff80829700 in hstTransferContext(0x1, 0x140005a78, 0x3ffc0439dc0, 0x4,
0x3ffc0438a00, 0x140011180) DebugInformationStrippedFromFile109:???
#2  0x3ff80813edc in dspDispatch(0x140009a10, 0x1400081a8, 0x140008030, 0x0,
0x140001760,
                       0x100000000) DebugInformationStrippedFromFile89:???
#3  0x3ff80817758 in pthread_mutex_block(0x1, 0x3ffc0433400, 0x3ffc0439dc0, 0x0,
 0x140001760, 0x0) DebugInformationStrippedFromFile95:???
#4  0x3ff8082b9f0 in __pthread_mutex_lock(0x3ffc0433400, 0x3ffc0439dc0, 0x0,
0x140001760, 0x0, 0x120002bd4) DebugInformationStrippedFromFile111:???
#5  0x120002bd0 in deposit(req_buf=0x140011184="2 25 25 200",
resp_buf=0x140035a18="") atm_svr_broken.c:418
#6  0x1200025cc in process_request(input_orderp=0x140011180) atm_svr_broken.c:230
#7  0x3ff80823e94 in thdBase(0x0, 0x0, 0x0, 0x1, 0x45586732, 0x3)
```

Example 6-3: Watching Threads Hang in the ladebug Debugger (continued)

```
DebugInformationStrippedFromFile101:???
(ladebug) quit
%
```

We see that there are two active application threads, one of which is the *main* thread. The *where* command tells us that the *main* thread (Thread 1) is in its normal hangout, waiting on *select* in *server_comm_get_request*. The *where* on Thread 4 shows us that it is our *process_request* thread (stack entry #6) and that it's waiting in the depths of *pthread_mutex_lock* (stack entry #4). It will stay there forever, because the thread that should have unlocked the mutex terminated sometime ago!

Debugging a race condition caused by a missing lock

In the debugging session in Example 6-3, we looked at the results of a forgotten *pthread_mutex_unlock* call. In Example 6-2, a unlock was forgotten and caused a deadlock. Our efforts to debug the missing unlock were fairly straightforward. We placed breakpoints at the beginning and end of the thread-starting routine and examined the state of the mutexes at each. What if we had forgotten a *pthread_mutex_lock* call in one of our threads? What would be the symptoms of this problem, and how would we proceed to debug it?

Our ATM server starts getting into trouble as its clients issue more and more requests for the same account. The more worker threads that are accessing this account at the same time, the more likely our server is to encounter a race condition on the account's data. More likely than not, we would discover such race conditions by running the server under a suitable test suite that simulates a heavy client load. It would be unfortunate if we had to wait for a race condition to surface from the disastrous effects our server might have on our customers' real-world data. Our tests would know what results we expect from all our threads combined and be able to compare the final state of account data against their expectations.

As we proceed to debug a race condition, our first step will be to identify the data that is being corrupted. Once we've found the victim, we'll ask questions that are very much like those you'd ask during a good game of Clue: "Which threads knew the victim?" "When was their last contact with the victim?" and "Do they have an alibi?" Those threads that approached the account holding a mutex lock (and released the lock when leaving) have an alibi that's air tight.

Assume that our test suite detected an account corruption problem in the ATM server. In the server, threads access accounts by calling the *retrieve_account* routine and release them by calling *store_account*. Before it calls *retrieve_account*, a thread should be holding the account's mutex; it should release it after it calls *store_account*.

In the case of the ATM server, it's easier to find the missing *pthread_mutex_lock* call by closely inspecting our code than by using the debugger. The *retrieve_account* routine is called from only three places: *deposit*, *withdraw*, and *balance*. These three routines themselves are called from only one place: *process_request*. Checking these four routines for correctly paired lock and unlock calls would quickly reveal the source of the error.

When confronted with a race condition in a more complex application, you may find it easier to start with the debugger and then move on to code inspection. You might use the debugger to set a watchpoint on a piece of shared data or to set breakpoints at those program statements that change the data. While the program is stopped at a breakpoint, you can identify the active thread and determine whether or not it holds the lock required for the account it's accessing.

Performance

If well-designed and well-written, a multithreaded program can outperform a similar nonthreaded application. However, if you make bad design decisions (trying to force concurrency on a large set of strictly ordered tasks is a very basic bad design decision) or poorly execute a good design, you may wind up with a program that fares worse than what you started with. At the very end of Chapter 1, *Why Threads?*, we discussed which types of applications are good candidates for threading. Here, we'll look at those decisions you must make once you've selected the application and begun your design work.

The Costs of Sharing Too Much — Locking

There's an unspoken tradition in our neighborhood that's beyond belief, but we'll tell you about it anyway. Without exception, the parents raise their children so that they're mindful of the virtues of sharing, which will surely be a benefit to them as they grow older and socialize. On any given Saturday night, herds of kids wheel about the streets on bicycles, skateboards, roller blades, scooters, and the like. When a boy tires of his bike, he exchanges it for a girl's skateboard; when a girl tires of her roller blades, she trades them for a boy's scooter; and so it goes. What the tradition seems to be is that any kid will share his or her wheels with any other kid, as long as the borrower's Dad hauls the stupid thing from the middle of the street back to its owner at the end of the evening. Anyone who has seen the neighborhood Dads out on the streets at 10 p.m. on a weekend night will learn this piece of wisdom: sharing is nice, but it's often inefficient—and inelegant.

Concurrency may give a multithreaded program its greatest performance advantage over other styles of programming. However, the more its threads share, the more its performance is pulled back to that of the rank and file. Shared data (and the associated locks) is both the greatest asset and the biggest curse in multithreaded programming. That threads in the same process have equal access to a common set of resources, including the process's address space, allows them to communicate with each other much faster than independent processes can. When they need to share a particular resource, they don't have to copy it from one process's memory to another, nor do they need to use System V shared memory functions. Normal memory accesses work fine. Unfortunately, as we've seen, sharing isn't entirely free. It's as if multithreading allows you to go a bit faster than traditional speed limits, but data sharing is the speed trap in the bushes. We must apply a lock to brake a bit while we pass through, but once we're through we can cruise once again.[*] Although we took a performance hit, we'll still reach our destination sooner than we would've otherwise.

Locks reveal the dependencies among the threads in our program: at each lock point, either threads share data, or one thread must wait for another to finish some task. The impact of each lock on our program's performance is twofold:

- There's the time it takes for a thread to obtain an unowned lock. This has little impact on our program's concurrency, so it's usually acceptable. The few calls required to lock and unlock a lock are minimal overhead.

- There's the time a thread spends while waiting for a lock that's already held by another thread. Because it keeps the thread from accomplishing its task, this delay may cause a significant loss of concurrency. The loss can become magnified if other threads depend on the results of the blocked thread.

Applications are suitable for threading only if access to shared data is a small part of them. If you find that your threads regularly block on locks and spend a lot of time waiting for shared data to become free, something's wrong with your program's design.

As a rule, you should ensure that, when your threads do hold locks, they hold them for the shortest possible time. This allows other threads to obtain the locks more quickly, avoiding the long waits that are the major hits to a program's concurrency. Examine each block of code framed by *pthread_mutex_lock* and *pthread_mutex_unlock* calls for instructions that don't require the special synchronization and could well be performed elsewhere.

---

[*] None of the authors (nor anyone else affiliated with the publication of this book) actually drives this way. The appearance of this metaphor in this book is not meant to favor any particular driving style over another.

In the following series of examples, we'll show you some common errors in using locks and suggest ways that you can avoid similar problems in your code. In Example 6-4, let's look at some code with poor locking placement.

Example 6–4: Code with Poor Locking Placement (badlocks.c)

```
pthread_mutex_t count_lock = PTHREAD_MUTEX_INITIALIZER;
int count = 0;

void r1(char *fname, int x, char **bufp)
{
  double temp;
  int fd;
  .
  .
  .
  pthread_mutex_lock(&count_lock);
  temp = sqrt(x);
  fd = open(fname, O_CREAT | O_RDWR, 0666);
  count++;
  *bufp = (char *)malloc(256);
  pthread_mutex_unlock(&count_lock);
  .
  .
  .
}
```

If *count* is the only piece of shared data used by this code, we can make the code considerably more efficient by rearranging the *pthread_mutex_lock* and *pthread_mutex_unlock* calls as shown in Example 6-5.

Example 6–5: Code with Poor Locking Placement, Improved (goodlocks.c)

```
pthread_mutex_t count_lock = PTHREAD_MUTEX_INITIALIZER;
int count = 0;

void r1(char *fname, int x, char **bufp))
{
  double temp;
  int fd;
  .
  .
  .
  temp = sqrt(x);
  fd = open(fname, O_CREAT | O_RDWR, 0666);

  pthread_mutex_lock(&count_lock);
  count++;
  pthread_mutex_unlock(&count_lock);


  *bufp = (char *)malloc(256);
```

Example 6–5: Code with Poor Locking Placement, Improved (goodlocks.c) (continued)

```
        .
        .
        .
    }
```

Finding poor locking policies is not often this simple. In Example 6-6, we'll look at the more complex situation in which the code references the shared data (*count*) from within a loop.

Example 6–6: Code with Poor Locking Placement in a Loop (badlocks.c)

```
pthread_mutex_t count_lock = PTHREAD_MUTEX_INITIALIZER;
int count = 0;

void r2(char *fname, int x, char **bufp)
{
  double temp;
  int i, reads;
  int start = 0, end = LOCAL_COUNT_MAX;
  int fd;

  pthread_mutex_lock(&count_lock);
  for (i = start; i < end; i++) {
      fd = open(fname, O_CREAT | O_RDWR, 0666);
      x = x + count;
      temp = sqrt(x);
      if (temp == THRESHOLD)
         count++;
      .
      .

      .
      /* Lengthy I/O operations */
      .

      .
      .
  }
  pthread_mutex_unlock(&count_lock);
}
```

When examining this code, we must first decide whether or not we should move the lock calls from outside the loop to the inside. If the loop spends most of its processing time performing operations on shared data, or if its total processing time is quite short, it's probably most efficient to keep the lock calls outside. This would leave the whole loop in the critical section. On the other hand, we'd move the lock calls inside if the loop has a lengthy processing time and doesn't reference shared data. We need to be mindful that the lock calls themselves take time. We don't really want to pay the cost of the lock calls each time we go through the loop unless, in doing so, we significantly reduce the time we spend blocking other threads. We'll assume that the code in Example 6-7 pays off in that way.

Example 6-7: Code with Poor Lock Placement in a Loop Improved (goodlocks.c)

```
pthread_mutex_t count_lock = PTHREAD_MUTEX_INITIALIZER;
int count = 0;

void r2(char *fname, int x, char **bufp)
{
  double temp;
  int i, reads;
  int start = 0, end = LOCAL_COUNT_MAX;
  int fd;

  for (i = start; i < end; i++) {
      fd = open(fname, O_CREAT | O_RDWR, 0666);
      pthread_mutex_lock(&count_lock);
      x = x + count;
      temp = sqrt(x);
      if (temp == THRESHOLD)
          count++;
      pthread_mutex_unlock(&count_lock);
      .
      .

      .
      /* Lengthy I/O operations */
      .
      .

      .

  }
}
```

Once you've arranged it so that threads hold locks for the shortest time possible, you should then focus on reducing the amount of data protected by any one lock (that is, reducing the lock's granularity). The smaller the unit of data a lock protects, the less likely it is that two threads will need to access it at the same time. For instance, if your program currently locks an entire database, consider locking individual records instead; if it currently locks records, try locking fields.

For example, suppose we've set up locks like this:

```
pthread_mutex_t data_lock;
struct record {
        int code;
        int field1;
        .
        .

        .

} data[DATA_SIZE];
```

Here, a single mutex, *data_lock*, protects the whole array. In the following code, we'll rearrange our record's structure so that each record contains its own lock. Now our threads can lock each record individually.

```
struct record {
        pthread_mutex_t data_lock;
        int code;
        int field1;

        .

        .

        .

} data[DATA_SIZE];
```

Be careful when following this course. As you tune your locks to finer and finer granularity, you must know when to stop. Eventually, you pass the point at which it's useful to break down the data a lock protects. In fact, at some point, your efforts may result in your threads performing more locking operations—and unnecessary ones at that. Performance tests and profiling can help you determine the granularity at which you should impose locking on your program's data. Good tests can clearly identify how often data is being accessed and what percentage of its execution time a program spends waiting for locks on the data.

Now that you've reduced the size of the code a thread executes while holding a lock, and reduced the size of the data each lock protects, you should consider whether some locks might in fact synchronize more efficiently if they were condition variables. Here's the rule of thumb: use locks to synchronize access to shared data, use condition variables to synchronize threads against events—those places in your program where one thread needs to wait for another to do something before proceeding.

It's easy to get mixed up. The beginning threads programmer will often rough out a bit of code like that in Example 6-8.

Example 6–8: Using a Mutex to Poll State (polling.c)

```
pthread_mutex_t db_lock = PTHREAD_MUTEX_INITIALIZER;
int db_initialized;

.

.

.

pthread_mutex_lock(&db_lock);
while (!db_initialized)

        pthread_mutex_unlock(&db_lock);
        sleep(1);
        pthread_mutex_lock(&db_lock);
}
pthread_mutex_unlock(&db_lock);

.

.

.
```

However, when we think a little harder about what we want this code to do, we realize that our threads are polling on the value of the *db_initialized* flag to determine when the database-initialization event has occurred. When this event occurs, our threads can proceed. When looked at in this light, it becomes clear that we should be using a condition variable instead of the mutex, as in Example 6-9.

Example 6-9: Replacing a Mutex with a Condition Variable (polling.c)

```
pthread_mutex_t db_lock = PTHREAD_MUTEX_INITIALIZER;
pthread_cond_t db_init_cv = PTHREAD_COND_INITIALIZER;
int db_initialized;

pthread_mutex_lock(&db_lock);
while (!db_initialized) {
        .
        .
        .
        pthread_cond_wait(&db_init_cv, &db_lock);
}
        .
        .
        .
pthread_mutex_unlock(&db_lock);
```

Using the condition variable, we can spare our threads the cycles it would take for them to continually lock a flag and check for the event. Instead, we'll wake them only when the database has actually been initialized.

After trying these methods to reduce lock contention, you might want to take a last look at the tasks you've delegated to the program's threads. Some tasks you've assigned to different threads may be linked so tightly that they can't be separated without introducing some strained and perhaps impossible locking requirements. If this is so, you might be able to increase the program's overall performance by joining the tasks and having them performed by a single thread.

Thread Overhead

Although the cost of creating and synchronizing multiple threads is less than that of spawning and coordinating multiple processes, using threads does involve overhead nonetheless.

When a thread is created, the Pthreads library (and perhaps the system) must perform database searches and allocate new data structures, synchronizing the creation of this thread with other *pthread_create* calls that may be in progress at the same time. It must place the newly created thread into the system's scheduling queues. In a kernel thread–based implementation, this requires a system call. The result is that the operating system allocates resources for the thread that are similar to those it allocates for a process.

You can minimize this overhead by avoiding the simplistic one-thread-per-task model. For instance, our initial version of the ATM server example was rather wasteful in that it created a thread for each client request and then let the thread exit when it completed the request. The version of the server we developed at the end of Chapter 3, *Synchronizing Pthreads*, was more efficient. When it started, it created a pool of worker threads and let them block on a condition variable. When a new request arrived for processing, the boss would signal on the condition variable, waking the workers. As they complete requests, workers would return to sleep on the condition variable.

Reusing existing threads is an excellent way to avoid the overhead of thread creation. You may need to experiment a little to determine how many threads can run efficiently at the same time. At length, you should create the maximum number of threads at initialization time so that a thread's creation expense is not billed against the request the thread is meant to process.

Thread context switches

Once they've been created, threads must share often limited CPU resources. Even on a multiprocessing platform, the number of threads in your program may easily exceed the number of available CPUs. Regardless of whether you're using a user space or kernel thread–based implementation, scheduling a new thread requires a context switch between threads. The running thread is interrupted and its registers and other private resources are saved. A new thread is selected from the scheduler's priority queues, and its registers and private context are brought in from swap space.

Some context switches are voluntary. If a thread is waiting for an I/O call to complete or a lock to be freed, it's just as if the thread has asked the operating system to remove it from execution and give another thread a chance to run. Others are involuntary. Maybe the thread has exceeded its quantum, and to be fair, it must yield the CPU. Maybe a higher priority thread has become runnable and is being given the CPU. In a perfect world (the same one in which threads never wait for other threads to unlock a mutex), no thread would be suspended involuntarily. Be that as it may, we'll look toward reducing the number of involuntary context switches as a good way to avoid the overhead of unnecessary context switches and improve our program's performance.

The most common cause of involuntary context switches among threads is the normal expiration of time quanta. If your platform's scheduler uses a round-robin scheduling policy, one good place to start reducing the number of context switches is by increasing the quantum value. Be careful, though. Because time quanta are meant to more fairly distribute CPU cycles among runnable threads, you may need to cope with some side effects on certain types of operations. For instance, if a user clicks on a box to request a quick operation, he or she may need to wait longer than before because a thread performing a slow operation has yet to use up its quantum.

Some Pthreads implementations allow you to control their scheduling policy, allowing you to ensure a quicker response time for high priority threads that are performing important tasks. There's a trade-off here, too, of course. The overall application might run slightly slower than under the default policy, because the favorable treatment enforced for high priority threads is causing more involuntary context switches.

Finally, too many context switches may simply mean that your program has too many threads. Try running the program with fewer threads, and see if the program speeds up. Eventually, you should determine when the system reaches its saturation point and limit the number of concurrent threads accordingly.

Synchronization Overhead

Each synchronization object (be it a mutex, condition variable, once block, or key) requires that the Pthreads library create and maintain some data structures and execute some code (possibly even a system call). Consequently, creating large numbers of such objects has its own cost. The cost can be magnified by the way in which you deploy the synchronization objects. For instance, if you create a lock for each record in a database, you increase the disk space required to store the database as well as the memory required to hold it while a thread is running. Nevertheless, the overhead could be worthwhile if the database must support different client requests simultaneously, and establishing fine-grained lock points at the record level allows it to do so efficiently.

How Do Your Threads Spend Their Time?

Profiling a program is a good first step toward identifying its performance bottlenecks. To track the time a program's threads spend using the CPU or waiting for locks and I/O completion, we can use any profiling tool that supports threads. (On Digital UNIX, the standard profiling tools, *prof* or *pixie*, can provide per-thread profiling data.)

By examining the profiling data, you'll get an idea of your threads' behavior. You should look for answers to the following questions:

- *Do the threads spend most of their time blocked, waiting for other threads to release locks?*

This is a sign that the tasks the threads perform aren't really independent of each other or that locking is applied too coarsely to the shared data.

- *Are they runnable for most of their time but not actually running because other threads are monopolizing the available CPUs?*

  In this case, the number of CPU-intensive threads is outstripping the number of CPUs in the system. (This can also happen to multiprocess applications.) Use the *W* and *xload* utilities to obtain the system's load factor: that is, the average number of processes and threads waiting to access the CPU. Use *vmstat* and *iostat* to determine the percentage of time the CPU is running in user space, is running kernel-mode code, or is idle. If the load factor is constantly high, or the amount of idle time is negligible, then you have too many processes or threads for your CPU.

- *Are they spending most of their time waiting on the completion of I/O requests?*

  In this case, most of your I/O may be directed at a single disk and that disk is becoming quickly saturated. Thereafter, requests sent to it will wind up queued in the driver or at the disk. To avoid this bottleneck, you must spread the data across other available disks. Use the *iostat* tool to list the I/O transaction rates to the devices on your system. If you cannot utilize additional disks, you may need to reorganize your application so that it requires fewer disk writes.

Performance in the ATM Server Example

Let's return to our ATM server and look at its performance. We'll create a specialized client program that can send the server a stream of requests and measure its response time. The test client measures the total time the server takes to complete a large set number of account transactions.

As shown in Figure 6-4, the ATM test parent program can start multiple test client processes to issue requests to the server across multiple connections. It can also specify how often a test client process accesses a specially designated "hot-spot" account. Finally, we can adjust the ATM server itself so that the work it performs to satisfy a client's request is more or less I/O intensive or CPU intensive.

To find out exactly how useful threads are, we created two additional versions of the ATM server—a serial server (one that doesn't use threads at all) and a multiprocess server.

We didn't optimize any of these programs in any sense and have often added code specifically to increase the amount of I/O or CPU work performed by the server. Our tests are meant to highlight common high-level aspects of multithreaded program performance and are not intended to be specific benchmarking results for the platform on which we ran them. Results will vary across different platforms.

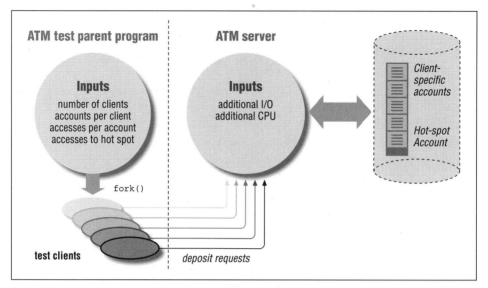

Figure 6–4: The ATM performance test setup

We recorded the results we'll present in this section on a single-CPU Alpha-processor-based DEC 3000 M300 workstation with 32 megabytes of memory, running Version 3.2C of the Digital UNIX operating system. The programs we used were Pthreads Draft 4 versions of our ATM server programs.

Performance depends on input workload: increasing clients and contention

The ATM is a classic server—it receives multiple concurrent requests. It performs I/O both to obtain the requests and to process them. As we'll show in the following test runs, the multithreaded version of the server generally outperforms the other versions. But even so, the tests show that the results depend heavily on the type of input the server receives and the characteristics of the work the server performs to service the requests. The input can vary, based on the number of clients that are simultaneously active and how often clients request access to the same account at the same time. The server's response to a client's request can involve different amounts of I/O and more or less CPU-intensive tasks.

First, let's see whether our multithreaded server or our serial server fares better as the number of clients increases. During this test run, we'll increase the number of active clients from 1 to 15, while keeping the net amount of work the server performs constant. All the clients access their own accounts and never access the hot-spot account. We'll run the test on our uniprocessor under the following conditions:

Contention for accounts	None
Number of clients	Increasing
Total accounts accessed	30
Total accesses to accounts	240
Type of accesses	Deposits
Server work	50/50 I/O and CPU

Figure 6-5 shows the results (in terms of the ratio of the execution time of the multithreaded server over that of the serial server).

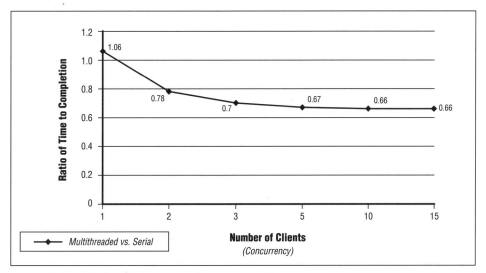

Figure 6–5: Multithreaded server with increasing clients

When we increase the number of clients, the results show:

- When there's just one client, the serial server outperforms the multithreaded server.

- When there's more than one client, each requesting transactions on different accounts, the multithreaded server bests the serial server.

When there's only one client, the server has only one request to process at any given time. After it issues a request, each client waits for a response before making another. In this situation, the actions taken by the multithreaded server to create a new thread and synchronize access to data are pure overhead. Because this overhead is not offset by any gain from concurrency, the multithreaded server's performance when only one client is active is, at best, close to that of the serial server. We could eliminate some overhead if we used a thread pool, effectively moving thread creation from the server's transaction-processing path to its initialization routine.

When there are multiple clients, the worker threads that are processing client requests can work concurrently. While one thread waits for the completion of an I/O operation to a database account, other threads can continue their tasks and issue I/O requests to other accounts. In this test run, we made sure that no two threads would access the same account. As a result, our threads suffer the overhead of locking, but they never block on a lock that's held by another thread.

Now let's see what happens to our servers when we ask the clients to modify the same account. During this test run, we'll gradually increase the percentage of the total requests that each client makes to the hot-spot account. Here, too, we'll keep the net amount of work the server performs constant. We'll run the test on our uniprocessor under the following conditions:

Contention for accounts	Increasing
Number of clients	5
Total accounts accessed	30
Total accesses to accounts	240
Type of accesses	Deposits
Server work	50/50 I/O and CPU

Figure 6-6 shows the results.

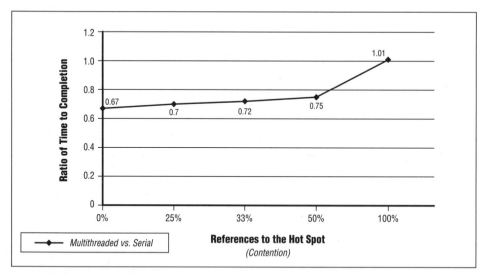

Figure 6–6: Multithreaded server with increasing contention

When we increase the amount of contention, the results show that, when multiple clients are accessing a single hot-spot account, the serial server outperforms the multithreaded server.

As the number of requests from different clients to the hot-spot account increases, the performance of our multithreaded server declines. When all requests from all clients are directed at the same account, the server loses all concurrency; each worker thread must wait to obtain the lock, on the account and it's almost always held by another thread. When there's this amount of contention among threads, it's clear that we're asking the threads to perform tasks that are not independent. They're related by the shared data of the single account.

The results of this test run demonstrate that multithreaded programs perform best when contention is the exception and not the rule. Consequently, when you're trying to determine whether or not an application would benefit from threads, look for tasks that can be performed independently, without interference from other tasks. Moreover, after you've designed the threads, minimize the amount of data they must share.

Performance depends on a good locking strategy

Now we'll look at how different locking strategies affect the performance of our multithreaded ATM server. We'll test three different locking designs:

- No locks at all (We'll disregard the inevitable race-conditions.)
- One lock for the entire database
- One lock for each account in the database

As in our last test run, we'll gradually increase the percentage of the total requests that each client makes to the hot-spot account. However, in this test run, we'll track the extent to which a locking strategy impacts the server's performance. We'll compare the two versions of the server that use locks (one using a single lock on the whole database and one using a lock for each account) against an ideal version that uses no locks. We'll run the test on our uniprocessor under the following conditions:

Contention for accounts	Increasing
Number of clients	5
Total accounts accessed	30
Total accesses to accounts	240
Type of accesses	Deposits
Server work	50/50 I/O and CPU

Figure 6-7 shows the results.

The results show that, when a lock is assigned to each account in the database, performance is better than when a single lock protects the entire database.

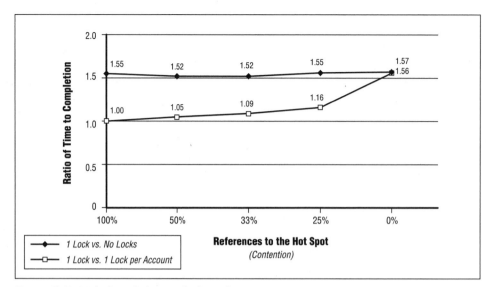

Figure 6-7: Multithreaded server locking designs

When a single lock is used for the database, performance is uniformly bad, regardless of the amount of contention. Because all worker threads must obtain the one and only lock whenever they access any account in the database, they cannot concurrently access accounts. It matters little whether they're accessing different accounts or the same hot-spot account.

When we use one lock per account, we see better performance because multiple threads can now independently access different accounts. When we reach the extreme of targeting all client requests to the hot-spot account, the single-lock and multilock versions perform about the same. Here, the hot-spot account lock is acting like the single global lock because it's the only one being used.

The results of this test demonstrate that careful distribution of a larger number of locks can have less performance impact than the use of a single lock for which all threads contend. In another sense, the fewer locks threads can fight over the better.

Performance depends on the type of work threads do

Now we'll look at the types of work threads perform.

When we add threads to an application it's to concurrently perform a set of computational tasks. Each task has a certain average time to complete and a certain mix of I/O and CPU-intensive activity. In our ATM server, the task that is being performed by worker threads is a deposit to an account in a bank's database.

We've adapted our server so that we can supply startup arguments that increase either its I/O activity or CPU-intensive activity. We increase I/O activity by forcing threads to write changed accounts to disk multiple times; we increase CPU-intensive activity by causing them to spin in a simple counting loop. Using these arguments, we'll adjust the combination of CPU and I/O work a thread must perform to complete a deposit transaction.

In our test run, we'll move from a completely I/O-intensive workload to a completely CPU-intensive workload and record the results. We'll run the test on our uniprocessor under the following conditions:

Contention for accounts	None
Number of clients	5
Total accounts accessed	30
Total accesses to accounts	240
Type of accesses	Deposits
Server work	Varying I/O and CPU workloads (work per transaction 4x other tests)

Figure 6-8 shows the results.

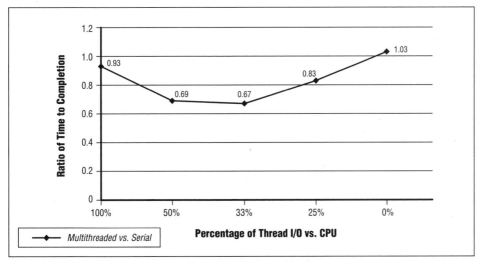

Figure 6–8: Multithreaded server with varying I/O and CPU workloads

The results demonstrate:

* In a uniprocessor configuration, the serial server outperforms the multi-threaded server on a pure CPU-intensive workload.

- On a mixed workload, the multithreaded server outperforms the serial server.

As the server's work becomes completely CPU intensive, threads no longer provide a performance benefit. The single CPU becomes a bottleneck for the many threads waiting to perform CPU-bound tasks. Think of the CPU as a resource with a single lock for which all threads contend.

Key performance issues between using threads and using processes

We'll now use our ATM server test program to highlight the ways in which performance differs between multithreaded and multiprocess versions of the same servers. Threads and processes are alike in many respects, although using processes results in more overhead than using threads. Processes are more expensive to create, and once created, they use more resources than threads to intercommunicate.

If we replaced the multithreaded server in the previous tests with a multiprocess one, the basic curve of the test results would remain essentially the same. However, the point at which the performance of the multiprocess server would exceed that of the serial server would be further out than the point we charted for the multithreaded server. In fact, to justify using a multiprocess server, we'd need more clients, more contention at shared data, or less CPU-intensive work than we'd need to justify writing a multithreaded server.

First, let's see how our multithreaded server and multiprocess server compare as the number of clients increases. As in the earlier test run, we'll increase the number of active clients from 1 to 15, while keeping constant the net amount of work each server performs. All the clients access their own accounts and never access the hot-spot account. We'll run the test on our uniprocessor under the following conditions:

Contention for accounts	None
Number of clients	Increasing
Total accounts accessed	30
Total accesses to accounts	240
Type of accesses	Deposits
Server work	50/50 I/O and CPU

Figure 6-9 shows the results.

The results demonstrate that the multithreaded server outperforms the multiprocess server, regardless of the number of clients.

The difference between the multithreaded and multiprocess servers is in the relative costs of creating threads vs. creating processes. Although both threads and processes must obtain locks to access shared data, they don't have to wait on

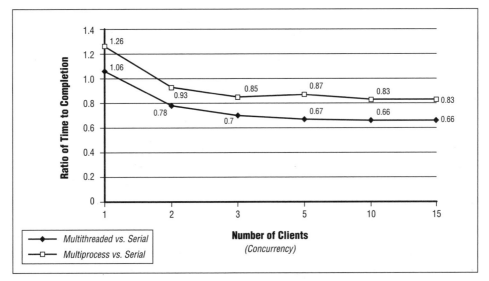

Figure 6-9: Multithreaded vs. multiprocess server performance with increasing clients

locks because this test run eliminates contention for the data.

Now let's introduce the contention, and see how our servers fare. As in the earlier test run, we'll ask the clients to modify the same account and gradually increase the percentage of the total requests that each client makes to this account. Here too we'll keep constant the net amount of work the server performs. We'll run the test on our uniprocessor under the following conditions:

Contention for accounts	Increasing
Number of clients	5
Total accounts accessed	30
Total accesses to accounts	240
Type of accesses	Deposits
Server work	Default (I/O Intensive)

Figure 6-10 shows the results.

The results show that the synchronization mechanisms used by the multithreaded server are more efficient than those used by the multiprocess server.

Where the multithreaded server uses mutex locks to control access to shared data, the multiprocess server uses System V semaphores. When there is little contention among threads for account data, the multithreaded server operates more efficiently because the Pthreads mutex-locking calls operate within user space. On the other hand, the multiprocess server's semaphore-locking calls are system calls and involve the operating system's kernel. As client contention for the hot-spot account

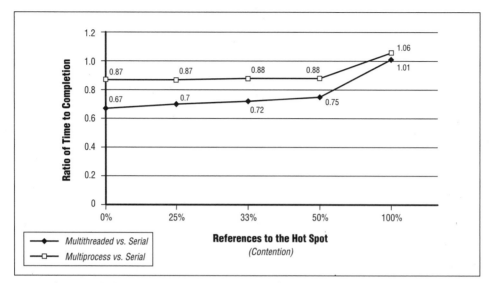

Figure 6-10: Multithreaded vs. multiprocess server performance with increasing contention

increases, the multiprocess server starts catching up to the multithreaded server. It no longer matters that the Pthreads synchronization primitives are lighter in weight than the multiprocess ones. Because worker threads and child processes alike are blocked waiting for account access, neither server is able to provide any concurrency.

One last difference between multithreaded and multiprocess servers that would be worth examining is the ways in which they share data. Whereas threads exchange data by simply placing it in global variables in their process's address space, processes must use pipes or special shared memory segments controlled by the operating system. Because we did not design the threads in our ATM server to share data, we have no good way of testing the performance of the servers' data communication mechanisms.

Conclusion

Back at the beginning of Chapter 1, we claimed that multiple threads were more efficient than multiple processes at performing the same amount of work. Now that we've reached the end of the book, we've shown this to be true—by our examples throughout and, objectively, by the performance measurements we've just discussed.

Efficient is an odd word to use. It hints of speed, and let's face it, speed is what we want from our programs. (Our programs give correct results, let's leave it at that!) However, speedy performance is only part of the story. We want to make it clear that threads not only streamline the many tasks in our programs, but they also allow us to make optimal use of our platform's processing cycles.

Why should we spend CPU time running the operating system when we don't have to? When we choose threads over processes to multitask our programs, the CPUs spend less time in system scheduling code, managing the grand tectonic plate shifts that process context switches often seem to be (the many swap I/O requests, the allocation of memory for child processes, the copies of parent data to a child's address space). We avoid the system calls that establish and manage shared memory regions. Although we cannot forego the expense of synchronizing access to our shared data, this is a liability for both thread and process multitasking models. (Judicious use of shared data and well-placed synchronization calls are key to any well-designed multitasking program.) All in all, multithreading benefits not just our program, but anyone else who is sharing the CPUs with us.

A

Pthreads and DCE

The Distributed Computing Environment (DCE), developed by the Open Software Foundation (OSF), consists of a toolkit and library that simplify the creation of secure, portable, and distributed applications for heterogeneous environments. Although DCE contains a great number of programming tools and server programs (and even supplies its own file system), we'll focus on its programming library and run-time environment in this appendix.

DCE-based applications consist of client programs and server programs that use remote procedure calls (RPCs) to communicate with each other. Their client-server structure makes DCE applications natural candidates for threading. In fact, thread support is tightly integrated into the DCE libraries and services. We'll use this appendix to give you an idea of the role threads can play in a DCE-based application.

DCE currently provides and uses the Draft 4 Pthreads interface. Check out Appendix B for a summary of the differences between the final Pthreads standard (which this book describes) and Draft 4.

The Structure of a DCE Server

A DCE server performs the same type of work as other servers. It waits for client requests on a communication channel and processes requests as they arrive. In fact, a DCE server looks just like any of the boss-worker style servers that we've presented elsewhere in this book, but it can take advantage of DCE library routines that:

- Automate the task of generating the more mundane server components.

- Transparently perform any data conversions that are required when servers or clients running on different platforms intercommunicate.

- Integrate RPC services with other important DCE services, such as the security service and the name service (which locates resources for your program on remote systems).

To allow a DCE server to process multiple requests concurrently, its engine uses POSIX threads.

Let's look back at the ATM server program we've been using as an example. Figure A-1 illustrates the components of our original version of the server; Figure A-2 shows how the server would look in a DCE implementation.

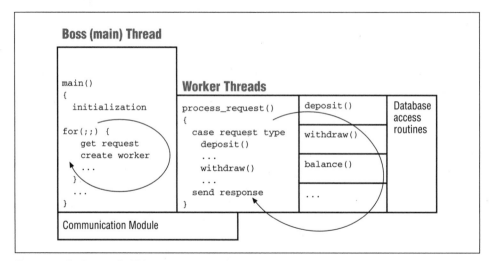

Figure A-1: Original ATM server components

We can map each component in the original ATM server to a similar component in the DCE version of the server, as shown in Table A-1. We'll compare each component of the original server with its corresponding component in the DCE version in the following sections of this appendix.

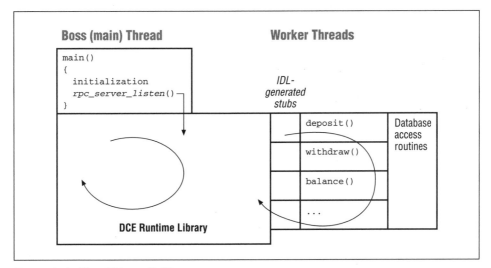

Figure A–2: The ATM as a DCE server

Table A–1: ATM Server Components: Original Version vs. DCE Version

Task	Original Server Component	DCE Server Component
Communicating with clients	Home-grown communication module that uses BSD sockets	DCE run-time library's transport layer interface
Waiting for clients	Boss thread's request-processing loop in *main* routine	Boss thread calls *rpc_server_listen* DCE library routine
Performing tasks	Worker thread routines	Server management routines
Unmarshaling and marshaling client/server messages	Boss thread's request-processing loop in *main* routine and worker threads' start routine.	Stub routines

What Does the DCE Programmer Have to Do?

One of the most difficult aspects of using threads under DCE—especially for the novice—is that DCE hides much of what is going on. If you're new to using threads, this may be somewhat confusing. It may appear that several critical steps are missing. For instance, in a DCE server you never need to call a *pthread_create* routine, specify thread attributes, or detach threads. The *rpc_server_listen* routine does all of this for you.

This must delight you experienced threads programmers (who appreciate the value of a free lunch). What do you need to do to complete a multithreaded application that you've designed under DCE?

Primarily, your job is to ensure that worker thread accesses to shared data are appropriately synchronized. To do so, you'd add the necessary calls to the functions *pthread_mutex_lock*, *pthread_mutex_unlock*, *pthread_cond_wait*, and *pthread_cond_signal* in the server management routines (and any submodules or libraries they call).

Although we've discussed only basic server tasks in this appendix, DCE applications do use threads for other purposes. For instance, you might explicitly call *pthread_create* to add threads to a DCE server for such tasks as:

- Renewing security credentials
- Handling signals
- Background processing

Example: The ATM as a DCE Server

Because our ATM server is a distributed application based on a client/server model, it's well suited for conversion to DCE. We'll do so in this section.

In Example A-1, we'll create an IDL (Interface Definition Language) file that defines all possible client calls. DCE will use this file to generate the stubs the *rpc_server_listen* routine will use to marshal and unmarshal client/server messages.

Example A-1: The IDL File for the DCE Version of the ATM Server

```
interface atm
{
    void open_account(
            [in]  handle_t  handle,
            [out] long      *id,
            [out] long      *success,
            [out] long      *passwd,
            [out] char      estring[20]);

    void deposit(
            [in]  handle_t  handle,
            [in]  long      *id,
            [in]  long      *password,
            [in]  long      *amt,
            [out] long      *success,
            [out] char      estring[20]);

    void withdraw(
            [in]  handle_t  handle,
            [in]  long      *id,
```

Example A-1: The IDL File for the DCE Version of the ATM Server (continued)

```
                    [in]  long      *password,
                    [in]  long      *amt,
                    [out] long      *success,
                    [out] char      estring[20]);

        void balance(
                    [in]  handle_t  handle,
                    [in]  long      *id,
                    [in]  long      *password,
                    [out] long      *success,
                    [out] long      *cur_balance,
                    [out] char      estring[20]);
    }
```

In Example A-2, we'll modify our server itself. We'll add some DCE-specific initialization calls to its *main* routine, set the maximum number of worker threads, and
call *rpc_server_listen*. At that point, the *main* routine enters the DCE run time for
the duration of its run.

Example A-2: The main Routine of the DCE Version of the ATM Server

```
#define SINTERFACE_SPEC            atm_v1_0_s_ifspec
#define MAX_CONC_CALLS_PROTSEQ     1
#define MAX_CONC_CALLS_TOTAL       10

extern int
main(argc, argv)
int argc;
char **argv;
{
  unsigned32              status;
  rpc_binding_vector_t    *binding_vector_p;

  /***********************************************/
  /* DCE Runtime and Communication Initialization */
  /***********************************************/

  /* Register with runtime */
  rpc_server_register_if(SINTERFACE_SPEC, NULL, NULL, &status);

  /* Designate a protocol sequence */
  rpc_server_use_all_protseqs(MAX_CONC_CALLS_PROTSEQ, &status);

  /* Obtain binding vector from runtime */
  rpc_server_inq_bindings(&binding_vector_p, &status);

  /* Register bindings with endpoint mapper */
  rpc_ep_register(SINTERFACE_SPEC, binding_vector_p, NULL,

  (unsigned_char_t *)EP_ANNO, &status);

  /* Export binding information to name service */
```

Example A-2: The main Routine of the DCE Version of the ATM Server (continued)

```
rpc_ns_binding_export(rpc_c_ns_syntax_dce,

(unsigned_char_t *)SERVER_NAME,

SINTERFACE_SPEC,

binding_vector_p, NULL, &status);

/***********************************************/
/* Initialization Routine for the ATM Server */
/***********************************************/
atm_server_init(argc, argv);

/***************************************************/
/* Jump to runtime listening loop, (Boss for(;;)) */
/***************************************************/
rpc_server_listen(MAX_CONC_CALLS_TOTAL, &status);
return 0;
}
```

In Example A-3, we'll fix up our worker thread routines—that is, the server management routines that will be triggered when our clients make an RPC to our server. We specified the interface to these routines in the IDL file. If we were writing these routines from scratch, we'd need to ensure that they contained appropriate synchronization code. However, because we added the synchronization calls in Chapter 3, *Synchronizing Pthreads*, we can simply reuse the existing routines.

For example, the code for the *deposit* server management routine remains pretty much the same, with the exception of the few IDL hooks at the beginning. Notice, too, that we've removed all the low-level code dealing with communication from our source code. DCE will take care of this for us. Our routine can now focus on its particular role in our application—that is, access to the bank account database.

Example A–3: The DCE ATM Server Deposit Server Management Routine

```
void deposit(
  rpc_binding_handle_t handle,       /* in */
  idl_long_int *id,                  /* in */
  idl_long_int *password,            /* in */
  idl_long_int *amount,              /* in */
  idl_long_int *success,             /* out */
  idl_char estring[20])              /* out */
{
  int rtn;
  int temp;
  account_t *accountp;

  /* Check inputs */
  if ((*id < 0) || (*id >= MAX_NUM_ACCOUNTS)) {
    *success = TRANS_FAILURE;
    strncpy((char *)estring,ERR_MSG_BAD_ACCOUNT, ERR_MSG_SIZE);
    return;
  }

  pthread_mutex_lock(&account_mutex[*id]);

  /* Retrieve account from database */
  if ((rtn = retrieve_account( *id, &accountp)) < 0) {
    *success = TRANS_FAILURE;
    strncpy((char *)estring,atm_err_tbl[-rtn], ERR_MSG_SIZE);

  /* Check password */
  }else if (*password != accountp->password)  {
    *success = TRANS_FAILURE;
    strncpy((char *estring, ERR_MSG_BAD_PASSWORD, ERR_MSG_SIZE);

  /* Add new balance */
  }else {
    (accountp->balance) = *amount;

    /* Store back to database */
    if ((rtn = store_account(accountp)) < 0) {
      *success = TRANS_FAILURE;
      strncpy((char *)estring,atm_err_tbl[-rtn], ERR_MSG_SIZE);

    /* Everything OK */
    }else {
      *success = TRANS_SUCCESS;
    }
  }
  pthread_mutex_unlock(&account_mutex[*id]);
}
```

B

Pthreads Draft 4 vs. the Final Standard

So you've read the book that describes the final Pthreads standard and now discover that you must support or port a multithreaded program that's based on the interfaces defined by Draft 4. Help!

The Pthreads interfaces and library implementations adopted by many vendors at Draft 4 can be significantly different from those the same vendors supply now in compliance with the final standard. We'll help you sort out the differences in this appendix.

To help you track down the changes that particularly affect your program, we've organized this appendix into sections corresponding to the major activities of a multithreaded program. In each section, we've classified differences as relating to either *features* or *syntax*. (Of course, if a Draft 4 feature was removed in the final standard, you may need to make a syntax change in your program to remove an undefined call or constant.)

Detaching a Thread

Feature: Draft 4 doesn't allow you to create a thread in a detached state; the final standard allows you to do so by using an attribute object. (See the section on thread attributes later in this appendix.)

Syntax: In an implementation that conforms to the final standard, you specify the argument to the *pthread_detach* function as a *pthread_t*; in a Draft 4 implementation, you specify the same argument as a pointer to a *pthread_t* (**pthread_t*).

Mutex Variables

Feature: In the final draft, mutexes have both defined and optional attributes (the priority-scheduling attributes and the process-shared attribute we discussed in Chapter 3, *Synchronizing Pthreads*). Draft 4 defines no mutex attributes. As a result, the mutex attribute calls listed below and the compile-time constants PTHREAD_PROCESS_SHARED and PTHREAD_PROCESS_PRIVATE have no meaning in a Draft 4 implementation.

- *pthread_mutexattr_getshared*
- *pthread_mutexattr_setshared*
- *pthread_mutexattr_setprotocol*
- *pthread_mutexattr_getprotocol*
- *pthread_mutexattr_setprioceiling*
- *pthread_mutexattr_getprioceiling*

Feature: Because Draft 4 doesn't allow you to statically initialize mutexes (with PTHREAD_MUTEX_INITIALIZER), you may need to use the *pthread_once* function in a Draft 4 implementation to avoid library initialization problems.

Syntax: When dynamically initializing a mutex in a Draft 4 implementation, you use the *pthread_mutexattr_default* constant to request default attributes. In an implementation that conforms to the final standard, you specify NULL.

Condition Variables

Feature: In the final draft, condition variables have both defined and optional attributes (the process-shared attribute we discussed in Chapter 4, *Managing Pthreads*). Draft 4 defines no condition variable attributes. As a result, the condition variable attribute calls (which are *pthread_condattr_getshared* and *pthread_condattr_setshared*) and the compile-time constants (which are PTHREAD_PROCESS_SHARED and PTHREAD_PROCESS_PRIVATE) have no meaning in a Draft 4 implementation.

Feature: Because Draft 4 doesn't allow you to statically initialize condition variables (using the PTHREAD_COND_INITIALIZER constant), you may need to use the *pthread_once* function in a Draft 4 implementation to avoid library initialization problems.

Syntax: When dynamically initializing a condition variable in a Draft 4 implementation, you use the *pthread_condattr_default* constant to request default attributes. In an implementation that conforms to the final standard, you specify NULL.

Thread Attributes

Feature: In the final draft, threads have stack-address and detached-state attributes (as discussed in Chapter 4). Draft 4 doesn't define these thread attributes. As a result, the thread attribute calls (*pthread_attr_setstackaddr*, *pthread_attr_getstackaddr*, *pthread_attr_setdetachstate*, and *pthread_attr_getdetachstate*) have no meaning in a Draft 4 implementation.

Feature: Draft 4 does not define a way for you to set the scheduling scope of a thread. (See the section on scheduling later in this appendix.)

Syntax: To destroy a thread attribute object in a Draft 4 implementation, you call *pthread_attr_delete*; in an implementation that conforms to the final standard, you call *pthread_attr_destroy*.

Syntax: The Pthreads library calls you use to change thread-scheduling attributes have different names in Draft 4 and the final standard. (See the section on scheduling later in this appendix.)

Syntax: In draft four a constant pthread_attr_default is defined that can be used as the second argument in the pthread_create routine when you want the default attributes for a thread. In the final standard the constant no longer exists and if you want default attributes you pass NULL.

The pthread_once Function

Syntax: Whereas Draft 4 defines the constant pthread_once_init (in lowercase letters) to represent the initialized value of a once block, the final standard defines the constant PTHREAD_ONCE_INIT (in uppercase letters).

Keys

Feature: Draft 4 has no equivalent to the *pthread_key_delete* function that's defined in the final standard.

Syntax: To initialize a key in a Draft 4 implementation, you call *pthread_keycreate*; in an implementation that conforms to the final standard, you call *pthread_key_create.*

Cancellation

Syntax: To set the cancellation state of a thread on an implementation that conforms to the final standard, you call *pthread_setcancelstate* with either the PTHREAD_CANCEL_ENABLE or PTHREAD_CANCEL_DISABLE constant. In a Draft 4 implementation, you call *pthread_setcancel* with either the CANCEL_ON or CANCEL_OFF constant (to enable or disable cancellation, respectively).

Syntax: To set the cancellation type of a thread on an implementation that conforms to the final standard, you call the *pthread_setcanceltype* function with either the PTHREAD_CANCEL_ASYNCHRONOUS or PTHREAD_CANCEL_DEFERRED constant. In a Draft 4 implementation, you call *pthread_setasynccancel* with either the CANCEL_ON or CANCEL_OFF constant (to asynchronous cancellation or deferred cancellation, respectively).

Scheduling

Feature: Draft 4 does not define a way for you to set the scheduling scope of a thread. As a result, the scheduling scope calls (*pthread_attr_setscope* and *pthread_attr_getscope*) have no meaning in a Draft 4 implementation.

Feature: Draft 4 defines a number of symbolic constants (for example, PRI_FIFO_MAX) to represent the maximum and minimum scheduling priorities of threads. These constants have been removed from the final standard. As a result you must call POSIX.1b functions such as *sched_get_priority_max* to obtain scheduling priority limits.

Feature: In a Draft 4 implementation, a thread calls the *pthread_yield* function to surrender the CPU to another runnable thread. In an implementation that conforms to the final standard, a thread calls the thread-specific POSIX.1b function *sched_yield.*

Syntax: In a Draft 4 implementation, you use the *pthread_setscheduler* and *pthread_setprio* functions together to dynamically set a thread's scheduling characteristics; in an implementation that conforms to the final standard, you use just one—*pthread_setschedparam.*

Syntax: In a Draft 4 implementation, you use the *pthread_attr_setprio* and *pthread_attr_getprio* functions to set and get a thread's scheduling-priority attribute; in an implementation that conforms to the final standard, you use *pthread_attr_setschedparam* and *pthread_attr_getschedparam.*

Syntax: In a Draft 4 implementation, you use the *pthread_attr_setsched* and *pthread_attr_getsched* calls to set and get a thread's scheduling policy; in an implementation that conforms to the final standard, you use the *pthread_attr_setschedpolicy* and *pthread_attr_getschedpolicy* calls.

Signals

Feature: Whereas the final standard requires vendors to provide the *pthread_kill* function, Draft 4 left it optional. If a given Draft 4 implementation supports it, the compile-time constant _POSIX_THREADS_PER_THREAD_SIGNALS_1 is true.

Syntax: To manipulate per-thread signal masks in a Draft 4 implementation, you call the POSIX.1 *sigprocmask* function. (Draft 4 defined a thread-specific version of this call.) In an implementation that complies with the final standard, you call *pthread_sigmask*. Note that the final standard leaves the behavior of *sigprocmask* in a multithreaded program undefined.

Threadsafe System Interfaces

Feature: In Draft 4, threadsafe system interfaces are optional; if the interfaces are supported on a given implementation, the compile-time constant _POSIX_REENTRANT_FUNCTIONS is TRUE. On an implementation that supports the final standard, this constant, when defined, must always be TRUE.

Feature: The Draft 4 version uses the term *reentrant* more often than it does *threadsafe*.

Feature: Draft 4 and the final standard vary in their lists of those library functions and system calls that don't need to be made threadsafe and those calls that require new, alternative reentrant versions.

Feature: Draft 4 does not define the *ftrylockfile* call.

Syntax: In Draft 4, the names of the faster versions of the threadsafe character-cell I/O calls have the form *unlocked_<xxx>*; in the final standard, the names have the form *<xxx>_unlocked*.

Error Reporting

Feature: In Draft 4, Pthreads library functions use the `errno` global to indicate the reason (that is, the error number) for an unsuccessful function call. The final standard specifies that Pthreads library functions should not use `errno`. Instead, most Pthreads library functions provide the error number as the return value of an unsuccessful call.

System Interfaces and Cancellation-Safety

Feature: Draft 4 requires implementations to make some ANSI C routines, but no POSIX.1 routines, cancellation-safe; the final standard doesn't require that any ANSI C or POSIX.1 routines be cancellation-safe.

Feature: Draft 4 doesn't require any system or library call to act as a cancellation point; the final standard requires many calls to be cancellation points.

Process-Blocking Calls

Feature: Draft 4 lists *creat, close,* and *tcdrain* as calls that must block only the calling thread, not the entire process. The final standard doesn't specify the behavior of these calls.

Process Management

Feature: Draft 4 doesn't define the *pthread_atfork* call.

Feature: Draft 4 leaves as undefined the behavior of a multithreaded process when one of its threads calls *exec.*

C

Pthreads Quick Reference

In this appendix, we'll provide a brief listing of the C language bindings of the Pthreads library routines:

pthread_atfork( )

```
int pthread_atfork (
void (*prepare)(void),
void (*parent)(void),
void (*child)(void));
```

Declares procedures to be called before and after a *fork* call. The *prepare* fork handler runs in the parent process before the *fork*. After the *fork*, the *parent* handler runs in the parent process, and the *child* handler runs in the child process.

pthread_attr_destroy( )

```
int pthread_attr_destroy (
pthread_attr_t *attr);
```

Destroys a thread attribute object.

pthread_attr_getdetachstate( )

```
int pthread_attr_getdetachstate (
const pthread_attr_t *attr,
int *detachstate);
```

Obtains the setting of the detached state of a thread.

pthread_attr_getinheritsched( )

```
int pthread_attr_getinheritsched (
const pthread_attr_t *attr,
int *inheritsched);
```

Obtains the setting of the scheduling inheritance of a thread.

pthread_attr_getschedparam( )

```
int pthread_attr_getschedparam (
const pthread_attr_t *attr,
struct sched_param *param);
```

Obtains the parameters (for instance, the scheduling priority) associated with the scheduling policy attribute of a thread.

pthread_attr_getschedpolicy( )

```
int pthread_attr_getschedpolicy (
const pthread_attr_t *attr,
int *policy);
```

Obtains the setting of the scheduling policy of a thread.

pthread_attr_getscope( )

```
int pthread_attr_getscope (
const pthread_attr_t *attr,
int *scope);
```

Obtains the setting of the scheduling scope of a thread.

pthread_attr_getstackaddr( )

```
int pthread_attr_getstackaddr (
const pthread_attr_t *attr,
void **stackaddr);
```

Obtains the stack address of a thread.

pthread_attr_getstacksize( )

```
int pthread_attr_getstacksize (
const pthread_attr_t *attr,
size_t *stacksize);
```

Obtains the stack size of a thread.

pthread_attr_init( )

```
int pthread_attr_init (
pthread_attr_t *attr);
```

Initializes a thread attribute object. A thread specifies a thread attribute object in its calls to *pthread_create* to set the characteristics of newly created threads.

pthread_attr_setdetachstate( )

```
int pthread_attr_setdetachstate (
pthread_attr_t *attr,
int detachstate);
```

Adjusts the detached state of a thread. A thread's detached state can be join-able   (PTHREAD_CREATE_JOINABLE)   or   it   can   be   detached (PTHREAD_CREATE_DETACHED).

pthread_attr_setinheritsched( )

```
int pthread_attr_setinheritsched (
pthread_attr_t *attr,
int inherit);
```

Adjusts the scheduling inheritance of a thread. A thread can inherit the scheduling   policy   and   the   parameters   of   its   creator   thread (PTHREAD_INHERIT_SCHED) or obtain them from the thread attribute object specified in the *pthread_create* call (PTHREAD_EXPLICIT_SCHED).

pthread_attr_setschedparam( )

```
int pthread_attr_setschedparam (
pthread_attr_t *attr,
const struct sched_param *param);
```

Adjusts the parameters (for instance, the scheduling priority) associated with the scheduling policy of a thread. The scheduling priority parameter (as speci-fied in the *struct sched_param*) depends upon the selected scheduling policy (SCHED_FIFO, SCHED_RR, or SCHED_OTHER). Use *sched_get_priority_max* and *sched_get_priority_min* to obtain the maximum and minimum priority set-tings for a given policy.

pthread_attr_setschedpolicy( )

```
int pthread_attr_setschedpolicy (
pthread_attr_t *attr,
int policy);
```

Adjusts the scheduling policy of a thread. Pthreads defines the SCHED_FIFO, SCHED_RR, and SCHED_OTHER policies.

pthread_attr_setscope( )

```
int pthread_attr_setscope (
pthread_attr_t *attr,
int scope);
```

Adjusts the scheduling scope of a thread. A thread can use system-scope scheduling (PTHREAD_SCOPE_SYSTEM), in which case the operating system compares the priorities of all runnable threads of all processes systemwide in order to select a thread to run on an available CPU. Alternatively, it can use process-scope scheduling (PTHREAD_SCOPE_PROCESS), in which case only the highest priority runnable thread in a process competes against the highest priority threads of other processes in the system's scheduling activity.

pthread_attr_setstackaddr( )

```
int pthread_attr_setstackaddr (
pthread_attr_t *attr,
void *stackaddr);
```

Adjusts the stack address of a thread.

pthread_attr_setstacksize( )

```
int pthread_attr_setstacksize (
pthread_attr_t *attr,
size_t stacksize);
```

Adjusts the stack size of a thread. The stack size must be greater than or equal to PTHREAD_STACK_MIN.

pthread_cancel( )

```
int pthread_cancel (
pthread_t thread);
```

Cancels the specified thread.

pthread_cleanup_pop( )

```
void pthread_cleanup_pop (
int execute);
```

Removes the routine from the top of a thread's cleanup stack, and if *execute* is nonzero, runs it.

pthread_cleanup_push( )

```
void pthread_cleanup_push (
void (*routine)(void *),
void *arg);
```

Places a routine on the the top of a thread's cleanup stack, and when the routine is called, ensures that the specified argument is passed to it.

pthread_condattr_destroy( )

```
int pthread_condattr_destroy (
pthread_condattr_t *attr);
```

Destroys a condition variable attribute object.

pthread_condattr_getpshared( )

```
int pthread_condattr_getpshared (
pthread_condattr_t *attr,
int *pshared);
```

Obtains the process-shared setting of a condition variable attribute object.

pthread_condattr_init( )

```
int pthread_condattr_init (
pthread_condattr_t *attr);
```

Initializes a condition variable attribute object. A thread specifies a condition variable attribute object in its calls to *pthread_cond_init* to set the characteristics of new condition variables.

pthread_condattr_setpshared( )

```
int pthread_condattr_setpshared (
pthread_condattr_t *attr,
int pshared);
```

Sets the process-shared attribute in a condition variable attribute object to either PTHREAD_PROCESS_SHARED or PTHREAD_PROCESS_PRIVATE.

pthread_cond_broadcast( )

```
int pthread_cond_broadcast (
pthread_cond_t *cond);
```

Unblocks all threads that are waiting on a condition variable.

pthread_cond_destroy( )

```
int pthread_cond_destroy (
pthread_cond_t *cond);
```

Destroys a condition variable.

pthread_cond_init( )

```
int pthread_cond_init (
pthread_cond_t *cond,
const pthread_condattr_t *attr);
```

Initializes a condition variable with the attributes specified in the specified condition variable attribute object. If *attr* is NULL, the default attributes are used.

pthread_cond_signal( )

```
int pthread_cond_signal(
pthread_cond_t *cond);
```

Unblocks at least one thread waiting on a condition variable. The scheduling priority determines which thread is awakened.

pthread_cond_timedwait( )

```
int pthread_cond_timedwait (
pthread_cond_t *cond,
pthread_mutex_t *mutex,
const struct timespec *abstime);
```

Atomically unlocks the specified *mutex*, and places the calling thread into a wait state. When the specified condition variable is signaled or broadcast, or the system time is greater than or equal to *abstime*, this function reacquires the mutex and resumes its caller.

pthread_cond_wait( )

```
int pthread_cond_wait (
pthread_cond_t *cond,
pthread_mutex_t *mutex);
```

Atomically unlocks the specified *mutex*, and places the calling thread into a wait state. When the specified condition variable is signaled or broadcasted, this function reacquires the mutex and resumes its caller.

pthread_create( )

```
int pthread_create (
pthread_t *thread,
const pthread_attr_t *attr,
void *(*start_routine)(void *),
void *arg);
```

Creates a thread with the attributes specified in *attr*. If *attr* is NULL, the default attributes are used. The thread argument receives a thread handle for the new thread. The new thread starts execution in *start_routine* and is passed the single specified argument.

pthread_detach( )

```
int pthread_detach (
pthread_t thread);
```

Marks a thread's internal data structures for deletion. When a detached thread terminates, the system reclaims the storage used for its thread object.

pthread_equal( )

```
int pthread_equal (
pthread_t t1,
pthread_t t2);
```

Compares one thread handle to another thread handle.

pthread_exit( )

```
void pthread_exit (
void *value);
```

Terminates the calling thread, returning the specified *value* to any thread that may have previously issued a *pthread_join* on the thread.

pthread_getschedparam( )

```
int pthread_getschedparam (
pthread_t thread,
int *policy,
struct sched_param *param);
```

Obtains both the scheduling policy and scheduling parameters of an existing thread. (This function differs from the *pthread_attr_getschedpolicy* function and the *pthread_attr_getschedparam* function in that the latter functions return the policy and parameters that will be used whenever a new thread is created.)

pthread_getspecific( )

```
void *pthread_getspecific (
pthread_key_t key);
```

Obtains the thread-specific data value associated with the specified *key* in the calling thread.

pthread_join( )

```
int pthread_join (
pthread_t thread,
void **value_ptr);
```

Causes the calling thread to wait for the specified thread's termination. The *value_ptr* parameter receives the return value of the terminating thread.

pthread_key_create( )

```
int pthread_key_create (
pthread_key_t *key,
void (*destructor)(void *));
```

Generates a unique thread-specific key that's visible to all threads in a process.

Although different threads can use the same key, the value any thread associates with the key (by calling *pthread_specific*) are specific to that thread alone and persist for the life of that thread. When a thread terminates, its thread-specific data value is destroyed (but the key persists until *pthread_key_destroy* is called). If a *destructor* routine was specified for the key in the *pthread_key_create* call, it's then called in the thread's context with the thread-specific data value associated with the key as an argument.

pthread_key_delete( )

```
int pthread_key_delete (
pthread_key_t key);
```

Deletes a thread-specific key.

pthread_kill( )

```
int pthread_kill (
pthread_t thread,
int sig);
```

Delivers a signal to the specified thread.

pthread_mutexattr_destroy( )

```
int pthread_mutexattr_destroy (
pthread_mutexattr_t *attr);
```

Destroys a mutex attribute object.

pthread_mutexattr_getprioceiling( )

```
int pthread_mutexattr_getprioceiling (
pthread_mutexattr_t *attr,
int *prioceiling);
```

Obtains the priority ceiling of a mutex attribute object.

pthread_mutexattr_getprotocol( )

```
int pthread_mutexattr_getprotocol(
pthread_mutexattr_t *attr,
int *protocol);
```

Obtains the protocol of a mutex attribute object.

pthread_mutexattr_getpshared( )

```
int pthread_mutexattr_getpshared(
pthread_mutexattr_t *attr,
int *pshared);
```

Obtains the process-shared setting of a mutex attribute object.

pthread_mutexattr_init( )

```
int pthread_mutexattr_init (
pthread_mutexattr_t *attr);
```

Initializes a mutex attribute object. A thread specifies a mutex attribute object in its calls to *pthread_mutex_init* to set the characteristics of new mutexes.

pthread_mutexattr_setprioceiling( )

```
int pthread_mutexattr_setprioceiling (
pthread_mutexattr_t *attr,
int prioceiling);
```

Sets the priority ceiling attribute of a mutex attribute object.

pthread_mutexattr_setprotocol( )

```
int pthread_mutexattr_setprotocol(
pthread_mutexattr_t *attr,
int protocol);
```

Sets the protocol attribute of a mutex attribute object. There are three valid settings: PTHREAD_PRIO_INHERIT, PTHREAD_PRIO_PROTECT, or PTHREAD_PRIO_NONE.

pthread_mutexattr_setpshared( )

```
int pthread_mutexattr_setpshared(
pthread_mutexattr_t *attr,
int pshared);
```

Sets the process-shared attribute of a mutex attribute object to PTHREAD_PROCESS_SHARED or PTHREAD_PROCESS_PRIVATE.

pthread_mutex_destroy( )

```
int pthread_mutex_destroy (
pthread_mutex_t *mutex);
```

Destroys a mutex.

pthread_mutex_init( )

```
int pthread_mutex_init (
pthread_mutex_t *mutex,
const pthread_mutexattr_t *attr);
```

Initializes a mutex with the attributes specified in the specified mutex attribute object. If *attr* is NULL, the default attributes are used.

pthread_mutex_lock( )

```
int pthread_mutex_lock (
pthread_mutex_t *mutex);
```

Locks an unlocked mutex. If the mutex is already locked, the calling thread blocks until the thread that currently holds the mutex releases it.

pthread_mutex_trylock( )

```
int pthread_mutex_trylock (
pthread_mutex_t *mutex);
```

Tries to lock a mutex. If the mutex is already locked, the calling thread returns without waiting for the mutex to be freed.

pthread_mutex_unlock( )

```
int pthread_mutex_unlock (
pthread_mutex_t *mutex);
```

Unlocks a mutex. The scheduling priority determines which blocked thread is resumed. The resumed thread may or may not succeed in its next attempt to lock the mutex, depending upon whether another thread has locked the mutex in the interval between the thread's being resumed and its issuing the *pthread_mutex_lock* call.

pthread_once( )

```
int pthread_once (
pthread_once_t *once_block,
void (*init_routine) (void);
```

Ensures that *init_routine* will run just once regardless of how many threads in a process call it. All threads issue calls to the routine by making identical *pthread_once* calls (with the same *once_block* and *init_routine*). The thread that first makes the *pthread_once* call succeeds in running the routine; subsequent *pthread_once* calls from other threads do not run the routine.

pthread_self( )

```
pthread_t pthread_self (
void);
```

Obtains the thread handle of the calling thread.

pthread_setcancelstate( )

```
int pthread_setcancelstate (
int state,
int *oldstate);
```

Sets a thread's cancelability state. You can enable a thread's cancellation by specifying the PTHREAD_CANCEL_ENABLE state, or disable it by specifying PTHREAD_CANCEL_DISABLE.

pthread_setcanceltype( )

```
int pthread_setcanceltype (
int type,
int *oldtype);
```

Sets a thread's cancelability type. To allow a thread to receive cancellation orders only at defined cancellation points, you can specify the PTHREAD_CANCEL_DEFERRED type; this is the default. To allow a thread to be canceled at any point during its execution, you can specify PTHREAD_CANCEL_ASYNCHRONOUS.

pthread_setschedparam( )

```
int pthread_setschedparam (
pthread_t thread,
int policy,
const struct sched_param *param);
```

Adjusts the scheduling policy and scheduling parameters of an existing thread. (This function differs from the functions *pthread_attr_setschedpolicy* and *pthread_attr_setschedparam* in that they set the policy and parameters that will be used whenever a new thread is created.)

pthread_setspecific( )

```
int pthread_setspecific (
pthread_key_t key,
void *value);
```

Sets the thread-specific data value associated with the specified *key* in the calling thread.

pthread_sigmask( )

```
int pthread_sigmask (
int how,
const sigset_t *set,
sigset_t *oset);
```

Examines or changes the calling thread's signal mask.

pthread_testcancel( )

```
void pthread_testcancel (
void);
```

Requests that any pending cancellation request be delivered to the calling thread.

Index

About the Authors

Brad Nichols is a freelance do-anything-computerish-for-a-buck kind of guy who works out of Milford, NH. He earned a B.S. degree in Mechanical Engineering from the University of New Hampshire in 1985 and an M.S. degree from Worcester Polytechnic Institute (WPI) in 1991. He started his computer career working on very hard hardware (fuel pumps and valves). He worked his way up through the hardware layers into software on projects involving embedded avionics systems at Textron Lycomming and United Technologies Hamilton Standard Division. Brad left these jobs to learn more about AI at WPI, but instead caught the Mach fever, and was introduced to threads programming in UNIX. While at WPI he also worked on an OSF/1 performance project for the Open Software Foundation (OSF). After attending WPI, Brad taught training seminars to software developers on the Mach kernel interfaces. He then joined Digital Equipment Corporation to work on the port of the OSF's Distributed Computing Environment's Distributed File System (OSFDCEDFSDU for short) to Digital UNIX. Now, Brad is once again on his own and spends most of his time teaching software engineers about technologies with much shorter acronyms—such as Pthreads.

When not working, Brad spends time at home trying to synchronize with his wife, Susan, and three little threads, Dan (who's 7), Tim (5), and Cecelia (3). And, oh yes, there's the lawn and dump things on weekends too.

Dick Buttlar is a consulting writer in the UNIX Engineering Group at Digital Equipment Corporation, where he currently contributes to the cluster documentation effort. He specializes in documentation for application and kernel programmers, although he has fond memories of the daisy-wheel printer manuals he wrote for Wang Laboratories when he had more hair and dressed nicely. He has a B.A. in English from Boston College and an M.A. in English from the University of Wisconsin at Madison.

He lives in Nashua, NH, with his wife, Connie, and three children. He enjoys playing pirates with his son Tom, taking his daughter Maggie fishing, and listening to Rancid with his daughter Jenn. He likes nothing better than hanging out on the Maine seacoast, cooking a nice meal for himself and his wife, while hummingbirds feed outside the kitchen window, the ocean rolls in at the cove, and Miles Davis's "Flamenco Sketches" softly plays on the boombox on the counter.

Jacqueline Proulx Farrell has been a software engineer with Digital Equipment Corporation since 1986 and is currently a principal software engineer.

She leads development of the DCE products for Digital UNIX. Jackie has a B.S. in applied math from the University of Vermont (1986), and studied distributed computing at Cornell University (MEng degree, 1993). Her previous projects at Digital include RT-11, DECtrade, and DCE CDS development.

Jackie is happily married to Bernard Farrell, also a software warrior as well as the father of three amazing children, Eleanor, Lee, and Hayley. Jackie and Bernard are soon to be parents of baby Mingzhu, who waits patiently for them in Yunnan Province, China.

Colophon

Our look is the result of reader comments, our own experimentation, and distribution channels. Distinctive covers complement our distinctive approach to technical topics, breathing personality and life into potentially dry subjects. UNIX and its attendant programs can be unruly beasts. Nutshell Handbooks help you tame them.

The animal featured on the cover of *Pthreads Programming* is a silkworm. Silkworms produce silk when they secrete a fine, strong filament while spinning their cocoons. According to legend, the Empress Ling-chi discovered how to unwind the filament approximately 3000 years ago B.C., and thus produced the world's first silk fabric. Silkworms survive exclusively on certain strains of mulberry leaves. The cultivated silkworm no longer exists in the wild. Although silkworms have been cultivated on a relatively small scale elsewhere, few places have both the warm climate and the abundance of mulberry trees that silkworms require, and so Asia, specifically China, continues to be the main producer of silk.

Hanna Dyer designed the cover of this book, based on a series design by Edie Freedman. The image is a 19th-century engraving from the Dover Pictorial Archive. The cover layout was produced with Quark XPress 3.3 using the ITC Garamond font. Whenever possible, our books use RepKover™, a durable and flexible lay-flat binding. If the page count exceeds RepKover's limit, perfect binding is used.

The inside layout was designed by Edie Freedman, Jennifer Niederst, and Nancy Priest. Text was prepared by Erik Ray in SGML DocBook 2.4 DTD. The print version of this book was created by translating the SGML source into a set of gtroff macros using a filter developed at ORA by Norman Walsh. Steve Talbott designed and wrote the underlying macro set on the basis of the GNU troff -gs macros; Lenny Muellner adapted them to SGML and implemented the book design. The GNU groff text formatter version 1.09 was used to generate PostScript output. The text and heading fonts are ITC Garamond Light and Garamond Book. The illustrations that appear in the book were created in Macromedia Freehand 5.0 by Chris Reilley. This colophon was written by Clairemarie Fisher O'Leary

How to stay in touch with O'Reilly

1. Visit Our Award-Winning Web Site

http://www.oreilly.com/

★"Top 100 Sites on the Web" —*PC Magazine*
★"Top 5% Web sites" —*Point Communications*
★"3-Star site" —*The McKinley Group*

Our web site contains a library of comprehensive product information (including book excerpts and tables of contents), downloadable software, background articles, interviews with technology leaders, links to relevant sites, book cover art, and more. File us in your Bookmarks or Hotlist!

2. Join Our Email Mailing Lists

New Product Releases

To receive automatic email with brief descriptions of all new O'Reilly products as they are released, send email to:
listproc@online.oreilly.com
Put the following information in the first line of your message (*not* in the Subject field):
subscribe oreilly-news

O'Reilly Events

If you'd also like us to send information about trade show events, special promotions, and other O'Reilly events, send email to:
listproc@online.oreilly.com
Put the following information in the first line of your message (*not* in the Subject field):
subscribe oreilly-events

3. Get Examples from Our Books via FTP

There are two ways to access an archive of example files from our books:

Regular FTP

- ftp to:
  ftp.oreilly.com
  (login: anonymous
  password: your email address)
- Point your web browser to:
  ftp://ftp.oreilly.com/

FTPMAIL

- Send an email message to:
  ftpmail@online.oreilly.com
  (Write "help" in the message body)

4. Contact Us via Email

order@oreilly.com
To place a book or software order online. Good for North American and international customers.

subscriptions@oreilly.com
To place an order for any of our newsletters or periodicals.

books@oreilly.com
General questions about any of our books.

software@oreilly.com
For general questions and product information about our software. Check out O'Reilly Software Online at **http://software.oreilly.com/** for software and technical support information. Registered O'Reilly software users send your questions to: **website-support@oreilly.com**

cs@oreilly.com
For answers to problems regarding your order or our products.

booktech@oreilly.com
For book content technical questions or corrections.

proposals@oreilly.com
To submit new book or software proposals to our editors and product managers.

international@oreilly.com
For information about our international distributors or translation queries. For a list of our distributors outside of North America check out:
http://www.oreilly.com/www/order/country.html

5. Work with Us

Check out our website for current employment opportunites:
www.jobs@oreilly.com
Click on "Work with Us"

O'Reilly & Associates, Inc.
101 Morris Street, Sebastopol, CA 95472 USA
TEL 707-829-0515 or 800-998-9938
     (6am to 5pm PST)
FAX 707-829-0104

International Distributors

UK, EUROPE, MIDDLE EAST AND AFRICA (EXCEPT FRANCE, GERMANY, AUSTRIA, SWITZERLAND, LUXEMBOURG, LIECHTENSTEIN, AND EASTERN EUROPE)

INQUIRIES
O'Reilly UK Limited
4 Castle Street
Farnham
Surrey, GU9 7HS
United Kingdom
Telephone: 44-1252-711776
Fax: 44-1252-734211
Email: information@oreilly.co.uk

ORDERS
Wiley Distribution Services Ltd.
1 Oldlands Way
Bognor Regis
West Sussex PO22 9SA
United Kingdom
Telephone: 44-1243-779777
Fax: 44-1243-820250
Email: cs-books@wiley.co.uk

FRANCE

INQUIRIES
Éditions O'Reilly
18 rue Séguier
75006 Paris, France
Tel: 33-1-40-51-52-30
Fax: 33-1-40-51-52-31
Email: france@editions-oreilly.fr

ORDERS
GEODIF
61, Bd Saint-Germain
75240 Paris Cedex 05, France
Tel: 33-1-44-41-46-16 (French books)
Tel: 33-1-44-41-11-87 (English books)
Fax: 33-1-44-41-11-44
Email: distribution@eyrolles.com

GERMANY, SWITZERLAND, AUSTRIA, EASTERN EUROPE, LUXEMBOURG, AND LIECHTENSTEIN

INQUIRIES & ORDERS
O'Reilly Verlag
Balthasarstr. 81
D-50670 Köln
Germany
Telephone: 49-221-973160-91
Fax: 49-221-973160-8
Email: anfragen@oreilly.de (inquiries)
Email: order@oreilly.de (orders)

CANADA (FRENCH LANGUAGE BOOKS)

Les Éditions Flammarion ltée
375, Avenue Laurier Ouest
Montréal (Québec) H2V 2K3
Tel: 00-1-514-277-8807
Fax: 00-1-514-278-2085
Email: info@flammarion.qc.ca

HONG KONG

City Discount Subscription Service, Ltd.
Unit D, 3rd Floor, Yan's Tower
27 Wong Chuk Hang Road
Aberdeen, Hong Kong
Tel: 852-2580-3539
Fax: 852-2580-6463
Email: citydis@ppn.com.hk

KOREA

Hanbit Media, Inc.
Chungmu Bldg. 201
Yonnam-dong 568-33
Mapo-gu
Seoul, Korea
Tel: 822-325-0397
Fax: 822-325-9697
Email: hant93@chollian.dacom.co.kr

PHILIPPINES

Global Publishing
G/F Benavides Garden
1186 Benavides Street
Manila, Philippines
Tel: 632-254-8949/637-252-2582
Fax: 632-734-5060/632-252-2733
Email: globalp@pacific.net.ph

TAIWAN

O'Reilly Taiwan
No. 3, Lane 131
Hang-Chow South Road
Section 1, Taipei, Taiwan
Tel: 886-2-23968990
Fax: 886-2-23968916
Email: taiwan@oreilly.com

CHINA

O'Reilly Beijing
Room 2410
160, FuXingMenNeiDaJie
XiCheng District
Beijing, China PR 100031
Tel: 86-10-66412305
Fax: 86-10-86631007
Email: beijing@oreilly.com

INDIA

Computer Bookshop (India) Pvt. Ltd.
190 Dr. D.N. Road, Fort
Bombay 400 001 India
Tel: 91-22-207-0989
Fax: 91-22-262-3551
Email: cbsbom@giasbm01.vsnl.net.in

JAPAN

O'Reilly Japan, Inc.
Yotsuya Y's Building
7 Banch 6, Honshio-cho
Shinjuku-ku
Tokyo 160-0003 Japan
Tel: 81-3-3356-5227
Fax: 81-3-3356-5261
Email: japan@oreilly.com

ALL OTHER ASIAN COUNTRIES

O'Reilly & Associates, Inc.
101 Morris Street
Sebastopol, CA 95472 USA
Tel: 707-829-0515
Fax: 707-829-0104
Email: order@oreilly.com

AUSTRALIA

Woodslane Pty., Ltd.
7/5 Vuko Place
Warriewood NSW 2102
Australia
Tel: 61-2-9970-5111
Fax: 61-2-9970-5002
Email: info@woodslane.com.au

NEW ZEALAND

Woodslane New Zealand, Ltd.
21 Cooks Street (P.O. Box 575)
Waganui, New Zealand
Tel: 64-6-347-6543
Fax: 64-6-345-4840
Email: info@woodslane.com.au

LATIN AMERICA

McGraw-Hill Interamericana
Editores, S.A. de C.V.
Cedro No. 512
Col. Atlampa
06450, Mexico, D.F.
Tel: 52-5-547-6777
Fax: 52-5-547-3336
Email: mcgraw-hill@infosel.net.mx

O'REILLY®